FOREIGN LABOR
IN NAZI GERMANY

FOREIGN LABOR
IN NAZI GERMANY

EDWARD L. HOMZE

PRINCETON UNIVERSITY PRESS

PRINCETON, NEW JERSEY

1967

Publication of this book has been aided
by the Whitney Darrow Publication Reserve Fund
of Princeton University Press

Printed in the United States of America
by Princeton University Press, Princeton, New Jersey

To Alma

PREFACE

WITH the outbreak of war in 1939, it was commonly assumed that lack of manpower would be one of the major limiting factors in Nazi Germany's war economy. By 1937, Germany had already achieved a state of full employment and, in fact, had experienced a shortage in certain labor specialities. Despite this seemingly critical labor shortage, records captured after the war indicated that Germany was able to draft from her economy nearly thirteen million men for her armed services from 1939 to 1945. At the same time she not only maintained, but steadily increased, the level of her total war production until the autumn of 1944. This remarkable achievement was accomplished by three means: the total war measures advocated by Albert Speer and executed by Joseph Goebbels, the Speer reforms that rationalized German production, and the foreign labor program. The foreign labor program alone recruited well over eight million new workers for the Reich during the course of the war, until foreign workers represented one-fifth of the total labor force in Germany at the end of 1944. The importance of these millions of foreign workers to Nazi Germany's war economy from a numerical standpoint can scarcely be denied.

It is the purpose of this study to describe the inception, organization, and administration of the Nazi foreign labor program and the relationship of the program to the Nazi war economy and government. This study differs in emphasis and documentation from the earlier explorative study, *The Exploitation of Foreign Labour by Germany* (Montreal: International Labour Office, 1945), by John H. E. Fried. Mr. Fried's study, which is based on published materials appearing during the war, emphasizes the foreign worker himself: his living and working conditions, wages, contracts, social insurance, and provisions for dependents. The present study relies extensively on captured German records and reports and stresses the governmental administration of the foreign labor program rather than the handling of individual foreign workers.

Three large collections of captured German documents deposited in the National Archives, Washington, D.C., were used in preparing this study. They are the files, working papers, and reports of the United States Strategic Bombing Survey (USSBS); the files and published sets of the Nuremberg Trials collection; and the voluminous collection of documents microfilmed at Alexandria, Virginia. A description and evaluation of these impressive collections will be found in the bibliographical essay concluding this book. However, a few brief notes at this point concerning my use of these documents might be helpful to the reader. Although I believe I have examined the important original German statistics on the foreign labor program, it seemed preferable to cite, whenever possible, the uniform labor statistics of the USSBS, which were compiled and reconstructed from original sources. There are many reasons for this choice. Captured German documents revealed numerous but unreliable labor statistics for the period from 1939 to 1945. For example, the most comprehensive set of labor statistics was the *Kraeftebilanz*, or manpower balance, computed annually at the end of May by the Reich Statistical Office (*Statistisches Reichsamt*). The *Kraeftebilanz* covered persons gainfully employed in the Reich but omitted party officials and home workers until 1944. Statistics from the Reich Labor Ministry (*Reichsarbeitsministerium*) were based on the holders of work books, yet few foreign workers apparently accepted work books, nor did every employed German have one. Statistics compiled from the health insurance agencies (*Krankenkassen*) and industrial plants such as the *Beschaeftigtenmeldung* and *Industrieberichterstattung* indicated the same shortcomings. Then, too, the accounting concept of German

viii

agencies changed as Germany incorporated various occupied areas into the Reich.

Most of these statistical difficulties were resolved by the large and impressive staff of the USSBS, which, under the direction of such gifted economists as John K. Galbraith and Burton H. Klein, adjusted German statistics and reconstructed a set of uniform labor statistics for Nazi Germany. As a result, USSBS alterations of the original German statistics were used in this study, and are noted with the phrase "as adjusted by the USSBS." The concept of the "Reich" used in the text was that employed by USSBS—namely, prewar Germany including Austria and the Sudetenland, but excluding the Protectorate. The procedure of listing German Jews as foreign workers, started by the Nazi accounting agencies, was also accepted by the USSBS and this study. This investigation does not include in its definition of foreign labor the rather sizable number of concentration camp inmates, for they were under the separate jurisdiction of Heinrich Himmler's SS (*Schutz Staffel*)—or, more properly speaking, the SS Security Service, the *Sicherheitsdienst*, or SD.

Citing individual German records from the extensive collection of documents microfilmed at Alexandria, Virginia— well over ten million frames at this time of writing—presented another difficulty to author as well as to reader. The German records were collected under a general classification and assigned a coded "T" number. The records were then filmed in rolls under this general classification. For example, a citation of "T-71, Roll 7" would indicate material taken from the seventh roll of microfilm under the general classification T-71, the code number for records of the Reich Ministry of Economics. The index for the individual rolls of microfilm appears in the *Guides to German Records Microfilmed at Alexandria, Virginia*, listed in the bibliography. Throughout the text, I have chosen to cite the general name of the

German document, the date, the coded "T" number, and the roll and frame numbers. Thus, a typical reference to micro-filmed material might be "Letter from Sauckel to Speer, dated April 2, 1943, on T-71, Roll 7, Frame 1234567." By elimi-nating the serial number, provenance information, item and folder numbers, the bulk of the footnotes has been sizably reduced for the general reader, while inclusion of the frame number has preserved the accuracy so important for the specialist.

The present book is an enlargement and extensive revision of a doctoral dissertation submitted to The Pennsylvania State University. During the research and writing I received advice and assistance from many individuals and institutions. I wish to express my thanks to Professors Alfred G. Pundt, Ira V. Brown, and Grover Platt for their suggestions in form-ulating the basic study. I am grateful to Mr. John Taylor and Mr. Robert Wolfe of the National Archives, Washing-ton, D.C., for their zeal and resourcefulness in answering many unusual requests. The patience and understanding of Professor William H. Seiler during the completion of the manuscript were greatly appreciated.

The assistance I received from the following organizations made continuous work on the study possible: The Interna-tional Institute for Education, for the Freie Universitaet-Berlin Award; The Pennsylvania State University, for a Graduate School Fellowship; and the Danforth Committee, for a Summer Grant. The skills of Mrs. Joyce Witham Fleeker who typed the manuscript and Mr. J. G. Cross who assisted me in Washington are appreciated.

I am grateful to the excellent editorial staff of Princeton University Press for their assistance in the final preparation of the book.

I appreciate the permissions from publishers to use ma-terial from the following books: *Hitler's Secret Conversa-tions*, translated by Norman Cameron and R. H. Stevens,

Farrar, Straus and Young; *The Goebbels Diaries*, edited and translated by Louis P. Lochner, Doubleday and Co., Inc.; *The Diary of Pierre Laval*, translated by Josée Laval, Charles Scribner's Sons; *Germany's Economic Preparations for War* by Burton H. Klein, Harvard University Press; *German Rule in Russia* by Alexander Dallin, St. Martin's Press, Inc., Macmillan & Co., Ltd.; *Berlin Diary* by William L. Shirer, Alfred A. Knopf, Inc.; and *Dictators Face to Face* by Dino Alfieri, translated by David Moore, New York University Press.

Lastly, I am deeply indebted to two people whose abilities, encouragement, and assistance made this book possible— Professor Kent Forster and Alma, my wife. Needless to say, final responsibility for this study, with its views and shortcomings, rests with no one but the author himself.

Lincoln, Nebraska   E.L.H.
May 1966

CONTENTS

xiii

CONTENTS

TABLES

xvii

FOREIGN LABOR
IN NAZI GERMANY

ABBREVIATIONS

DAF	Deutsche Arbeitsfront (German Labor Front)
GBA	Generalbevollmaechtiger fuer den Arbeitseinsatz (Plenipotentiary General for the Utilization of Labor)
IMT	Trials of the Major War Criminals before the International Military Tribunal (Nuremberg, 1948)
NCA	Nazi Conspiracy and Aggression (American Series from the Nuremberg Trials)
OKH	Oberkommando des Heeres (Supreme Command of the Army)
OKW	Oberkommando der Wehrmacht (Supreme Command of the Armed Forces)
OMi	Ostministerium (East Ministry)
OT	Organisation Todt (Major Construction Unit)
RSHA	Reichssicherheitshauptamt (Central Security Office)
SD	Sicherheitsdienst (Security Service)
SS	Schutzstaffel (Elite Guard of the Nazi Party)
USSBS	United States Strategic Bombing Survey
Wi Rue Amt	Wehrwirtschafts- und Ruestungsamt (Military, Economic and Armament Office)
Wi Stab Ost	Wirtschaft Stab Ost (Economic Staff East)

CHAPTER I

Foreign Labor and German Mobilization
for War

FROM the founding of the German Reich in January 1871 until the present, foreign labor has been vital to the German economy. During the rapid industrialization of Imperial Germany in the 1870's and 1880's, the familiar pattern of labor migration from rural to urban areas was taking place. The landowners, especially those with extensive holdings in eastern Germany, increasingly replaced the migrating German workers with seasonal foreign workers. By the outbreak of World War I, nearly one-half million foreign agricultural workers annually crossed the German frontier. Few of the foreigners remained the year around to work in the mines and factories of Germany; the power of organized labor prevented it. However, this situation changed with the outbreak of World War I.

During the first few months of the war Germany experienced a brief unemployment crisis, but by 1915 it was apparent that the shortage of labor was Germany's most fundamental and chronic economic weakness. To correct this situation, women and children, prisoners of war, and foreigners were put to work. Still the labor shortage grew and became more ruinous the longer it persisted. Finally, in desperation, Quartermaster-General Erich Ludendorff ordered the forced deportation of Belgian workers to Germany on October 3, 1916. The deportation decree caused such a wave of indignation throughout the world that the German government modified and then finally abandoned it.

Germany managed to secure some volunteers from European countries in addition to Belgium, but prisoners of war offered a much better source of labor during World War

3

I. By 1916, there were 600,000 prisoners of war employed in the Reich, compared with 348,917 civilian foreign workers.[1] The Kaiser's modest attempt to recruit foreign labor during the war became a portent of what a later, less sensitive, German government would do.

After the war, the unsettled economic conditions of Germany, the loss of territory, inflation, reparations, the breakup of the large estates, and the depression severely reduced the number of foreign workers that came into the country. By 1933, the trickle of foreign workers dried up. Germany had five million unemployed and was bordering on civil war. Under these desperate conditions, Adolf Hitler and the Nazi party seized control of the German state.

LABOR CONTROLS IN NAZI GERMANY

The Nazi party's philosophy and policies regarding labor were fundamentally shaped by the circumstances of its maturation, especially the German inflation and depression. Therefore, it is necessary to examine the legislative actions of the Nazi party after it assumed power in 1933 to show the type and degree of controls that the Nazis established over the German workers prior to the war and subsequently extended to the foreign workers, and to illuminate some of the later inconsistencies in the foreign labor program.

In the early years of Nazi rule, Hitler himself repeatedly rejected any specific economic blueprint. Economic policy remained subservient to political goals. The insistence on the primacy of politics over economics kept the Nazi party from achieving a basic economic orientation. Repeatedly, from 1933 to 1945, party leaders emphasized this attitude. National Socialism was a political protest against the economic realities of the twentieth century. Bernhard Koehler,

---

[1] Eberhard Trompke, *Der Arbeitseinsatz als Element deutscher Wehr- und Kriegswirtschaft* (Rostock: Carl Hinstorffs Buchdruckerei, 1941), p. 92.

formerly the chairman of the economic committee of the party, expressed the Nazi revulsion from economic theory when he wrote, "From the very beginning, National Socialism was a revolt of the living feelings of the people against the fact that the whole life of the people was determined by economics, by material existence."[2] Thus, just as the Communists view the world through Marxian-colored spectacles, so too the Nazis viewed the world through their politically distorted lenses. As a result, the Nazis often transposed economic problems into political ones.

In the labor field, the initial actions of the new Nazi government in 1933 reflected the primacy of political goals over all others. In the spring of that year the Nazi government eliminated the political power of German labor. The trade unions, backbone of the Social Democratic party, were immediately abolished. The newspapers, funds, and property of the unions were incorporated into the monolithic Nazi-controlled *Deutsche Arbeitsfront* (DAF). The political parties representing labor were ruthlessly crushed. German labor, stripped of political and economic bargaining power, lay ready for molding by the Nazi party.[3]

The immediate labor problem was unemployment. The Nazi methods of reducing unemployment were neither unique nor unusual. Accompanied by a loud propaganda campaign, massive public work projects, like the *Reichsautobahn*, were started to stimulate the general level of business. All levels of government in Germany were encouraged to begin con-

[2] As quoted in Franz Neumann's *Behemoth* (New York: Oxford University Press, 1942), p. 232. In discussing this Nazi aversion to formal theoretical economics, Neumann uses the apt expression that the Nazis had "an economy without economics."

[3] For an account of the destruction of the German trade union movement, see Hans-Gerd Schumann's *Nationalsozialismus und Gewerkschaftsbewegung: Die Vernichtung der deutschen Gewerkschaften und der Aufbau der Deutschen Arbeitsfront* (Hanover and Frankfurt a/M: Norddeutsche Verlagsanstalt O. Goedel, 1958).

struction projects. The Nazi party set a good example by ordering construction of new party offices and public buildings. This aspect of the Nazi recovery policy has been widely discussed by various economists and publicists.[4] It is sufficient here to note two things. First, the amount of deficit spending in Germany was never as great as imagined by outside observers. Germany's budget was substantially in balance until 1938, when armament expenditures were increased.[5] Second, the political advantages derived by the Nazis from the public work projects were just as important as the economic ones.

The Nazis also tried to reduce unemployment by pressuring individual employers in regard to their uses of manpower and machinery. Employers were encouraged to hire as much labor as possible. At the same time there is some evidence that the Nazis sought to curb the introduction of labor-saving machinery in German industry.[6] It might seem that these

[4] See Kenyon E. Poole, *German Financial Policies, 1932-1939* (Cambridge: Harvard University Press, 1939); Gustav Stolper, *German Economy, 1870-1940* (New York: Reynal, 1940); Otto Nathan and Milton Fried, *The Nazi Economic System* (Durham: Duke University Press, 1944); Claude W. Guillebaud, *The Economic Recovery of Germany from 1933 to 1938* (Toronto: Macmillan & Co., 1939); Karl Dietrich Bracher, Wolfgang Sauer, Gerhard Schulz, *Die nationalsozialistische Machtergreifung*, Schriften des Instituts fuer Politische Wissenschaft, Vol. 14 (Cologne: Westdeutscher Verlag, 1960); and General Georg Thomas, *Grundlagen fuer eine Geschichte der deutschen Wehr- und Ruestungswirtschaft*, manuscript in the USSBS files and also on T-77, Roll 635, Frame 1828397 ff. [henceforth cited as *Studie der Wehrwirtschaft*].

[5] See Burton H. Klein, *Germany's Economic Preparations for War* (Cambridge: Harvard University Press, 1959), p. 8. Klein used many captured German documents to prove that the Nazi fiscal policies were ultra-conservative until the dismissal of Schacht.

[6] Herbert Block, "German Methods of Allocating Labor," *Research Project on Social and Economic Controls in Germany and Russia*, No. 2, Graduate Faculty of Political and Social Sciences organized under the New School for Social Research, 1942, pp. 2-5. (Mimeographed copy deposited with the U.S. Commerce Department Library, Washington, D.C.)

6

measures would be opposed by the average manufacturer, yet most manufacturers accepted them in context with the total recovery program of the Nazi government. The program included a number of things that the manufacturers wanted: destruction of the trade unions, stabilization of the mark at a high value, price and wage controls, and market division policies.[7] Thus, in a sense, Nazi policy encouraged inefficient production in order to promote employment. During the war, part of the difficulty of the Reich government in the rationalization of industry could be traced to these earlier policies and, of course, to the monopolistic organization of German business.[8]

Besides encouraging the creation of new jobs, the Nazi government took drastic measures to control the flow of labor into the market. Through the National Labor Service (*Reichsarbeitsdienst*), young workers were kept out of the market.[9]

[7] Klein, in *Germany's Economic Preparations*, pp. 7-16, thinks that the fear of inflation was an important factor in explaining the rather unusual economic measures that the Nazis took in the depression. Although the Nazis enjoyed the support of many industrialists, they still were anti-capital in their outlook. As the war progressed, they became even more hostile. The opposite view is presented by Juergen Kuczynski in *Die Geschichte der Lage der Arbeiter unter dem Kapitalismus; Studien zur Geschichte des staatsmonopolistischen Kapitalismus in Deutschland 1918 bis 1945*, Vol. 16 (Berlin: Akademie-Verlag, 1963), pp. 187-188. He insists that the big industrial combines gradually infiltrated the whole Reich economy and by the war years effectively controlled Nazi economic policy. Arthur Schweitzer, in *Big Business in the Third Reich* (Bloomington: Indiana University Press, 1964), pp. 552-555, presents the thesis that a bilateral structure of power between the Nazis and big business existed during the first stage of Nazi power. Only after 1937 did the Nazis achieve preeminence in the economy and establish full fascism.

[8] There is no adequate study of how the organization of German business handicapped rationalization, although numerous writers hint at it.

[9] The National Labor Service, previously on a voluntary basis, was made compulsory in June 1935. All men between the ages of eighteen and twenty-five were to serve for a period of six months.

Further, the reduction of working hours was encouraged and the retirement of eligible overaged workers was mandatory. To check the flow of rural labor into the cities, an order was passed which empowered labor authorities to ask non-agricultural employers to dismiss any workers who had been in agricultural employment within the past three years. In 1934, all laborers were frozen in their jobs, and the Reich labor offices were given exclusive authority to allocate labor within their areas.[10] This latter action had serious repercussions during the war; labor offices resisted continually the free flow of labor in and out of their jurisdictions.[11]

Of all the early Nazi labor actions, none had as serious aftereffects as the campaign to remove women from all gainful employment. Soon after the Nazis assumed power, they launched an intensive propaganda campaign to release women from industry. The virtues of motherhood were extolled. Women were constantly being told that their proper role was in the home. Monetary incentives like the marriage loans were enacted.[12] Generous allowances were later granted

---

The conscripted men worked at a variety of jobs, ranging from agriculture to reclamation projects, road building, and construction work on military projects. In later years, the Labor Service became almost an integral part of military training.

[10] *Reichsgesetzblatt*, 1934, Part I, p. 381 and p. 202. In spite of the decrees restricting workers to agriculture, nearly 400,000 migrated into industry from 1933 to 1939, states Klein in *Germany's Economic Preparations*, p. 73. See also Eduard Willeke's article on the migration of labor, "Der Arbeitseinsatz im Kriege," in *Jahrbuecher fuer Nationaloekonomie und Statistik*, Vol. 154 (1941), pp. 177-201.

[11] After the war, Albert Speer reported that the autonomous attitudes of the labor offices cost him a 10 per cent reduction of his labor force because he could not transfer labor from one labor office's district to another. See Interview No. 11 of Albert Speer, May 18, 1945, in the unpublished files of the USSBS, National Archives, Washington, D.C.

[12] Marriage loans were granted to politically reliable couples, provided that the bride had been employed and, upon marriage, would

to soldiers' wives; as a result, many women refused to work. Klein noted that these measures were only too successful in inculcating the idea that women should remain in the home, "for their effects persisted into the period when labor became scarce."[13]

Naturally, the campaign to remove women from industry cannot be explained exclusively in economic terms. The Nazi philosophy, imbued with the concept of racial supremacy, dictated that every effort should be made to increase the population. The German birth rate had been steadily declining since the 1870's, as it had in all of western Europe, and the Nazis wanted to arrest this decline. They were extremely successful not only in arresting the decline, but also in rapidly increasing the birth rate by the end of the 1930's. During the war, at the precise moment when they desperately needed adult labor, Germany experienced the converging of two birth-rate trends. On one hand, the size of the military age classes was smaller than usual—reflecting the sharp notch caused by the First World War's mobilization and deaths—and, on the other hand, German women had more children than ever before.[14] Even if many German women

give up working. In connection with the high birth-rate policies of the Nazis, one-fourth of the marriage loan was cancelled at the birth of each child.

[13] Klein, *Germany's Economic Preparations*, p. 60. Juergen Kuczynski, in *Die Geschichte der Lage der Arbeiter unter dem Kapitalismus; Studien zur Geschichte der Lage der Arbeiterin in Deutschland von 1700 bis zur Gegenwart*, Vol. 18 (Berlin: Akademie-Verlag, 1963), pp. 253-256, claims that in spite of the pious pleadings about the virtues of womanhood, the Nazis were, in fact, deliberately pursuing a policy of lowering the status of women in society. Kuczynski cites as an example the ruthless removal of German working women from the economy in 1933-1934.

[14] Dudley Kirk, "Population Trends in Postwar Europe," *Annals of the American Academy of Political and Social Science*, CCXXXVII, January 1945, pp. 45-56; and USSBS, *The Effects of Strategic Bombing on the German Economy*, Overall Economic Effects Division, October 31, 1945, p. 35.

wanted to enter war work (an assumption by no means proven), it was often impossible for them to do so because of the proportionally large number of young children in Germany.

The social policy of the Nazis regarding German women and their role in society had a direct bearing on the Nazi decision to mobilize foreign labor during the war. Rather than attempting to intensify the mobilization of native, especially female, labor, the Nazis followed a seemingly easier course; they recruited millions of foreigners.

All of these Nazis measures—the stimulation of business through spending, the pressure on employers, and the control of labor—sharply reduced unemployment and quickly encouraged a higher level of business activity. By 1936, unemployment shrank to nearly a predepression level and industrial production had topped the 1928 mark. In fact, the Nazi measures were so successful that a shortage of labor developed in some industries—notably, the metal industries —as early as 1935. A year later, the Nazis were busy reversing their programs, beginning with those dealing with the early retirement of workers.

Another indication of the growing shortage of labor by 1935 was the severe restrictions placed on the control of labor, especially skilled labor. In February of 1935, the work book (*Arbeitsbuch*) law required every wage earner to register with his local labor office.[15] Through the work books, it was possible for the government to have absolute control over the mobility of the workers. The work books also made

[15] The work book contained general information on the worker, plus specific technical information such as vocational training, jobs held, wage and rating, and disciplinary measures taken against the worker. The worker had to present his work book to his employer when he accepted employment. Another copy was held by the local labor office. Later regulations allowed the employer to keep a worker's work book for the duration of any contract, thus insuring that any worker who broke a contract could not find another job.

available a variety of data concerning the workers, thus facilitating better overall planning and allocation of labor by the national government. By January 1936, presentation of a work book was a prerequisite for employment in a large number of jobs, ranging from free domestic services to heavy industries.[16] In addition to the work book law, specific regulations were passed making it impossible for the skilled worker to leave the Reich.[17]

With the introduction of the Four Year Plan under Hermann Goering in November of 1936, the last shreds of the Nazi depression policy were abandoned. Women who had received marriage loans were no longer barred from taking work.[18] The tight restrictions placed on foreign labor were relaxed. Instead of being curbed, the basic work week was expanded. The much-vaunted 40-hour work week of the Nazi party was ignored, although the 48-hour work week was not officially recognized until August of 1938. Everywhere, the emphasis was on higher productivity by the individual worker and, simultaneously, the stabilization of the wage level.[19]

The urgent needs of rearmament and the possibility of a general European war removed the remaining few aspects of freedom for the German worker. In June 1938, the Compulsory Labor Decree (*Dienstverpflichtverordnung*, as amended in February 1939) was passed. By this decree, any inhabitant of the Reich had to accept work assigned to him any place in the Reich or undergo any kind of vocational training the labor office requested. His conscription was either

[16] In 1939, every German wage earner had to have a work book. In 1943, the "privilege" of the work book was extended to foreign workers in the Reich.

[17] Block, "German Methods of Allocating Labor," p. 6.

[18] *Reichsgesetzblatt*, 1939, Part I, p. 400.

[19] Neumann, *Behemoth*, p. 340; and Gerhard Bry, *Wages in Germany, 1871-1945* (Princeton: Princeton University Press, 1960), pp. 260-263.

11

for a limited period, during which the worker was on leave from his former job, or for an unlimited one. If it was for an unspecified length of time, all previous labor contracts were automatically abrogated. In addition, by terms of the Emergency Service Decree (*Notdienstverordnung*) of October 1938, the police authorities had the right to conscript any person for a short duration to meet emergencies—i.e., fires, civil defense—and, in the event of war, to clear away air-raid damage.[20]

Another series of labor decrees was aimed at German youth who had not already entered the labor market. The Reich Labor Service was made compulsory for all men between eighteen and twenty-five. This labor service usually preceded the term of military training. The labor service for women remained voluntary until September 1939, when it was made compulsory. All unmarried women between the ages of seventeen and twenty-five were required to spend six months in labor service. In August 1941, the labor service for women was extended for six additional months. Originally, the work for women was chiefly in agriculture or domestic service; however, later amendments allowed work in munition factories or so-called War Auxiliary Services to count as labor service.[21]

Probably one of the most interesting decrees for German youth was designed to help alleviate the shortage of skilled workers. Goering's Fifth Directive, which initiated the Four Year Plan, compelled industrial concerns to train workers in various skills.[22] The number to be trained by the individual firms was set by the local labor office. Those companies unable or unwilling to train workers were fined 50 RM per

[20] *Reichsgesetzblatt*, 1939, Part I, pp. 206, 403, and 1330.
[21] Willeke, "Der Arbeitseinsatz im Kriege," p. 199.
[22] See "Anordnung zur Durchfuehrung des Vierjahresplans ueber die Sicherstellung des Bedarfs an Metallarbeitern fuer staats und wirtschaftspolitisch bedeutsame Auftraege der Eisen- und Metallindustrie," in *Reichsarbeitsblatt*, 1937, Part I, p. 247.

12

month per apprentice. By the end of the fiscal year 1938, approximately 156,000 apprentices were being trained in this program. This figure represented one-third of the total number of all young men leaving school that year. Goering's control over labor allocation to individual plants was so detailed that one of the Four Year Plan Directives prohibited plants in the metal industries from increasing their total staff by more than ten metal workers every three months without written permission of the local labor office.[23] On February 11, 1937, this directive was extended to all plants in the metal industries and covered all skilled and unskilled metal workers, foremen, technicians, and supervisors.[24]

It is readily apparent that Germany had a far more comprehensive system of labor control than any other country in Europe, with the possible exception of the Soviet Union. This thorough system was one of the major reasons that Germany could effectively absorb millions of foreign workers during the war with so few disruptive effects. However, it would be incorrect to conclude that Germany had achieved a high degree of manpower mobilization because she had eliminated unemployment and had developed a comprehensive system of labor control. In fact, the actual extent of mobilization of German manpower was very different from that planned by the Nazis.

GERMAN PLANS AND THE OUTBREAK OF WAR

The German foreign labor program during World War II was an emergency solution to the manpower shortage. A thorough search of documents after the war uncovered no masterplan for a comprehensive foreign labor program. The labor officials had no plans for the utilization of foreign labor comparable to the German Army leaders' plans to secure

[23] *Reichsanzeiger*, November 9, 1936, as quoted in Block, "German Methods of Allocating Labor," pp. 8-10.
[24] Block, "German Methods of Allocating Labor," pp. 6-9.

strategic raw materials from occupied areas.[25] However, in spite of the lack of plans, the German leaders were aware of the possibilities of using foreign labor, especially in light of their World War I experiences. The meager preparations for the use of foreign labor indicated that the labor officials were relying on Hitler's general strategy of a short war.

Hitler did not envision a long war in which additional labor would be needed; he preferred the blitzkrieg concept. *Der Fuehrer* had counted on his modest but rapid rearmament program to give him quick, cheap victories and, thereby, a decisive advantage over the Western democracies.[26]

The decision of Hitler to conquer Europe with a minimum of expenditures was not a hasty one. Many of Hitler's advisers, such as General Georg Thomas, felt that Germany's armament program had to be one of depth instead of just breadth. Thomas argued for a program that would increase the capability of German industry and protect it through an extensive stockpile of critical materials.[27] The Four Year Plan had reflected this viewpoint, but Hitler was impatient with his economic planners. In 1939, he thought the time propitious to strike; Poland was isolated. It was hoped that England and France would back down as they had at Munich. The directive for the attack against Poland confirmed this, for it stated: "Our policy aims at confining the war to Poland, and this is considered possible in view of the internal

[25] Economic mobile units were organized in the German Army under General Georg Thomas' office (*Wirtschafts- und Ruestungsamt, OKW*). These units were to move into occupied areas, inventory, and secure critical raw materials.

[26] Klein, *Germany's Economic Preparations*, pp. 25-27, 173-175; and USSBS, *The Effects of Strategic Bombing*, pp. 15-18.

[27] Cf. Thomas, *Studie der Wehrwirtschaft*. Klein, *Germany's Economic Preparations*, pp. 56-59, estimated that Germany had only from a three to six months' supply of oil stocks when the war started. Stocks of ferro-alloys were only slightly better.

14

crisis in France and British restraint as a result of this."[28]
As events proved, Hitler had become hypnotized by his own
analysis, for England and France went to war. This was not
the first nor the last time that Hitler fell victim to his own
theories, but even this development did not fundamentally
alter his strategy. He was confident of Germany's ability to
win a quick victory.

There were two other possible reasons that may have affected Hitler's decision to gamble on rapid rearmament to
achieve quick victory. First, Germany would be spared the
disruptive effects that large-scale war preparations would
have on the Reich's ability to reenter international markets
after the conclusion of the war. Second, Germany would re-
tain its comparatively high living standard—an important
consideration for a man who had preached for twenty years
that Germany had lost World War I through a collapse of
the home front.[29]

To understand the foreign labor program, it is essential to
remember Hitler's war strategy and the possible explanations
for it. The first known time that Hitler mentioned the utilization of vast numbers of foreign workers was at a meeting on
May 23, 1939. Hermann Goering, Erich Raeder, and Wilhelm Keitel, representatives of the German armed services,
were present. According to the minutes of the meeting, Hitler
stated that he intended to attack Poland at the first suitable
opportunity. He further stated:

. . . If fate brings us into contact with the West, the
possession of extensive areas in the East will be advan-
tageous. We shall be able to rely upon record harvests,
even more in time of war than in peace.

[28] *Nazi Conspiracy and Aggression*, 10 vols. (Nuremberg, 1947-
1949), VI, 935 [henceforth cited as *NCA*].
[29] Arthur Schweitzer, "Business Power Under the Nazi Regime,"
Zeitschrift fuer Nationaloekonomie, October 1960, pp. 422-432.

The population of non-German areas will perform no military services, and will be available as a source of labor.[30]

Hitler's meaning was not lost on Goering. Among the multiplicity of posts that he held, Goering was Chief of the Four Year Plan. In this position, he had jurisdiction over the labor allocation to all of Germany's war industries. By 1939, Goering had, in fact, usurped most of the power of the Reich Ministry of Labor.[31] Goering had already begun to plan for the heavier labor requirements of a war economy. On January 28, 1939, he sent a series of directives to the Supreme Command of the Armed Forces, the OKW (*Oberkommando der Wehrmacht*). In the event of war, the directives envisioned the employment of prisoners of war in large groups. The prisoners of war would live in large compounds of 10,000 or more and would be sent to their work daily. From the terms of the directives, it was obvious that Goering had no conception of using prisoners of war on an individual basis in industrial plants.[32]

However, a more immediate labor situation in early 1939 was the shortage of agricultural workers. Labor officials counted on 90,000 Polish workers in the spring. When the political crisis between Germany and Poland deepened, the workers failed to appear. Quickly the Labor Ministry sent recruiters into eastern Europe and Italy in search of additional labor.[33] About 30,000 Italians and 85,000 Bohemians

[30] *NCA*, III, 798-799.
[31] Under the administration of the Four Year Plan, Goering established an Office for the Allocation of Labor. Dr. Friedrich Syrup, former President of the Reich Labor Office, was appointed head of this office. Syrup was to coordinate the efforts of all German administration offices connected with labor, including the Labor Ministry.
[32] *Trials of the Major War Criminals Before the International Military Tribunal*, 42 vols. (Nuremberg, 1947-1949), XXXVI, 545-549 [henceforth cited as *IMT*].
[33] Willeke, "Der Arbeitseinsatz im Kriege," p. 196; and *Sammlung*

16

and Moravians were recruited.[34] Normally this recruitment drive would have been sufficient for Germany's needs, but Germany went to war.

A detailed breakdown of total employment in Germany as of May 31, 1939, indicated that foreigners, including seasonal workers, contributed less than 1 per cent of the total labor force. (See Table I.)

INITIAL LABOR MOBILIZATION

The mobilization of the labor force of any nation for a war economy is a threefold process. First, the total size of the labor force can be increased by eliminating unemployment and by drawing into the economy persons not previously working, i.e., young workers, women, retired workers. Second, workers can be shifted from non-essential industries to essential war industries. This is usually done by transferring workers from the consumer and service industries to the armed forces, the basic raw material industries, and the war industries. Third, labor in all industries can be made more productive by the rationalization of working procedures, the introduction of new machines and methods, the creation of incentive programs, or simply by increasing the hours of work per worker. In summary, then, labor mobilization implies an increase in the relative size, distribution, and effectiveness of the manpower in a given economy. Normally, these three processes of mobilization are carried on simultaneously.

Immediately before the war, many German leaders propagandized the need for a thorough mobilization of men and materials. At the time of the Czech crisis, Goering told an

---

der Bestimmungen ueber den Einsatz auslaendischer Arbeiter in Deutschland (Berlin: Verlag der Deutsche Arbeitsfront, 1941), p. 4.

[34] P. Waelbroeck and J. Bessling, "Some Aspects of German Social Policy," *International Labour Review*, XLIII, 135.

TABLE I

DISTRIBUTION OF LABOR IN GERMANY ON MAY 31, 1939

(in thousands)

Economic Division	Germans		Foreigners[a]	Per cent[b]
1. Agriculture, forestry, fishing	11,103		120	1.1
2. Industry and transport	18,482		155	0.8
a. Industry		10,836	110	1.0
b. Handwork		5,307	29	0.5
c. Transport		2,109	16	0.7
d. Power		231	1	0.4
3. Trade, banking, insurance	4,595		8	0.2
4. Administration and services	2,670		7	0.3
5. Armed forces administration	689		2	0.3
6. Domestic service	1,575		7	0.4
Total[c]	39,114		301	0.8

[a] Including Jews of all nationalities.
[b] Foreigners as a percentage of total labor force.
[c] Figures rounded off.
SOURCES: *Kriegswirtschaftliche Kraeftebilanz* for 1944, from the *Statistisches Reichsamt* (Abteilung VI), as adjusted by the USSBS. A copy of the original document can be seen on Roll 2074 in the files of the USSBS, National Archives, Washington, D.C.

audience at the Air Ministry that he was "going to make barbaric use of his plenipotentiary power which was given to him by *Der Fuehrer*."[35] All the wishes and plans of the state, party, and other agencies which were not in line with total mobilization were going to be rejected. When the war started, Goering and Walter Funk again stated that Germany was going to have a rigorous war economy. They promised the sharpest limitation of consumption and civilian

[35] *NCA*, III, 902-903.

income.[36] In the meantime, Hitler came to the political conclusion that the previously planned large-scale mobilization
of the economy was unnecessary. On September 2, 1939,
Hitler ordered that the mobilization would only be partially
executed. In discussing this action of Hitler, General Thomas
wrote:

> The Supreme Commander was of the opinion that a
> war with Poland did not necessitate a general mobiliza-
> tion, and any other form of mobilization was out of the
> question for political reasons. . . . This was especially
> applicable as far as the economy was concerned. . . . The
> preparations, covering many years of work, for the mobi-
> lization of the economy were consequently, for the most
> part, useless.[37]

The quick conquest of Poland changed the atmosphere in
Germany. The Goebbels' propaganda office claimed that
Nazi planning had avoided the usual impact of war on the
economy. The General Plenipotentiary for the Economy,
Funk, confirmed this opinion in a speech on October 14. He
said that the prewar mobilization plans would not have to be
implemented because the war had not disrupted the German
economy to the degree anticipated.[38] The slogan "Business
as usual" was adopted and encouraged. Germany was going
to have, in the words of Burton Klein, a "peacelike war economy."[39] The question remained how this was to be
accomplished.

However, even partial German mobilization had a tremendous effect on the labor economy. From May 1939 to
May 1940, 4.4 million workers were drafted out of the economy into the armed forces. Thus, the total German civilian

---

[36] Rolf Wagenfuehr, *Rise and Fall of the German War Economy,
1939-1945*, manuscript in the files of the USSBS, p. 8.
[37] Klein, *Germany's Economic Preparations*, p. 186.
[38] Wagenfuehr, *Rise and Fall of the German Economy*, p. 9.
[39] See Chapter VIII in Klein's *Germany's Economic Preparations*.

19

labor force dropped from 38.8 million to 34.4 million.[40] Divisions of the labor economy that required heavy manual labor, such as agriculture and industry, lost the largest number of men.

The first method of meeting the deficit in agriculture and industry was through the internal transfer of workers. Workers could have been shifted from non-essential to war-essential industries. However, one difficulty with this method was that Germany was already at full employment. The non-essential industries realized that there were no replacements for their workers once they had been transferred. Another difficulty in the transfer of workers lay in the Army draft policies. Unlike most other countries, the German military services called up military manpower themselves, often without much consultation with outside organizations until February 1942. Consequently, it was very difficult for industries to protect their skilled workers. Immediately, the draft requirements created labor shortages in critical occupational fields, such as motor repairs and electrical work.[41] The industries covered these shortages by internal redistribution, but the system was far from satisfactory.

Besides the lack of coordination between the military and civilian agencies, there was another difficulty in the transference of labor. The labor and production policies of the civilian agencies themselves were poorly coordinated. It was not until Speer became Reich Minister of Munitions in 1942 that production programs could control labor allocation. Even then the system failed to function smoothly.[42] The highly

[40] See OKW/Wi Rue Amt/Rue IV (a), report dated January 1943, titled *Erfahrungsbericht ueber die Entwicklung auf dem Gebiet der Personalbewirtschaftung in der Zeit vom Winterbeginn 1941/ 1942 bis zum Winterbeginn 1942/1943*, on T-77, Roll 440, Frames 1600355-405.

[41] Thomas, *Studie der Wehrwirtschaft*, pp. 173-174.

[42] Although Funk had been given control over raw materials, labor allocation, and production programs in the event of war, he quickly

organized totalitarian state found coordination as difficult to achieve as did the democratic states.

Many hoped that the natural rhythm of mobilization would also facilitate the distribution of labor. The original mobilization plans had called for an industrial and personnel evacuation from the Polish and French borders in two stages; this would have released some labor. The swiftness of the Polish campaign precluded an evacuation in the East, and apparently little was done in the West.[43] Very little labor was released in this manner.

Another hope was that the immediate curtailment of raw materials would sharply contract employment in non-war pursuits, such as trade, private construction, and non-war manufacturing. The shortage of some raw materials resulted in a slight increase of 220,000 workers flowing into the critical metal manufacturing and mining industries; but it was not nearly what had been expected. The construction industry was particularly disappointing. The World War I experience in construction offered an instructive parallel. During the First World War, construction was restricted immediately and nearly one-half of the workers engaged in construction were released to other fields.[44] In the Second World War, construction was curtailed gradually. Only in 1942 was Speer able to persuade Hitler to stop unnecessary public construction, especially projects dear to the party.[45]

The second general method of meeting the deficit in agriculture and industry was to draft women. Although General Thomas and others continually advised this, their sugges-

---

was deprived of these powers. Speer attempted to reorganize the economy in 1942 along the lines that had been planned for Funk, but he was never completely able to bring labor allocation under his control.

[43] Thomas, *Studie der Wehrwirtschaft*, pp. 174-179.
[44] *Ibid.*, pp. 175-177.
[45] Klein, *Germany's Economic Preparations*, p. 105.

tions were rejected by the Nazi hierarchy. The drafting of women and other total war measures were, in the words of Reich Minister Funk, "unbearable to the party for psychological reasons during the years 1939 to 1942."[46] The voluntary program for women workers was a bitter disappointment. By the end of March 1940, there were about 500,000 fewer women employed than in September 1939.[47] The total number of employed women dropped slowly until 1943, when a new compulsory law was applied. The reason for this sharp drop in women workers at the beginning of the war was obvious. Franz Seldte, Reich Minister of Labor, wrote a letter to Hans Lammers on March 21, 1940, explaining the situation, in which he said, "The new regulations covering family support issued in the fall of 1939 not only tended to keep women who received support from taking up work, but has also resulted in the fact that numerous women, who have been granted support through war marriages, have given up the work which they formerly carried out."[48] Postwar investigations bear out Seldte's contention that the immediate effect of family allowances was to drive the marginal woman worker out of employment.

The general war plans of the Nazis, the partial mobilization of the economy, the Nazis' unwillingness to demand a heavier sacrifice from their own people, the lack of coordination and organization of the party and government, and the Nazi reluctance to draft women all pointed to one solution. The immediate manpower shortage had to be solved with foreign labor. In September of 1939, with a slashing three-week onslaught, the *Wehrmacht* delivered such a pool of labor.

[46] Thomas, *Studie der Wehrwirtschaft*, p. 190.
[47] *Ibid.*, pp. 331-332.
[48] *Trials of War Criminals Before the Nuremberg Military Tribunals Under Control Council Law No. 10*, 15 vols. (Washington, D.C., 1951-1953), XIII, 956-957 [henceforth cited as *Minor Trials*].

THE QUICK UTILIZATION OF POLISH LABOR

The timing, the speed, and the success of the attack on Poland probably contributed as much to the inception of the foreign labor program as anything else. The attack came in September, the height of the harvest in Germany. Anxiety over the harvest was expressed in many quarters; the shortage of labor in agriculture seemed critical. At the same time, the military campaign in Poland succeeded beyond all expectations. The first week's operation was decisive, although Warsaw did not surrender until September 27, 1939. The entire Polish Army, numbering nearly a million, fell captive to the *Wehrmacht*. A vast labor pool of both war prisoners and civilians was ready for exploitation. The Germans were not slow in using it.

Three days after the German Army crossed the Polish frontier, labor offices were in operation in the Polish towns of Rybnik and Dirshau. By September 15, nearly thirty labor offices were recruiting Poles for work in Germany. Close cooperation between the OKW and the labor offices resulted in delivering 110,000 Polish civilian workers to the Reich by the end of October 1939.[49] In addition, nearly 300,000 Polish prisoners of war were used in the harvest of the 1939-1940 crop.

Circulars which provided for the employment of Polish prisoners of war had been issued by the Reich Minister of Labor on the 26th of September, and by the Food Ministry on the 4th and 5th of October. These circulars stipulated that the Polish prisoners of war were to be used in agriculture first. Later, some of them were to be used in mining (principally lignite, ore, and potash mining), railroad maintenance, cable-laying, and road construction. They were to be employed in groups of fifty or more under the control of the Army. The employers of the prisoners of war were to pay

[49] Willeke, "Der Arbeitseinsatz im Kriege," p. 201.

army camp authorities 60 per cent of the normal German wages for time-work and 80 per cent for piece-work minus deductions for room and board. The labor and food offices were to arrange the details of employment.[50]

The German effort to secure Polish labor was so successful that by May 31, 1940, the total number of foreigners at work in the Reich had increased 847,000 over the previous year. The vast majority of them were Polish. As Table II shows, most of the increase flowed into agriculture and industry.

TABLE II

DISTRIBUTION OF CIVILIAN LABOR IN THE REICH ON MAY 31, 1940
(in thousands)

Economic Divisions	Germans	Foreigners[a]	Per cent[b]
1. Agriculture, forestry, fishing	10,006	681	6.4
2. Industry and transport	15,857	402	2.5
a. Industry	9,551	256	2.6
b. Handwork	4,122	108	2.6
c. Transport	1,982	35	1.8
d. Power	202	2	1.0
3. Trade, banking, insurance	3,719	20	0.5
4. Administration and services	2,605	21	0.8
5. Armed forces administration	710	11	1.5
6. Domestic service	1,511	15	1.4
Total[c]	34,409	1,148	3.2

[a] Including Jews of all nationalities and prisoners of war.
[b] Foreigners as a percentage of total labor force.
[c] Figures rounded off.
SOURCE: *Kriegswirtschaftliche Kraeftebilanz*, as adjusted by the USSBS.

[50] Quoted from *Landswirtschaftliches Ministerialblatt*, 1939, Nos. 39 and 41, in *International Labour Review*, XLI, 396.

Of the 1.1 million foreigners, about 344,000 were prisoners of war. Of the 800,000 civilian workers, approximately 19 per cent were women.[51] Since German labor statistics did not identify workers by nationality, it is difficult to determine how many of these workers were Polish. However, personal accounts permit an approximation. Hans Frank, Governor General of Occupied Poland, noted on March 7, 1940, that 130,000 Polish civilian workers and 480,000 Polish prisoners of war were already at work in the Reich. A later entry in his diary mentioned that 210,000 civilian workers were in the Reich by May of 1940.[52] Considering the fact that Frank was ruling only a small part of what was prewar Poland, it is reasonable to estimate that perhaps from 700,000 to 800,000 Poles were already working in the Reich by May 31, 1940. Thus, with this increase of foreign labor from 1 per cent to 3 per cent of the Reich's labor force, the first significant step in mobilization of foreign labor had been taken.

[51] See OKW/Wi Rue Amt/Rue (Z St/IV f), report on the manpower situation as of May 31, 1941, on T-77, Roll 216, Frame 952917.
[52] *NCA*, IV, 886 and 889.

CHAPTER II

Poland: Laboratory for the Foreign Labor Program

THE conquest of Poland in 1939 opened new vistas for Nazi social and economic planners. For some planners, Poland was the beginning of the new German drive to the East and a solution to the *Lebensraum* problem. For other planners, Poland was a vast reservoir of labor and materials that could be harnessed for the immediate war needs of Germany. To others, the defeat of Poland vindicated the racial theory of Nazism. The Poles—an inferior race—had succumbed to the Germans—a superior race; therefore, according to the Nazi extension of Social Darwinism, the superior race had every right to exploit the inferior race to secure its goals. At times, German policy in Poland reflected one or more of these viewpoints simultaneously.

As early as October 1939, Hitler himself sketched out future German plans for Poland. He told General Keitel that under no circumstance would Poland be made into a model state under German rule. Poland was to be a connecting link to the eastern areas that Germany would one day have. The Polish people were to be reduced to a low standard of living, and they were to be used for labor. Poland was to be an *Arbeitsreich* for the *Herrenvolk*.[1]

German administrative plans called for a division of Poland. Since the Soviet Union received the eastern half of Poland under the terms of the 1939 Pact, Germany had to be contented with an immediate division of the western section of Poland. All the Polish land that had been Prussian before 1914 and a large strip of territory beyond the old frontier were incorporated into the Reich. This was done by extend-

[1] *IMT*, xxvi, 378.

ing the *Gau* of West Prussia slightly and creating a new *Gau*, *Wartheland* or *Warthegau*. The rest of the German share of Poland was organized into the "General-Government," an area not incorporated into Germany but regarded as a part of Greater Germany. The General-Government and the Protectorate of Bohemia-Moravia were alike in this respect. Coincidentally, in both the Protectorate and the General-Government, the name of Frank was prominent. Dr. Hans Frank was appointed Governor General in Poland and Karl Hermann Frank was Secretary of State in the Protectorate. There the similarity ended, for German policy in the Protectorate was vastly different from that in the General-Government.

In the Reich-incorporated areas of Poland, the Germans began a systematic program of evacuating the Poles and re-settling Germans and *Volksdeutsche* (Germans living outside the Reich) in their place. Prior to 1941, Germany had secured the repatriation of 600,000 Germans through treaties. About 400,000 came from the Soviet sphere of influence, 100,000 from the Italian sphere, and 100,000 from various other countries in southern Europe.[2] The Germans living in the General-Government area of Poland were also repatriated to create an ethnic division between the Poles and the Germans. Most of these repatriated Germans were scheduled to settle in the newly incorporated areas taken from Poland.[3] It was hoped that the newly acquired lands

[2] Eugene Michel Kulischer, *The Displacement of Population in Europe* (Montreal: International Labour Office, 1943), p. 11.

[3] René Kraus in *Europe in Revolt* (London: Macmillan & Co., 1942), p. 66, quotes *Gauleiter* Arthur Greiser of Warthegau when he received his fellow German colonizers on October 10, 1939. Greiser said, "In ten years there will not be a single non-German farmer left. All our living space in this province that has come home to the Reich belongs to German newcomers from the Baltic, Russia, South Tyrol and Rumania." Hans-Juergen Seraphim, in his article "Voelkliche Wirtschaftsgestaltung and nationalstaatliche Wirtschafts-politik im deutschen Osten," *Jahrbuecher fuer Nationaloekonomie*

27

would relieve some of the pressure for more land from the
farmers of Baden, the Rhineland, Wuerttemberg, Franken,
Sudetenland, and Silesia.[4] Although the ultimate aim of the
vast resettlement program was to establish German influence
and leadership over the newly acquired areas, an immediate
goal was to release Polish labor in these areas for recruitment to the Reich.[5] The coupling of the resettlement program
with the foreign labor program illustrated the dilemma of the
Germans. They were recruiting labor from outside the Reich
and at the same time sending thousands of Germans out of
the Reich to the vacated areas. At first, it seemed an advan-
tageous arrangement to the Germans, but later in the war
shifting so many people had a serious effect on the rational
utilization of manpower.

In the General-Government area of Poland, there was no
such conflict of interest. The Germans had no intention of
settling their people there. The entire emphasis was on the
exploitation of the material and human resources of the area.
Hitler gave Frank the following principles for its administration: "This territory in its entirety is booty of the German
Reich, and it thus cannot be permitted that this territory shall
be exploited in its individual parts, but that the territory in
its entirety shall be economically used, and its entire economic worth redound to the benefit of the German people."[6]

THE FOREIGN LABOR PROGRAM IN OPERATION

The first actions of the Germans in setting up the General-
Government were to repeal the Polish social legislation and

---

und Statistik, Vol. 152, p. 674, mentioned the plans to place 400,000
German families in the new German districts.

[4] The Nazis thought the farm holdings in these districts were too
small for modern economical farming. See Seraphim, "Voelkliche
Wirtschaftsgestaltung," pp. 650-676.

[5] Ibid., p. 674. For further information see Robert L. Koehl,
RKFDV: German Resettlement and Population Policy, 1939-1945
(Cambridge: Harvard University Press, 1957).

[6] NCA, iv, 906.

to abolish Polish labor organizations. Next, the Germans promulgated new laws and decrees concerning wages, hours, and other conditions of work. One of the first labor laws was announced by Frank on October 26, 1939. The laws were in the form of a decree called the *Arbeitspflicht*; it stated:

Section I. (1) Effective immediately all Polish inhabitants of the General-Government between the ages of eighteen and sixty shall be subject to compulsory public labor.

(2) A special decree will be issued with regard to Jews.

Section II. Persons who can prove permanent employment useful to the commonwealth shall not be called for the performance of public work service.

Section III. Compulsory public labor shall comprise, in particular, work in agricultural undertakings, the construction and maintenance of public buildings, the construction of roads, waterways, and railways, the regulation of rivers, and work on land improvements.[7]

The same day, special regulations for Jews introduced the concept of forced labor (*Arbeitszwang*).[8] Later, on December 14, 1939, the age limits for all Poles were extended to include the 14- to 18-year-old youths.[9] These compulsory labor decrees had the effect of mobilizing Polish labor for possible recruitment for the Reich. The actual recruitment for the Reich was initially on a voluntary basis, but decisions reached in Berlin in the winter of 1939-1940 made the use of force in recruitment a foregone conclusion.

[7] *Verordnungsblatt des Generalgouverneurs fuer die besetzten polnischen Gebiete*, No. 1, October 26, 1939, p. 6.

[8] *Dokumente der Deutschen Politik und Geschichte*, Vol. v; *Die Zeit der nationalsozialistischen Diktatur*, prepared by Johnnes Hohlfeld (Berlin: Dokumenten-Verlag, 1951), pp. 150-152.

[9] *Verordnungsblatt*, G.G.P., December 14, 1939, p. 224.

Early in January 1940, Goering notified Frank that in order to complete the Four Year Plan in the Reich, all long-term projects in the General-Government had to be rejected. Instead, Frank was to concentrate on fulfilling immediate and obtainable goals that would strengthen the war economy of Germany. One such goal was the ". . . supply and transportation of at least one million male and female agricultural and industrial workers to the Reich. . . . among them at least 750,000 agricultural workers of which at least 50 per cent must be women in order to guarantee production in the Reich and as a replacement for industrial workers in the Reich."[10]

Goering realized the difficulty of recruiting one million Polish workers voluntarily. In his opinion, coercion would probably be necessary. Furthermore, Goering thought that forced recruitment of the Poles would have the additional effects of subjugating them politically and decreasing the birth rate by separating the male and female population.[11]

Frank was understandably reluctant to apply force in recruiting a million Polish workers. Like all administrators, his first concern was the establishment of law and order. A huge forced recruitment drive would alienate the population and make the maintenance of law and order difficult for the new German government. Besides, Frank thought the volunteer labor program was a modest success. Even the Polish government in exile released information that many people in districts affected by unemployment and misery were offering to go to Germany.[12]

Berlin did not share Frank's views regarding the alienation of the Polish population or the success of the voluntary program. By the end of January 1940, the Four Year Plan

[10] NCA, IV, 926.
[11] Feliks Gross, The Polish Worker (New York: Roy Publishers, 1945), p. 225.
[12] The Black Book of Poland, prepared by the Polish Ministry of Information (New York: G. P. Putnam's Sons, 1943), p. 160.

Council ordered Frank to deliver daily from eight to ten trains containing 1,000 Polish workers each.[13] Frank's cautious voluntary program could not possibly meet this requirement. Nevertheless Frank, who was scarcely a man to oppose his superiors directly, wrote to Goering that he would do everything possible to accelerate the recruitment program.[14]

The German decision to step up the recruitment drive by coercion marked a milestone in the German occupational policies for Poland. It may be that this decision to ignore political repercussions in Poland and press for more labor was motivated by the traditional German dislike of the Poles and the Nazi racial hatred of them. However, a more plausible explanation for the German decision lay in the circumstances of Germany at the time. The proposed offensive in the West had been postponed until the spring and its outcome was in doubt. The Germans were feverishly mobilizing their Army and industries for the drive, and quick labor replacements were needed.[15] The whole situation seemed to dictate urgent, drastic measures. It did not appear important to assess the effects of the recruitment of a million Poles on future German plans and policies. The immediate problem was to secure the manpower for a quick victory.

The two leading exponents of the massive recruitment program in the Four Year Plan Council were Goering and Herbert Backe.[16] Goering, as previously noted, was interested in securing additional labor for the German industries. Backe, the German Food Controller, also needed Polish labor. On

---

[13] *Minor Trials*, viii, 328.   [14] *NCA*, iv, 885.

[15] Cf. Milton Shulman, *Defeat in the West* (New York: E. P. Dutton, 1948); and Klein, *Germany's Economic Preparations*.

[16] Backe's chief, in name only, was Walter Darré. Darré was the Nazi food leader but was removed from all responsibility through intrigues. Backe, a close friend of Goering, figured prominently in the plots against Darré. Backe committed suicide in the autumn of 1947, just before he was to face trial in the so-called "Minor Trials" of 1948-1949 against the high-ranking civil servants of Nazi Germany.

3 1

February 14, 1940, Backe explained to the Sixth Meeting of the Council for the Four Year Plan that German agriculture was in a critical situation. The winter of 1939-1940 had been a hard one. The weather had caused extensive damage, and the outbreak of the war in September had resulted in a late and incomplete cultivation of the land. It was absolutely necessary to plan on a careful spring cultivation. Backe would only vouch for the German food supply if the Council would immediately increase the delivery of seeds and fertilizers, allocate more tractors and horses and, most important of all, increase the size of the agricultural labor force.

Backe estimated that the 320,000 Polish POW's and 57,000 Polish civilian workers in the Reich would have to be strengthened with one million more Poles and 70,000 additional foreign workers for agriculture. In total, Backe requested 1,447,000 foreign workers for agriculture. The Council approved Backe's program, with the provision that he was to receive only 780,000 of the new Polish workers; the rest would go to industry.[17] With the tentative requirement of one million Polish workers, Frank pressed his recruitment drive. Immediately, he ran into difficulties.

The first group of Poles that Frank attempted to recruit were the refugees from the areas newly incorporated in the Reich. At the rate of 10,000 daily, nearly one million Poles and Jews had been removed from East and West Posen, Danzig, and Upper Silesia to the General-Government by the spring of 1940.[18] Most of these refugees could not find work in the already crowded General-Government. When the refugees approached the labor offices for unemployment compensation, they were told that they were ineligible under the new laws. The labor officials were ready, however, to secure work for them in the Reich with good pay and good living conditions. Many refugees accepted the offer, but not the vast numbers that Frank needed.

[17] *Minor Trials*, VIII, 324-329.   [18] *IMT*, XXIX, 363.

Frank knew that the majority of Polish workers for the Reich had to come from the General-Government proper. Few of the Polish workers from this area had ever worked in the Reich, even on a seasonal basis. Consequently, Frank's initial recruitment drive was difficult, but a combination of economic conditions in the General-Government was breaking down the Polish workers' resistance. The immediate dislocation of Polish industry and the lack of raw materials created extensive unemployment among the Polish workers. The food supply was deteriorating, and the shortage of food and other consumer products resulted in inflation. The real wages of the Polish workers were shrinking rapidly. The difficulties of the workers were in marked contrast to the bright picture of better wages and living conditions in the Reich portrayed by Frank's recruiters. Frank hoped that the dire economic conditions in the General-Government would supply enough incentive to recruit his one million quota.

By March 6, 1940, Dr. Max Frauendorfer,[19] the *Reichshauptamtsleiter* in the General-Government, reported that 73,000 Polish industrial workers had already been sent to the Reich. Nearly 4,000 workers were being transported daily.[20] Frauendorfer said that numerous letters from the workers in the Reich to their families at home indicated that the workers were very grateful for the treatment they were receiving in the Reich. Frank ordered that these letters be published; they might help in future recruitment.[21]

The next day, Frank called a conference to discuss the program of shipping agricultural workers to the Reich.

[19] Dr. Frauendorfer was the center of a controversy in early 1963. Wearer of the Nazi party's highest medal and former official with Himmler when the future SS leader was the chief of the Munich police, Frauendorfer was nominated by the Bavarian Christian Socialist Union party for a seat in the West German parliament. His nomination touched off a storm of protest from the Socialist party and several newspapers.

[20] *NCA*, iv, 886.   [21] *Ibid.*, 887.

Stabsleiter Reichert opened the conference with the remark that it was absolutely necessary to secure the million Poles for German agriculture. Since Backe had appointed Reichert to Frank's staff, Reichert spoke with authority. Dr. Frauendorfer then reported on the progress of the program. As of that date, only 81,477 Polish agricultural workers had been sent to the Reich. In Frauendorfer's opinion, the 154 special trains that had been dispatched to Germany since February 12 represented the utmost that could be accomplished at the moment. The addition of these 81,477 workers raised the total number of Polish civilian workers in the Reich to about 130,000—a far cry from the one million planned.

Frank suggested that the 480,000 POW's, many of whom were already working in the Reich, also be counted in the one million requirement. Reichert refused this proposal. He wanted the pace of the recruitment drive stepped up, even if it meant the use of force. Frank and his police chief, Friedrich W. Krueger, were both opposed to the introduction of compulsory service or the employment of force against the Polish agricultural worker at that time. They pointed out that the conditions of the railroads and highways made it impossible to use force in the countryside. Besides, there were not sufficient German police at their disposal to carry out such measures. Instead, Frank suggested that if any force were exercised, it should be limited to workers concentrated in urban districts, for they could be obtained with the minimum amount of effort.[22]

Although Frank could object to the widespread use of force in March of 1940, he knew that it was becoming increasingly difficult to secure Polish workers for the Reich. The Poles were beginning to evade the recruiters. Many had forged medical certificates or statements which declared that they were not fit for labor service. Others took refuge in the

[22] *Ibid.*, 886-887.

woods. Occasionally, they even fired upon the German recruiters. Even when recruited, many Poles refused to report
to the assigned railroad stations for shipment to the Reich.
Frank attributed these evasions to a "psychosis of anxiety"
among the population.[23]

In addition to all of these difficulties, Frank thought that
forced recruitment would create too much unfavorable propaganda abroad, especially in America. He wanted to avoid
the use of force if possible, but he felt that light pressure
could be exerted by stopping the payment of unemployment
relief to those who refused to work in the Reich. To apply
more force would only have the effect of further demoralizing
the Poles.[24]

Many leaders in Berlin thought that Frank was stalling;
Backe, in particular, held this view. Desperate for farm
workers, Backe even suggested that Nazi party members and
German schoolchildren would have to be drafted if Frank
did not secure Polish labor more energetically.[25] To Backe,
the arch-bureaucrat, the problem of recruiting, delousing,
vaccinating, and transporting a million unwilling Poles to
Germany could be solved by administrative fiats. Only
action was needed from Frank, the Army, and the German
railroads. Thus, according to the administrative rules of Nazi
Germany, Backe prevailed, for he was closest to the powers-
that-be and had the simplest solution. Orders were sent to
Frank that he was to use all necessary force to secure at once
Polish labor for the Reich.

In his diary notes for May 10, 1940, Frank revealed that
pressure from Berlin compelled him to allow the use of force
in labor recruitment. Up to that time, only 160,000 Poles
had been secured for work. Frank anticipated great difficulties in this new course of action. Therefore, he considered it
advisable to cooperate closely with district and town chiefs

[23] *Ibid.*, 889.   [24] *Ibid.*, 890.
[25] *Minor Trials*, VIII, 328.

and the police in executing force so that he could be sure the action would be reasonably expedient. The indiscriminate arresting of young Poles as they left church services or movies would incite too much national nervousness. Generally speaking, Frank had no objections at all to the "rubbish capable of work, yet often loitering about, being snatched from the streets."[26] But the best method would be the organization of swift systematic raids; then it would be absolutely justifiable to stop a Pole in the street, and ask what he was doing and where he was working. If his answers were not correct, he would be hauled off to work in the Reich.[27]

To help Frank speed up the recruitment drive, the Army embarked on a policy that was to be repeated throughout the war. The Army converted prisoners of war to civilian workers. On May 22, 1940, General Hermann Reinecke, who was in charge of all POW's, ordered the release of all Polish POW's capable of working. The released POW's were to report to their local police and labor offices when they returned home. The POW's already in the Reich were to be converted to civilian status by signing contracts similar to the ones signed by civilian workers. The exceptions to this directive were interesting, for they revealed part of the social policy that the Germans were preparing for the occupied areas. According to Reinecke's directive, the following Polish POW's were not to be released: those in operational areas or useful to the Army in any particular way; all officers and non-commissioned officers; members of the intelligentsia; minorities not yet transported home, such as Jews and Baltic peoples; the physically incapable of work; and prisoners who were lazy, unreliable, or undergoing punishment (the SS and Gestapo called them "asocial prisoners," a vague classification).[28]

[26] IMT, xxix, 376.   [27] Ibid., 377.
[28] See the order of the OKW, Freilassung polnischer Kriegsgefangener, dated May 22, 1940, on the conversion of POW's, on T-73, Roll 34, Frames 3164082-86.

Besides the program for the demobilization and conversion of POW's to civilian workers, the Army inaugurated another program in 1940. It aimed at utilizing POW's according to their former training and talents.[29] Throughout 1940, the Army began to reclassify and shift POW's from agriculture to industry. As Table III shows, POW's were about evenly

TABLE III

DISTRIBUTION OF WORKING POW's

(in percentages)

Occupation	January 1940	July 1940	January 1941
Agriculture	95%	65%	52%
Industry	5	35	48

SOURCE: *Reichsarbeitsblatt*, 1941, Part V, p. 257.

divided between agriculture and industry by January 1941.

The combination of the Army policy of conversion and the new policy of forced recruitment in the General-Government undoubtedly increased the number of Polish workers that were sent to the Reich. Even so, it was not until August 1942 that Frank could report that he had secured 800,000 workers.[30] This was an impressive sum, considering that the General-Government's population was only around 16,000,000. The total number of Poles from prewar Poland who worked in Germany probably ranged from 880,000 in October of 1940, to about 1,080,000 in the spring of 1942 before Fritz Sauckel came into power.[31]

The real importance of the two decisions in May 1940 to

[29] Willeke, "Der Arbeitseinsatz im Kriege," p. 330.
[30] *NCA*, IV, 912-913.
[31] *International Labour Review*, L, 470. This estimate may be low, since the ILR estimates were generally lower than the official German statistics found after the war. Unfortunately, there are no German statistics on the exact number of Poles in the Reich at this particular time.

37

start forced recruitment and conversion of POW's lies not so much in the number of Polish workers who were brought into the Reich, but rather in the effect that these decisions had later. The decisions of May 1940 marked the ascendancy of the believers in a "hard policy" over the believers in a more moderate policy. The hard policy advocates were characterized by their racial emphasis, their frankly opportunistic attitudes, and their unbelievable self-assurance in the quick and final victory of Nazi Germany. The moderates played down the racial aspects of Nazism, tried to assess the long-term effects of actions, and had much less confidence in a quick, final victory. The conflict between the advocates of these two policies kept the higher echelons of the German government divided. The resulting tension could be seen in every aspect of German policy—the foreign labor program, occupation policy, reorganization of the war economy, and final war aims.

The decision regarding POW's in May 1940 also marked another defeat of the Army at the hands of the Nazi party. By ignoring the Geneva Convention rules for prisoners of war, the Army condoned Nazi racial and political principles. There was a direct progression from the May 1940 decision to convert POW's and the infamous slaughter of POW's and political officers after the invasion of the Soviet Union.

The May decisions were the beginning of Frank's rapid decline in influence within the General-Government. Although he was given explicit promises that he would be free from outside intervention when he took the job in Poland, those promises were ignored. The May decisions were the first of a series of interferences by individuals and organizations in Frank's realm. The decisions also accelerated the decline in Frank's personal power within the Nazi party. Hitler and Goebbels became increasingly irritated with him, and finally Hitler was ready to dismiss him from his post.

Apparently to console himself, Frank turned to living scandalously like an oriental potentate.[32]

The decision to use force meant the beginning of government by compulsion and terror for the Polish people. The volunteer program was replaced by the forceful removal of Polish workers, with all of its attendant horrors. A pattern of handling occupied peoples was developed in Poland in 1940 that, when extended to vastly larger numbers of people in the East, contributed to the eventual collapse of Germany.

At the same time that orders were being sent to Frank for the use of force in labor recruitment, other decisions were being made within the Reich that increased the difficulty of recruiting more Poles. Although these decisions were made by different individuals and offices, they all shared the same viewpoint; the Poles were inferior people and had to be treated accordingly. The Poles were the first foreign people to experience the role of the *Untermensch* (literally, subhuman) in the Nazi state.

THE "UNTERMENSCH" PHILOSOPHY IN ACTION

The Poles were near the bottom of the Nazi racial scale. Below them were only the Jews and the gypsies. Nazi leaders never seemed to tire in their abuse of the Poles. Hitler had, on many occasions, called the Poles an inferior race, a race that would not work unless forced to. In Hitler's own words, the Poles ". . . are especially born for low labor. . . . There can be no question of improvement for them. It is necessary to keep the standard of life low in Poland and it must not be permitted to rise."[33] From the sheer repetition of the Nazi leaders' abuse of the Poles, an outside observer might conclude that the Nazis either had an abnormal hatred of the Poles, or were unable to convince the Germans that the Poles were inferior.

[32] Cf. *The Goebbels Diaries*, ed. and trans. by Louis P. Lochner (New York: Doubleday and Company, 1948).

[33] *IMT*, vii, 224-226.

Apparently, when the Poles first came into the Reich, there was no definite discrimination against them. In the desire to utilize Polish labor quickly in the harvest of 1939, the Nazi racial philosophy was largely ignored. Gradually, however, the Nazi leaders developed an elaborate policy of discrimination.

The first legal discriminations were proclaimed by Goering on March 8, 1940. All Poles in the Reich were to be issued a special labor permit containing their fingerprints and photos. They had to wear badges on their outer clothes indicating their nationality. The Poles were restricted from certain areas of Germany, such as the western frontier.[34] In October, Goering clarified this earlier decree by explaining that the badges were necessary for security purposes and that "no defamation is intended thereby."[35] As far as the German public's attitude toward the Poles was concerned, Goering went on to say that the presence of so many Poles in the Reich was "so unique and novel that no binding regulations can be made for Germans," and the party should instruct the people on how to behave. Generally, Goering thought that the Germans should keep their distance from the Poles. In line with this view, he suggested that the Poles be prohibited from all cultural life of the Germans and be segregated in their housing. Goering also thought that the number of Polish males and females should be balanced in any given area. If this could not be accomplished, Polish brothels should be established to protect Germans from blood pollution.[36]

On the same day that the Goering directive was issued, Himmler sent detailed instructions to his police units to implement the directive. The police were to arrest immediately all Germans who had sexual relations or love affairs with Poles. Himmler suggested that before the actual arrest, the police encourage some public humiliation of the offenders,

[34] NCA, viii, 251-252.   [35] Ibid., 252.
[36] Ibid., 253. See also Goebbels Diaries, p. 48.

such as cutting off their hair before the entire village.[37] After
the arrest, Himmler urged firm punishment for the Germans
in order to set an example for the rest of the population.
The actual punishment would be to send the Germans to
concentration camps. For those Germans who merely helped
Poles, Himmler suggested a short imprisonment.[38] Needless
to say, the punishment for a Pole for sexual offenses against
Germans was death. Ulrich von Hassel recorded in his diary
that Himmler once had "one hundred and eighty Polish farm
workers unceremoniously hanged because they had had inter-
course with German women."[39]

Himmler's order also stipulated that the Polish badge
should be a violet "P" on a yellow triangle. Failure to wear
this badge carried a stiff fine of 150 RM or six weeks in jail.
In addition, Himmler placed a curfew on Poles, restricted
their use of public conveyances, and prohibited them from
participating in German cultural, social, or church functions.
However, the SS leader did request that the Reich Minister
of Church Affairs provide for the spiritual welfare of the
Poles through special church services conducted by German
clergy only.[40]

The Poles were also discriminated against in wages and
working conditions. The Polish agricultural worker was paid
less than a German because ". . . the German worker is accustomed to a higher standard of living than that of Polish
workers."[41] In industry it was more difficult to discriminate
against Polish workers. If the Nazis allowed the Poles to work
for lower wages than the Germans or other foreign workers,
the factory owners would prefer cheap Polish labor. To evade
this problem, the German employers were required to pay

---

[37] *Ibid.*, 255. [38] *Ibid.*, 261-263.
[39] Ulrich von Hassel, *The Von Hassel Diaries, 1938-1944* (New
York: Doubleday, 1947), pp. 195-196.
[40] *Minor Trials*, II, 267.
[41] *International Labour Review*, XLIII, 337.

Polish workers the same wages that they paid German workers, but the Reich authorities collected a special 15 to 20 per cent tax from the Polish workers. This levy was called the *Sozialausgleichsabgabe*, or social equalization fee.[42] Thus, this special tax fulfilled all of the Nazi requirements: it kept Polish wages lower than German wages; it removed the chance of employers profiting from cheap Polish labor; and it fattened the Reich treasury.

The Polish industrial worker was also denied some of the fringe benefits the German worker had. In commenting on this, one German labor official explained that "because of the numerous atrocities and acts of cruelty by the Poles in this war, it was impossible to allow them to participate completely in our progressive social order."[43] Translated to hard reality, this meant that the Poles were paid only for work done.[44] They received no bonus nor did they receive per diem pay. Naturally, the Poles were ineligible for marriage, child, or death grants given to Germans.[45] However, Polish workers were allowed vacation and sickness pay.[46] Their wages were also insured for 90 per cent of time lost because of air raids and alarms.

At the same time that legal discriminations were ordered against the Poles, the Propaganda Ministry was busy preparing the German populace for the *Untermensch* philosophy. In January 1940, Goebbels issued a circular to the German newspapers containing instructions on how the papers should handle the treatment of Poles. Goebbels advised:

[42] Thomas Reveille, *The Spoil of Europe* (New York: W. W. Norton and Company, 1941), p. 270.

[43] Franz Mende, *Die Beschaeftigung von auslaendischen Arbeitskraeften in Deutschland* (Berlin: Verlag der DAF, 1942), p. 1 in section A II b.

[44] *Lagerfuehrer-Sonderdienst*, prepared by the *Amt fuer Arbeitseinsatz* (Berlin: Verlag der DAF, 1940), pp. 20-21.

[45] Mende, *Die Beschaeftigung*, p. 16 in Section A II a.

[46] *Lagerfuehrer*, p. 24.

It must be suggested to the reader that gypsies, Jews and Poles ought to be treated on the same level. This is all the more important since there is no doubt that for a long time we shall be obliged to employ Poles as agricultural laborers in Germany. It is therefore desirable to build up a defensive front in the heart of the German nation.[47]

The German press obediently followed the line of Goebbels, reminding the population that 58,000 Germans had been killed by the Poles. The German people were warned not to eat at the same table with the Poles, or visit and celebrate with them. The press continually mentioned the danger of espionage. Germans were admonished to maintain their distance from Poles and to keep the Nordic blood pure. A typical editorial was somewhat like the following:

> German people, never forget that the atrocities of the Poles compelled the Fuehrer to protect our German people by armed force! . . . The servility of the Poles to their German employers merely hides their cunning; their friendly behavior hides their deceit. . . . Germans! The Pole must never be your comrade! He is inferior to each German comrade on his farm or in his factory. Be just, as Germans have always been, but never forget that you are a member of the master race![48]

The press also played up reports of punishment meted out to Germans who had shown kindness to Poles. Noticeable was the preponderance of farmers and workers who were punished.[49]

Unwittingly, the Nazi *Untermensch* concept of the Poles propounded in the German press and in the decrees of Goer-

[47] *Black Book of Poland*, p. 424.

[48] William L. Shirer, *Berlin Diary* (New York: Alfred A. Knopf, 1941), p. 513.

[49] In *Black Book of Poland*, pp. 125-128, there are excerpts from German newspapers.

ing and Himmler was self-defeating for Germany in the long run. The more the Poles in the Reich were abused, either by words or actions, the more difficult became the task of recruiting additional Poles. Yet, the Nazi leaders were so confident that they chose to ignore the difficulties that the *Untermensch* concept entailed.

Besides revealing the practical difficulties in the *Untermensch* concept, the first experiences of the Nazis in starting a foreign labor program in Poland uncovered a number of problems that hampered them throughout the war. The foreign labor program was but one among many concerning the occupied areas. If any of these programs were to succeed, a priority system had to be established lest the Nazis dissipate all their energy. Someone had to determine which was more important, be it the resettlement program, the SS racial program, Frank's occupational program, or the foreign labor program. To allow each individual and organization to run its own programs in its own way without considering other factors was tantamount to chaos.

In addition, the Polish labor program revealed the weaknesses in German methods, procedures, and techniques. If the Nazis were to achieve a maximum utilization of foreign labor with a minimum amount of damage to the economy from which this labor was drawn, new and better methods had to be devised. It was not enough to seize labor wherever there was sufficient police force, nor was it enough to seize labor and send it to the Reich's farms regardless of former training. By 1941, the critical shortage in skilled labor made it imperative that more sophisticated methods of recruitment be employed.

CHAPTER III

The Voluntary Labor Program for Europe
(1940-1941)

BEFORE Frank had the opportunity to apply renewed force to the widespread recruitment of Polish labor, the urgency was gone. By June of 1940, the German Army's attack in the West was concluded. Hitler's blitzkrieg strategy achieved successes that staggered the world. Even the brilliant victories of Bismarck and von Moltke were eclipsed by the triumphs of Hitler. Denmark, Norway, the Lowlands, and France were conquered in less than ninety days. In the spring of 1941, more victories followed. Nazi Germany reached her apex of power.

The conquest of much of Europe opened new sources of wealth for the Germans. The rich mines of France and the Balkans, the coal of Belgium, the agricultural products of Holland and Denmark—the vast deposits of natural wealth of the continent were ready for German use. Not the least of the wealth of these countries was human labor. In the West, the labor was highly skilled in comparison with that in the East. A balance had seemingly been struck. The labor from the East would replenish German agriculture, and the labor from the West, German industry.

From the summer of 1940 until the winter of 1941, the German attempt to utilize this labor was characterized by modesty and restraint. Unlike their policy in Poland, the Germans were slow to introduce compulsory labor laws and delayed the use of force. It was not until late 1941 that labor laws were passed in western countries and although light pressure was applied in 1941, generally the foreign labor program was on a voluntary basis until 1942. The Germans were also much more selective in the workers they recruited.

45

They sought skilled workers in particular, and the placement of the workers reflected care in recruitment. In short, there was a certain leisure about the labor program during this period that was missing in the first frantic program in Poland. Moreover, the program was now much more comprehensive, for it was broadened to include not only the German-occupied territories, but also the other Axis nations and even the neutrals.

WEST EUROPEAN POW'S: THE READY-MADE LABOR SUPPLY

As in Poland, the first large group of foreigners from the West that the Germans brought into the Reich to work were POW's. Two months after the western offensive, there were 350,000 POW's engaged in work, primarily in agriculture.[1] By October of 1940, this number had increased to 1,000,000. The use of western POW's was so successful in agriculture in 1940 that the German Army felt able to demobilize and return to civilian status all but 80,000 of the Polish POW's that it held.[2]

The German system of handling western POW's was very simple. The POW's were collected in large camps in the occupied areas, where they were screened and processed. Officers, politically unreliable enlisted men, and Jews—all of whom were considered dangerous by the German Army and SS—were immediately segregated from the rest of the POW's and sent to special camps in the occupied areas or in the Reich. The remainder of the POW's, especially those from Denmark, Norway, and Holland, were then released with the provision that they were to report to their local police and labor offices once they arrived home. All of the released POW's had to promise not to bear arms against Germany.

[1] Willeke, "Der Arbeitseinsatz im Kriege," p. 201.
[2] *Ibid.*, p. 202. The figure for the Polish POW's appeared in the *International Labour Review*, L, 470.

They were also subject to recall in the event the German authorities deemed it necessary.

The Flemish-speaking Belgian POW's were released under these conditions, but the rest of the Belgian and French POW's were treated differently. About 80,000 French-speaking Belgian POW's were kept by the Germans and sent to the Reich to work. The reason for this division of Belgian POW's was obscure. Perhaps the Germans were making a racial concession to the Flemings in order to follow a calculated policy of dividing Belgium internally by playing the Flemings against the Walloons. Some French POW's were released, especially the German-speaking ones from Alsace and Lorraine, who now were considered German nationals, but the bulk of the French Army, well over a million men, was kept as insurance of French cooperation. The Germans realized how sensitive Pétain would be about these French POW's.

The POW's who were sent to work in the Reich were assigned to *Stalags*, or camps under the control of the Army. The *Stalag* functioned at first as a reception center and later as the permanent home camp of the POW's. In reality, the *Stalag* was only the administrative unit for most POW's, because once they had been processed through the *Stalag* they were quartered in a subcamp of the *Stalag* called a *Kommando*. The *Kommando* was usually within easy walking distance from the place where the POW's were to work. The size of the *Kommando* varied from ten to twenty POW's in rural areas to thousands in urban areas. Thus, the average POW only saw the main *Stalag* when he arrived, was sick or disciplined, or transferred to another *Stalag*. In all of the camps, the POW's were guarded either by the regular Army or by the police and militia in remote areas.

The individual German employer who wanted POW's for labor submitted his request to the local labor office or, if he was in agriculture, to the local Food Ministry office. The local

47

offices investigated and evaluated the merits of the request. If the request was approved, the local offices negotiated directly with the Army for the needed number of POW's. The Army could refuse the request if it did not like the conditions under which the POW's were to work. Often, large companies attempted to by-pass the local labor offices and negotiated directly with the Army for labor. This practice continued until 1942, when strict regulations were passed forbidding it. By then, however, the larger companies were by-passing the labor offices again by negotiating with the SS for concentration camp inmates. Until the latter half of 1941, the Army followed closely the Geneva Convention, which forbade the use of POW's in war industries.

This system of allocating POW's was cumbersome and wasteful. The local labor offices and the Army enjoyed too much authority within their own spheres for effective utilization of the POW's. There was a definite tendency for the local labor offices to resist any transfer of POW's once they had been assigned within the labor office's district. Later in the war, when heavy air-raid damages and extensive new armament programs necessitated the transfer of large numbers of workers and equipment, the local autonomy of the labor office created more difficulties.

The wage policy for the POW's was also unsatisfactory, especially to the German industrialists. The industrialists had to pay the Army equivalent German wages for the POW's labor, which usually was of poor quality. The Army in turn, gave the individual POW a small part of this sum, about one mark per day, for pocket money and kept the rest for expenses. The agricultural employers had a distinct advantage over the industrialists, for they had only to supply room and board plus a small cash wage for the use of the POW's. The combination of the Army's strict adherence to the Geneva Convention, the wage policies, and the difficulties of employing guarded workers discouraged many industrialists from requesting POW's. As a consequence, most of the POW's flowed into agriculture.

By May of 1941, Germany had about 1,300,000 POW's in the Reich.[3] Of these, about 80,000 were Polish, 80,000 were Belgian, and the rest were French and British. Of the total, 93.6 per cent were actively engaged in work, with 55.2 per cent in German agriculture.[4] The German use of POW's and the conditions imposed on them were to change radically after the Russian POW's started to flow into the Reich.

WEST EUROPEAN CIVILIAN WORKERS

Significantly, the foreign labor program in the West began while a bitter quarrel between the Foreign Office and Goering's office was in progress. The quarrel centered around which office in Germany would have control of the economies of the occupied western countries. Since these areas were not to be incorporated into the Reich, Joachim von Ribbentrop maintained that they were, in essence, foreign countries and therefore his office had the final jurisdiction. Goering felt that in his capacity as head of the Four Year Plan he alone should be responsible. Besides, the occupied countries were under military governments, and Goering was supreme in that area, too. The quarrel was eventually resolved in Goering's favor, but not without bitterness on both sides.[5]

While Goering and Ribbentrop struggled for the control of the captured economies, unemployment mounted. In the second half of 1940, Belgium and Holland each had a half million and France had a million unemployed.[6] With such a

[3] Dr. Walter Stothfang, "Der Arbeitseinsatz an der Jahreswende," *Monatshefte fuer NS-Sozialpolitik*, v (1941), 4.

[4] OKW/Wi Rue Amt/Rue (Z St/IV f), *Ergebnisse der volkswirtschaftlichen Kraeftebilanz vom 31. Mai 1941*, on T-77, Roll 216, Frames 952913-953. (This information is on Frame 952916.)

[5] *Documents on German Foreign Policy, 1918-1945* (Washington: U.S.G.P.O., 1956), x, 170-173 and 213-215.

[6] *IMT*, xv, 662-663.

tempting pool of workers, the Germans wasted little time in organizing a recruitment drive. A German propaganda campaign was started and promises of high salaries and good living conditions in the Reich flooded the occupied territories. Special German labor offices and some private firms started recruiting.[7]

The Germans inaugurated other policies that indirectly helped in the recruitment of labor. On June 20, 1940, they issued a decree in France prohibiting any increases in salaries or prices.[8] Similar measures were issued in other western European countries. Indicative of the German fear of inflation, these measures also helped to create social unrest in the occupied countries and thus encouraged the recruitment program. The Germans also removed much of the consumer goods from these countries by extensive governmental purchases and by artificially changing the discount rate to favor the mark over the local currencies. Inevitably, the remaining amounts of consumer goods flowed into the black market, where the average worker, whose wage was fixed, found himself in a decidedly disadvantageous position. The total effect of these German policies was to lower the real wages within the occupied countries and thereby encourage the recruitment of labor to the Reich.

In France, Germany had initiated two additional measures to insure French cooperation in all phases of the occupation, including the foreign labor program. The first was the artificial merger of the two northern departments of France with Belgium for administrative purposes. Both of these departments contained much of France's heavy industries, which were vital to the whole French economy. In the event that France proved unwilling to cooperate with the Germans, the

[7] Cf. German newspapers' accounts of recruitment in 1940, on T-81, Roll 511, Frames 5274445-782.

[8] Robert Aron, *The Vichy Regime, 1940-1944*, trans. by Humphrey Hare (London: Putnam, 1958), p. 187.

detachment of the two departments could be declared final by the Germans. A second pressure exerted by the Germans on the French was the control of the demarcation line that divided France. Neither the occupied zone of France nor Vichy France was able to live independent of the other. General Otto von Stuelpnagel explained to General Charles Huntziger in rather cavalier terms that the demarcation line ". . . is a bit we have put in the horse's mouth. If France bucks we shall tighten the curb chain. We shall loosen it in proportion as France behaves well."[9]

In France and the other occupied countries of the West, the actual recruitment was done by the Reich Ministry of Labor. Although the Labor Ministry had officials attached to the German Military Commands in the occupied countries, it operated in an independent manner. At first, the Labor Ministry rarely bothered to notify the Military Command or the native labor offices about the workers that were recruited.[10] However, later in the war, when compulsory recruitment occurred, closer cooperation developed between the German labor offices and the Military Command. In addition to the Reich Labor Office, large private firms in Germany, particularly those in the coal and chemical trusts, were actively recruiting labor in the West.

The German recruiters promised high wages ranging from .57 RM per hour in rural areas to 1 RM in large cities, with the average wage from .70 to .85 RM. The labor contracts usually called for a 60-hour work week and a duration of six, nine, or twelve months. Some industries such as construction paid the western workers per diem allowances of

---

[9] *Ibid.*, p. 189.

[10] Document SD-43, in the files of the Nuremberg Trials Collection, National Archives, Washington, D.C.; and *France During the German Occupation, 1940-1944*, trans. by Philip W. Whitcomb, Hoover Institution on War, Revolution and Peace (Stanford: Stanford University Press, 1957), I, 52 [henceforth cited as *France During Occupation*].

1 to 1.50 RM for family upkeep. Western workers were also promised a vacation every three months if married and every six months if unmarried.[11] Workers were allowed to send home up to 250 RM per month if married and 150 RM if unmarried. In addition to wages, the western workers were promised working conditions, food rations, fringe benefits (marriage and child loans excepted), and housing similar to those of the German worker.[12] Foreign workers were warned to bring their own clothes, since it was impossible to issue them ration stamps for clothes in the Reich.

Apparently the promises of some of the German recruiters in the occupied countries had to be tempered, for in the fall of 1940 the Reich Labor Office began issuing regulations prohibiting certain recruitment practices. On September 20, 1940, very exact and detailed regulations covering health inspection for foreign workers were ordered. These regulations were especially concerned with the foreign workers being sent into the armament industries.[13] The Labor Office also issued special regulations for specific industries. The records of the *Bezirksgruppe Steinkohlenbergbau Ruhr* indicated that the Labor Office expressly forbade the association from recruiting foreigners for an indefinite period. The association was, however, allowed to raise the minimum time for a contract from six months to one year. The same association was also ordered to give foreign workers a .15 to .30 RM per hour raise after the workers completed a short introductory training period.[14]

[11] See letter from Dr. H. Heise, the German Labor Ministry's Representative in Copenhagen, to the Foreign Office, dated December 16, 1941, on T-77, Roll 167, Frames 900811-816.

[12] Mende, *Die Beschaeftigung*, p. 4 in Section A ii a.

[13] See Labor Ministry's directive, *Einsatz auslaendischer Arbeitskraefte in der Ruestungsindustrie*, September 28, 1940, on T-77, Roll 167, Frames 900886-889 and 900908.

[14] Arbeitsamt Gelsenkirchen, *Merkblatt ueber die Beschaeftigung gewerblicher auslaendischer Arbeitskraefte*, October 14, 1940, on T-83, Roll 42, Frames 3407934-939 and 3407946-954.

Besides reports of abuses by German recruiters in the fall of 1940, the Reich Labor Ministry was flooded by complaints about foreign workers furnished by the local German labor offices. The labor offices complained that the foreign workers were lazy and unwilling to work, and some were engaging in black market operations. Many of them were leaving their jobs or feigning sickness in order not to work. The labor offices wanted the Gestapo to start imposing heavy fines or arresting foreign workers who were guilty of labor infractions.[15] The labor offices were displeased also with the productivity of many of the foreign workers. In November 1940, the Reich Labor Ministry sent to the local labor offices a summary report frankly appraising various aspects of the foreign labor program.[16] The report mentioned that false promises given to workers, especially the Dutch and Belgians, were causing difficulties in further recruitment in the western countries. In general, the report noted the usual grumblings by the foreign workers about wages and restrictions on life in the Reich, but it also stated that their morale and discipline were good. The effectiveness of the western foreign worker was the only disappointment. The Danish and Belgian workers were on a par with the German worker, but the French and Dutch workers were not. Although many local labor offices had commented on the splendid training of the French workers, the Labor Ministry's report noted that they were producing less than the Germans. There were also complaints about the French spreading Marxist propaganda among their fellow workers.

Of all the western workers, the Dutch seemed to cause

[15] See records of the Remscheid Labor Office in the unpublished material files of USSBS, February 1941 *Monatlicher Taetigkeitsbericht*. These "monthly activity reports" from the local labor offices offer an unusual insight into the problems of Germany during the war; not merely labor problems were reported.

[16] See *Reichsarbeitsministerium* report, dated November 9, 1940, on T-77, Roll 167, Frames 900876-879.

the Germans the most difficulty. German employers invariably characterized the Dutch workers as complaining, indifferent, undisciplined, and obstinate. Their work was good only when they were closely supervised. The Dutch, like the Danes, had a propensity for violating German labor decrees, especially the one that prohibited foreign workers from returning home on weekends. Rather than punish these Dutch and Danish workers, the Germans relaxed the restrictions on weekend travel a year later.[17] The Labor Ministry's report of November 1940 ended on a dour note; considering the difficulties involved in the foreign labor program, the German employers, recruiters, and general public would have to make a concerted effort to improve every aspect of the program in the coming year.[18]

In line with the recommendations of the Reich Labor Ministry's report, the German government established a special office in the German Labor Front to help solve many of the difficulties that had arisen. This special office was called the Office for Labor Allocation and was charged with

. . . the responsibilities of directing the allocation and care of all native and foreign workers in every respect not already covered by existing regulations of the Labor Administration. This office has the special responsibility of helping foreign workers negotiate and conclude labor contracts and wage scales; arrange transportation, transfer and care for foreign workers from their native lands to their place of work in the Reich; and for the protection and care of foreign workers in the Reich in all respects, i.e., feeding, housing and recreation. This office is to insure through the German Labor Front representatives that all regulations

[17] See *Ruestungs Insp. Wehrkreise X* (Kiel) report, dated October 23, 1941, on T-77, Roll 247, Frame 1066758.

[18] *Reichsarbeitsministerium* report, dated November 9, 1940, on T-77, Roll 167, Frame 900879.

dealing with foreign workers in the factories and camps are carried out.[19]

Later in 1941, the German Labor Front appointed one liaison man (*Verbindungsmann*) for every nationality that had more than twenty persons employed in a factory. These men were to work with the Labor Front and the agents of the factories to insure full cooperation. Only the Polish, Czech, and Russian nationalities were forbidden to have liaison men.[20] Indirectly, the decisions to organize a special office and establish liaison men introduced another powerful Nazi organization, the German Labor Front, into the already complicated operation of the foreign labor program.

The efforts of various German agencies to improve the labor program in the West appeared to be a modest success. German labor reports in the fall of 1941 indicated that the Germans were pleased with the performance of the western workers. The male French and Belgian workers were reported to be willing and industrious; they caused very few labor disciplinary problems for the Germans. The major fault that the Germans found with them was that their contracts were too short.[21] Too many of them were able to find work in their own countries. The Dutch and Danes also showed an improvement. However, this was not the case with French and Belgian female workers. German reports complained that they were a continual source of trouble. The women failed to work, and their constant socializing with German military personnel caused friction with the German women. The behavior of the French and Belgian women scandalized the Germans. The Stuttgart Labor Office wrote,

[19] *Reichsarbeitsblatt*, Part i, 1940, p. 513.

[20] Carl Birkenholz, *Der auslaendische Arbeiter in Deutschland* (Berlin: Verlag fuer Wirtschaftsschriftum, 1942), p. 204.

[21] *Ru/Insp. Wehrkreise X* report, dated October 23, 1941, on T-77, Roll 247, Frames 1066756-758.

"It is not an exaggeration when it's said that you rather rarely find a decent French woman." The Reutlinger Labor Office reported from fifteen to twenty cases of pregnancy and venereal disease among the 385 French and Belgian women assigned to the office.[22] But in spite of threats and warnings to both the German soldiers and French women, the situation could not be corrected.

Although the Germans had their difficulties with the western workers in the first year, they considered the labor program numerically a success. By the end of 1940, nearly 220,000 civilians from the occupied western countries were at work in the Reich.[23] Throughout 1941, the number of western workers in the Reich rose steadily, and by October 1, it had reached an impressive figure (Table IV).

GERMANY'S ALLIES AS A SOURCE OF LABOR

Italy, Germany's chief ally, figured prominently in the Nazi foreign labor program from 1939 to the fall of 1941. Two prewar incidents anticipated later German dependency on Italian labor. In the spring of 1939, when the Polish seasonal workers failed to come into the Reich, Germany turned immediately to Italy. The Reich Ministry of Labor dispatched *Ministerialrat* Dr. Franz Mende to Rome to negotiate for the needed labor. In March, Dr. Mende and Dr. Francisco Gerbasi of the Italian Foreign Office agreed that 30,000 Italians should enter the Reich.[24] Again, just prior to the beginning of the war, Hitler sent a request for additional labor. On August 26, 1939, he wrote to his friend Mussolini: "Now

[22] Report from *Kriminal-Obersekretaer* Stoeckle of Stuttgart and others to the SS office, dated October 31, 1941, on T-81, Roll 537, Frames 5306929-958.

[23] Dr. Letsch, "Der Einsatz gewerblicher auslaendischer Arbeitskraefte in Deutschland," *Reichsarbeitsblatt*, Part v, 1941, p. 43.

[24] Deutsche Arbeitsfront, Amt fuer Arbeitseinsatz, *Sammlung der Bestimmungen ueber den Einsatz auslaendischer Arbeiter in Deutschland* (Berlin: Verlag der DAF, 1941), p. 194.

56

TABLE IV

FOREIGN WORKERS FROM WESTERN OCCUPIED, ALLIED, AND
NEUTRAL NATIONS EMPLOYED IN THE REICH AS OF
OCTOBER 1, 1941

Country	Men	Women	Total
A. FROM WESTERN OCCUPIED NATIONS:			
Denmark	25,319	3,576	28,895
Holland	80,653	12,342	92,995
Belgium	106,832	14,669	121,501
France	34,042	14,525	48,567
Norway	620	384	1,004
Luxemberg	2,299	451	2,750
Total	249,765	45,947	295,712
B. FROM GERMANY'S ALLIES:			
Italy	249,972	21,695	271,667
Slovakia	53,993	26,044	80,037
Bulgaria	14,352	226	14,578
Hungary	25,390	9,600	34,990
Finland	241	102	343
Rumania	5,036	1,330	6,366
Total	348,984	58,997	407,981
C. FROM NEUTRAL NATIONS:			
Portugal	139	24	163
Sweden	606	402	1,008
Switzerland	11,668	5,302	16,970
Spain	1,089	211	1,300
Turkey	203	117	320
USA	1,308	543	1,851
Ireland and the United Kingdom[a]	491	452	943
All others	12,161	4,848	17,009
Total	27,665	11,899	39,564

[a] German records do not indicate the exact number of Irish or U.K. workers; presumably most were Irish, since the U.K. was not a neutral at the time.

SOURCE: Report dated October 9, 1941, from the *Oberkommando der Wehrmacht, Wehrwirtschafts- und Ruestungsamt*, Rue/IVd, T-77, Roll 243, Frames 985921-922. Apparently this report is from the Labor Ministry; the copy used here is from a broken file.

I have a big favor to ask you, Duce. You and your people could help me most in this hard struggle by supporting me with Italian manpower, manpower for industrial as well as agricultural purposes."[25]

The relationship between the two countries was cordial at first; they treated each other as equals and both were sensitive to criticism from the other. As the war progressed, however, a definite coolness crept into the relationship. The inability of Italy to match the German military effort forced Italy into a secondary position. Hard-pressed for basic raw materials such as oil and coal, and manufactured articles, Italy's bartering powers with Germany dwindled. More often than not, the only asset Italy had was her manpower, which Germany began extracting for concessions. As Dino Alfieri, the Italian Ambassador to Berlin, noted: "Since every new Italo-German trade and economic convention was coupled with a personal request from Hitler to Mussolini for a fresh contingent of Italian workers, the Duce always gave way in the end."[26]

The German demands for Italian labor were not very heavy in 1939 and 1940. Although Alfieri thought that there were about 300,000 Italians employed in the Reich at the end of 1940, others placed the figure at one-third of that.[27] The arrangements for the transfer of Italians were apparently conducted by Robert Ley's Labor Front and the Fascist Industrial Workers' Federation.[28]

As long as there were not a large number of Italians in the Reich, there were relatively few difficulties. The observant

[25] NCA, IV, 462.
[26] Dino Alfieri, Dictators Face to Face, trans. by David Moore (New York: New York University Press, 1955), p. 114.
[27] Willeke, in the article "Der Arbeitseinsatz im Kriege," estimated 70,000 Italians were in the Reich in 1940. The International Labour Review estimated 90,000 for the same period.
[28] Pre-trial interview of Robert Ley, taken at Nuremberg on October 2, 1945. A copy of the testimony is in the files of the USSBS.

German labor officials did note, however, the wide variation in the quality of the Italian workers. Northern Italians were considered able workers, but southern Italians were poor. In general, the labor officials praised the discipline of the Italian workers, and, at the same time, warned German employers to take special care of the "Italian sensitivity about their food," lest the Italians become alienated.[29]

The entrance of Italy into the war in June 1940 brought increased cooperation between the two allies and increased responsibilities. By the beginning of 1941, Germany was delivering large quantities of coal, oils, and other raw materials to Italy. German technicians were busy reorganizing and modernizing Italian industry. Germany was also granting large war contracts to the Italians. In return, Germany began demanding more Italian resources, both material and human.[30]

Early in January 1941, Berlin ordered Ambassador Hans Georg von Mackensen in Rome to make a secret survey of the Italian employment situation. On January 14, Mackensen reported to Berlin that, of 4.4 million Italian industrial workers, approximately 437,000 were without work. In addition, the ambassador thought that another 500,000 workers were employed only part-time. Mackensen estimated that Germany could easily draw 200,000 skilled workers and 500,000 unskilled workers out of Italy.[31] With this information, Berlin sent a delegation to negotiate with the Italians regarding the labor quotas for the year. The German delegation, headed by *Ministerialrat* Rolf Hetzell of the Reich Ministry of Labor, arrived in Rome on the 5th of February. Three days later, Hetzell and the Italian representative Gerbasi

[29] Cf. Labor Ministry's directives, dated September 20, 1940, on T-77, Roll 167, Frame 900879.

[30] Thomas, *Studie der Wehrwirtschaft*, p. 375.

[31] See the diplomatic report of Mackensen, on T-77, Roll 247, Frame 1066695.

reached the first of a series of agreements. The first called for the dispatch of 150,000 Italian industrial workers to the Reich. Of these, 50,000 were to be skilled metal workers, 30,000 trainees drawn from the unemployed, and 70,000 out of other Italian industries. A few days later, a second agreement was signed which called for an additional 54,000 Italian workers, mostly from the mining, chemical, and building industries. In all, Germany wanted 204,000 industrial workers from Italy for 1941. Besides the industrial workers, Germany contracted for 60,000 agricultural workers from Italy for the same year.[32] On February 12, 1941, the Italian newspaper *Corrière della sera* carried an account of the German-Italian negotiations. The newspaper mentioned that the new quota, added to the 54,000 Italians already in the Reich, would mean that approximately 320,000 Italians would work there in 1941. Many German officials were doubtful about Italy's ability to fulfill the 1941 quotas.[33]

The German Labor Ministry reported that 133,303 new Italian workers had arrived in the Reich by June 14, 1941.[34] On October 1, 1941, German records indicated that the total number of Italians working in the Reich had risen to 271,667.[35] It is highly probable that the Italians did fulfill their quota of 320,000 by the end of the year.

As soon as the first large batch of Italians arrived in the Reich in 1941, there were difficulties. German reports be-

[32] Records of these negotiations can be seen on T-77, Roll 586, Frames 1766902-972; T-77, Roll 247, Frames 1066701-737; and in Thomas, *Studie der Wehrwirtschaft*, pp. 375 ff.

[33] See the secret reports of the German delegation, on T-77, Roll 247, Frames 1066707-710, especially Dr. Letsch's report.

[34] Dr. Timm's report from the Reich Labor Ministry, dated June 14, 1941, on T-77, Roll 247, Frames 1066732-733.

[35] *Oberkommando der Wehrmacht, Wehrwirtschafts- und Ruestungsamt* report, dated October 9, 1941, on T-77, Roll 243, Frames 985921-922. This report probably originated in the Labor Ministry, but this reference is from a broken file in the OKW records.

came filled with criticism of the Italian workers. The earlier guarded German praise of the Italians vanished. The local labor office at Remscheid (Duesseldorf *Gau*), for example, reported that the Italians were completely undisciplined. In spite of all efforts by the Italian and German authorities, the workers caused difficulties. The Remscheid office added, "Unfortunately a part of these workers are not accustomed to regular work, but rather they view their stay in Germany as a vacation. Many believe they can pass their time by playing cards!"[36]

Individual private firms were equally critical. A typical firm, Kaeuffer & Co. in Wiesbaden, claimed that the Italians were not being properly tested. Many of those who signed contracts as welders turned out to be magazine salesmen. Of the fifty Italians assigned to the firm, only thirty-four had ever set foot in a metal factory, and yet all were collecting skilled metal workers' wages. Furthermore, continued the Wiesbaden firm, at the slightest criticism or pretext the Italians would indignantly run off to their representative in Frankfurt and would not be seen for days.[37] A German plant in Kiel reported that its Italian workers did nothing but loaf and conduct black market trade in Italian cigarettes and wine. The Kiel factory had to punish or release 173 of its 285 Italian workers between May and the end of August 1941.[38] The complaints spread to other factories, for the German armament inspectors reported that many plants wanted to refuse Italians for fear of upsetting their factories' peace. The inspectors dismissed these excuses by pointing out that

[36] Remscheid Labor Office, *Monatlicher Taetigkeitsbericht*, August 1941, in the unpublished material files of the USSBS.

[37] The Kaeuffer and Co. report is one of many from private firms in the Reich on their experiences with the foreign workers. This particular report is on T-77, Roll 247, Frames 1066747-751.

[38] Reports from the Kiel *Wehrkreise*, dated October 23, 1941, on T-77, Roll 247, Frame 1066757.

6 1

it was the responsibility of the employer to insure "industrial peace."[39] All German reports mentioned the same things: the Italians were lazy and poorly trained; they left their jobs for higher wages; they complained about the food; they never returned from leave; and they caused unrest among the other workers.[40] Even Alfieri admitted that some of the trade unions were probably sending their slackers to Germany.[41]

Besides getting into difficulties at work, the Italian workers, with their casual manners and appreciation of women, quickly ran into trouble with the local German populace and police. The Italians were regarded with suspicion by many Germans. Often they were brusquely refused cigarettes and other scarce items in German taverns.[42] But it was the Italian propensity for women to which the Nazis chiefly objected. Alfieri claimed to have known of numerous cases where German women were arrested or warned about associating with Italians. Moreover, Alfieri said, there were even cases when German girls had their hair cut off and were tarred.[43] When Alfieri protested such actions to the Foreign Minister, Ribbentrop told him he was "dramatizing the situation."[44]

There was an element of truth in Alfieri's assertion, for German directives bluntly stated that "relationships with Italians were unwelcomed."[45] In substance, the German attitude was, to paraphrase George Orwell, that the Germans and the Italians were equal but the Germans were more equal.

[39] See the directive of the *Wehrkreise* inspectors, dated June 12, 1941, on T-77, Roll 247, Frame 1066731.

[40] As an example, see the collection of reports from the *Reichstreuhaender der Arbeit fuer das Wirtschaftsgebiet Suedwestdeutschland*, on T-81, Roll 537, Frames 5306858-874.

[41] Alfieri, *Dictators*, p. 114.

[42] Cf. Alfieri, *Dictators*; and *Goebbels Diaries*.

[43] Alfieri, *Dictators*, p. 115.   [44] *Ibid.*, p. 117.

[45] See the complaints about the Italians from the Regensburg area, on T-77, Roll 248, Frames 166770-793.

The charges and countercharges between the Italian and German officials mounted steadily throughout 1941. The Italian government, including Mussolini, was shocked by the "concrete examples of misuse" of Italian workers by the Germans.[46] In response, the German officials repeated the complaints of the labor offices and factories. The situation became so tense that in August of 1941 Mussolini sent Dr. Carlo Lombrassa, President of the Italian Commission for Migration and Colonization, to Germany to rectify the situation.

Lombrassa had a series of conferences with the German officials, especially the representatives of the Labor Front, about improving cooperation between the two countries.[47] The results of the conferences were apparently not as good as the Italians expected. Mussolini and Ciano continued to receive reports about the mistreatment of their nationals in the Reich.[48] Finally, in November, Hitler intervened personally. He ordered all government and party agencies to attempt to improve immediately the conditions of the Italian workers in the Reich and to restrain their criticism of the Italians.[49] The foreign labor program had already placed a heavy strain on German-Italian relations before 1942.

Compared with Italy, the rest of Germany's allies played an insignificant part in the foreign labor program up to 1942. The Germans signed a series of agreements with their allies for the importation of labor, but the total number of workers involved was small and the concessions that the Germans gave these workers indicated that the agreements were token in nature. The German-Rumanian pact of December 3,

---

[46] Alfieri, *Dictators*, pp. 110-111.

[47] See the Reich Labor Office's report on Lombrassa's Berlin trip, on T-77, Roll 247, Frames 1066754-756.

[48] Count Galeazzo Ciano, *The Ciano Diaries, 1939-1943*, ed. by Hugh Gibson (Garden City, N.Y.: Doubleday, 1946), pp. 383 and 406.

[49] Alfieri, *Dictators*, p. 117.

1941, was typical. The terms of this agreement stated that
Rumania was to send 16,400 industrial workers to Germany.
In return, Germany promised that the workers were to receive the same wages and benefits accorded her own workers.
In addition, the Rumanian workers were to be housed privately instead of in camps, and they were to be employed in
factories in groups of twenty-five or more.[50] Although the
number of workers from some of the other minor allies of
Germany was somewhat larger, their combined total contribution was not as large as that of Italy (Table IV).

THE NEUTRALS

Germany made some attempts to enlist workers from the
neutral nations, but most of these nations were reluctant to
allow many of their workers to leave for the Reich. Consequently, the total contribution of the neutral nations to the
foreign labor program was slight. Although Germany
realized the difficulties of her position in relation to the neutrals, she had hoped that the war against the Soviet Union
would soften their attitude toward her. German propaganda
continually pointed out to the neutrals that she was in a
crusade against the godless forces of communism, and that
any aid given to her would help keep Europe free from the
Red menace. Germany hoped that both Spain and Turkey
would be influenced in this way, but the response of the neutrals was hardly overwhelming (see Table IV).

SUMMARY OF THE VOLUNTARY PROGRAM

From May 31, 1940, to October 1, 1941, Germany
achieved remarkable success with her labor program as the
total number of foreign workers and POW's rose from 1.1
million to 3.5 million (see Table V). However, Germany
had little to do with the initial mobilization of these foreign
workers. Most of them had been readied by their own gov-

[50] *Reichsarbeitsblatt*, Part v, 1942, p. 47.

TABLE V

FOREIGN WORKERS AND POW's EMPLOYED IN REICH
ON OCTOBER 1, 1941

Origin of Workers	Total Number	Per cent
Western occupied areas	295,712	8.4
Germany's allies	407,981	11.6
All neutrals	39,564	1.1
Protectorate	140,052	3.9
Poland	1,007,561	28.9
Yugoslavia	108,791	3.1
Greece	505	0.1
Russia	25,269	0.7
Stateless persons	114,118	3.2
POW's (all nationalities)	1,367,973	39.0
Total	3,507,526	100.0

SOURCE: Same as Table IV.

ernments (as soldiers, in the case of the POW's) and handed over to Germany. Germany had only to arrange their transportation and allocation to employers within the Reich. Thus, Germany escaped the problems of recruiting unwilling workers or injuring the economies of the countries supplying workers. In short, Germany was capitalizing on a ready-made situation.

This period can also be characterized as the time when Germany skimmed the cream of the unemployed from its occupied areas and its allies. Once it was gone, however, Germany soon found herself in trouble. In the occupied areas, Germany inherited all the problems involved in their economies. Decisions had to be made as to how many workers could be removed from these countries without affecting their economic ability to produce goods for themselves and for Germany. Increasingly Germany faced resistance from her allies as the war placed new demands on them. As for the neutrals, Germany's relationship with them fluctuated with the tides of war. As long as it appeared that Germany was going to be the arbiter of Europe's future, the neutrals were willing to help her with labor and raw materials. But once Germany's future position became doubtful, the neutrals, along with Germany's allies and the people in Germany's occupied areas, reacted accordingly.

CHAPTER IV

The Russian War and Labor

AFTER the German conquests of 1940 and the spring of 1941, only two major powers were left in Europe to oppose German dominance of the Continent. In the West was Britain; in the East, Russia. Britain offered no immediate threat to the German position. The British Army had been badly mauled in France, and the British homeland was bombed, isolated, and seemingly on the verge of defeat. Although Hitler had plans for an invasion of England in the fall of 1940 (Operation Sea Lion), circumstances forced him to postpone them and turn to his second adversary—the Soviet Union. Late in 1940, Hitler issued orders for the attack on Russia (Operation Barbarossa). The strategy was the same as the earlier German blitzkrieg campaigns in Poland, Norway, and France. Hitler's directive of December 18, 1940, clearly implied this when it stated: "The German Armed Forces must be prepared to crush Soviet Russia in a quick campaign before the end of the war against England."[1] Goering, head of the Luftwaffe, thought that the campaign in Russia could achieve all of its objectives within three months.[2] Even the delay of the offensive which was caused by the Balkan campaign did not seriously affect the German timetable. The war against the Soviet Union was scheduled for completion by the winter of 1941.

The decision to attack Russia implied hardly any new departures in the German economy. There were no massive preparations for the attack. German production of weapons and ammunition was increased slightly prior to the attack but then actually fell off when the Army achieved its initial

[1] *NCA*, iii, 407.
[2] USSBS, *Effects of Strategic Bombing*, p. 18.

6 7

successes. The production of munitions, in particular, never reached the level of 1940 when the French campaign was in progress. The total armament expenditure for 1941 was only 12.1 billion marks as compared with 12.0 in 1940.[3]

When Germany attacked the Soviet Union, her stock of weapons and ammunition was substantially above that of June 1940. Germany had, for example, 5,100 combat planes and 4,500 operational tanks at the time of the invasion in Russia. This was an increase of about 1,000 planes and 1,000 tanks over 1940. But considering the wider and heavier commitments of both the Air Force and the Army in 1941, the total increase of equipment was rather modest. Events in Russia quickly proved that the German supply of all kinds of armaments was inadequate.[4]

In any case, preparations for the attack brought no significant strain on the manpower front. Germany had drafted 5,808,000 men by May 1941, but this loss was partially regained by the foreign labor program, which added some 3,020,000 workers to the economy (see Table VI). Total employment was down four million from May 1939, but the decrease was borne mainly by consumer industries.

The most amazing aspect of the German labor economy before the attack on Russia was the growth of the foreign labor program from May 1940 to May 1941. The total number of foreigners increased from 1,148,000 in May 1940 to 3,020,000 a year later, an increase of 263 per cent. The largest gain was recorded in occupations directly related to the German war effort. Thus, the tendency to channel foreign labor into key war industries was already apparent by this early date and was to continue throughout the duration of the war.

The allocation of so many foreigners to the war industries

[3] *Indexziffern der Deutschen Ruestungsendfertigung*, prepared by the *Planungsamt*, Ministry for Armament and War Production, June 1944. A copy of this report is in the USSBS files.
[4] Klein, *Germany's Economic Preparations*, p. 191.

TABLE VI
DISTRIBUTION OF LABOR IN THE REICH AS OF MAY 31, 1941
(in thousands)

Economic Division	Germans	For- eigners[a]	% of Labor[b]	% of In- crease[c]
1. Agriculture, forestry, fishing	9,262	1,459	13.6	214
2. Industry and transport	15,206	1,379	8.3	342
a. Industry	9,200	965	9.5	377
b. Handwork	3,730	310	7.7	287
c. Transport	2,073	97	4.5	277
d. Power	204	7	3.3	350
3. Trade, banking, insurance	3,358	58	1.7	290
4. Administration and services	2,626	51	1.9	243
5. Armed forces administration	804	39	4.7	355
6. Domestic service	1,473	33	2.2	220
Total[d]	32,729	3,020	8.4	263

[a] Including Jews and prisoners of war of all nationalities.
[b] Foreigners as a percentage of total labor force.
[c] Percentage of increase of foreigners from previous year.
[d] Figures rounded off.
SOURCE: *Kriegswirtschaftliche Kraeftebilanz* for 1942, as adjusted by the USSBS.

was an obvious gamble taken by Germany. Since one-third of these foreigners were enemy POW's and most of the rest were from conquered countries, Germany faced a severe security problem. This difficulty became of increased importance when people from the Soviet Union arrived.

EARLY GERMAN PLANS FOR THE OCCUPIED SOVIET TERRITORIES

Under the terms of the 1939 Pact, Russia supplied Germany with extensive quantities of foodstuffs and raw materials vital to the German economy and virtually impossible to obtain elsewhere because of the British blockade. When Germany invaded the Soviet Union and the flow of Russian goods was halted, the Germans hoped to minimize the dangers of dislocating their economy by quick exploitation of captured Russian resources. The Germans reasoned that their blitzkrieg attack would inflict a quick and decisive defeat on Russia, thus allowing the Germans to reestablish the flow of Russian goods to the Reich. Once Germany was master of the Russian area west of the Ural Mountains, her economic position would be impregnable.

In the spring of 1941, German leaders issued two general plans of operation for the immediate exploitation of captured Russian resources. One plan came from General Thomas' office and the other from Goering's Four Year Plan Office. General Thomas' plan, the Oldenburg Plan, was the economic counterpart of the military operation orders for Barbarossa. It dealt primarily with the seizure of products immediately necessary for the German war economy, such as oil stockpiles, iron ore, and rare materials. It envisioned as German objectives in Russia the quick restoration and utilization of the full industrial and agricultural resources of the country without any major changes in its structure until the war was successfully concluded. This meant, in effect, that the collective organization of Russian agriculture and industry was not to be disturbed.[5]

The Goering plan was not strictly a plan, but a series of directives instructing German administrators on policy in the Soviet Union; it differed greatly from the Oldenburg Plan. The Goering directives, first circulated secretly in "The Green File" issued on May 22, 1941, indicated the tone of future German occupational policies for the Soviet Union. Political, racial, and economic objectives of the Nazis were

[5] *IMT*, xxvii, 32-38.

to be pursued simultaneously without any thought of restoring Russian industry or society. Russia was to be ruthlessly exploited for the betterment of the Third Reich. Even law and order, the minimum requirements for all human societies, were to be restored only in those invaded areas that had a surplus of agricultural products or crude oil. As for the other areas, "The Green File" gave this ominous advice:

Many tens of millions of people in the industrial areas will become redundant and will either die or will have to emigrate to Siberia. Any attempts to save the population in these parts from death by starvation through the import of surpluses from the Black Earth Zone would be at the expense of supplies to Europe. It would reduce Germany's staying power in the war and would undermine Germany's and Europe's power to resist the blockade. This must be clearly and absolutely understood.[6]

In June 1941, even before the wartime German civil government for Russia, the Eastern Ministry or *Ostministerium* (*OMi*), was established, Hitler ordered the Goering plan into operation. Hitler's decree allowed Goering's Four Year Plan Office to organize special independent agencies in Russia called the Economic Staff East (*Wirtschaft Stab Ost* or, as abbreviated, *Wi Stab Ost*). A branch of Goering's Economic Staff was attached to each rear area command and was composed of military and civilian personnel. The general purpose of this staff was to incorporate the Russian economy into the total economic scheme of the Reich.[7] Immediately, a sharp difference of opinion developed within the Economic Staff

[6] A complete copy of "The Green File" can be seen in the National Archives' Nuremberg Trials Collection. "The Green File" bears the code number EC 472.

[7] Otto Braeutigam, *Ueberblick ueber die Besetzten Ostgebiete waehrend des 2. Weltkrieges* (Tuebingen: Studien des Instituts Besatzungsfragen zu den deutschen Besatzungen in 2. Weltkrieg, 1954), p. 8 (mimeographed).

East over implementing "The Green File." A liberal wing of the staff thought that the Goering plan was impossible, and that a better procedure in the long run would be to aim at restoring and utilizing the full industrial and agricultural resources of the country. The opposite view was that Germany should extract everything possible from the country and consider long-range programs after the war was won. Thus, in Russia, as in Poland, a serious conflict occurred in German governmental circles over priority of goals.[8]

On July 7, 1941, Hitler delineated his eastern policy at a conference at his headquarters. German policy in the East was to have three general objectives. It should seek to dominate, administrate, and exploit the newly conquered areas for the greater good of the Reich. German control should be extended to the Urals, creating in this area an opportunity for German colonization. The native peoples were to be used for labor in Russia, but they were never to be allowed to bear arms for Germany or to enjoy any self-government.[9]

Hitler picked the party philosopher Alfred Rosenberg to carry out these broad principles in the East. Rosenberg was designated the head of the East Ministry and was directly responsible for all German civil government in the occupied areas of the Soviet Union. Administratively, Rosenberg divided his domain into Reich Commissariats, one for the Baltic countries and Northern Russia called the *Ostland*, and another for the entire Ukraine and southern Russia. The areas directly behind the front lines, extending sometimes two or three hundred kilometers, were administered by the Army. The chief German official in the *Reichskommissariat*

---

[8] Cf. Braeutigam, *Ueberblick*; Peter Kleist, *Zwischen Hitler und Stalin* (Bonn: Athenaeum Verlag, 1950); Alexander Dallin, *German Rule in Russia* (New York: St. Martin's Press, 1957); and Gerald Reitlinger, *The House Built on Sand* (New York: Viking Press, 1960).

[9] *NCA*, vii, 1090.

Ostland was Hinrich Lohse, *Gauleiter*[10] of Schleswig-Holstein since 1933. For the same post in the Ukraine, Rosenberg had suggested Fritz Sauckel, *Gauleiter* of Thuringia. Goering opposed the appointment of Sauckel and suggested that Erich Koch be given the job; Hitler agreed. The appointment of Koch marked the beginning of one of the most spectacular feuds in Nazi party circles. Rosenberg and Koch hated one another, and immediately the German administration in Russia was handicapped by the total lack of cooperation between the East Minister and the *Reichskommissar* for the Ukraine.[11]

DECISION TO USE RUSSIAN LABOR

While Hitler and Rosenberg were preparing grandiose plans for Russia, German agencies were debating the possible use of Russian labor in the Reich. But, unlike all the other countries that Germany had conquered, there was a real concern about bringing the Russians into Germany. Many party leaders pointed out that since the Russians were thoroughly disciplined and indoctrinated by the communist system, they would spread Marxist propaganda in the Reich and the German people might be affected. The Nazi party publicly praised the loyalty of the German people, but privately, like all totalitarian powers, it wondered how successful its own indoctrination had been.

[10] Nazi Germany was divided into 42 Gaus, or districts. Each *Gau* had a *Gauleiter*, who was the highest ranking party official in the district. This *Gau* system was purely a party organization, although the Nazis did try later in the war to incorporate the regional German Governmental Organization into the *Gau* structure. For ease in reading, the Anglicized plurals of *Gau* and *Gauleiter* (Gaus and Gauleiters) have been substituted for the less familiar German forms.

[11] *IMT*, xxxviii, 90-91. Accounts of Koch's appointment and its aftermath are in all the books cited in footnote 8. See also Alfred Rosenberg's *Letzte Aufzeichnungen* (Goettingen: Plesse Verlag, 1953).

Although Hitler had at first ruled against using Russians, the Munitions Ministry reported in a meeting on July 4, 1941, that *Der Fuehrer's* order might be relaxed. Apparently Hitler was willing to allow some Russian POW's in the Reich provided three conditions were met. First, there were to be no Mongolian or Asiatic POW's sent to the Reich. Second, only Russian-speaking POW's were to be admitted, thus minimizing the possibilities of communist propaganda. Third, all POW's were to be heavily guarded and used in large groups, never employed individually. With these conditions in mind, the Munitions Ministry and other Reich agencies notified the Army that they could use immediately 500,000 Russian POW's.[12]

In late August, an agreement was made between the OKW (*Ober-Kommando der Wehrmacht*, or Supreme Command of the Armed Forces) and the OKH (*Ober-Kommando des Heeres*, or Supreme Command of the Army) which called for screening and organizing Russian POW's into work companies.[13] Screening the POW's followed the usual Nazi racial and political lines. All POW's were separated into five groups. The first group consisted of POW's who were racially close to the Germans or who could be used politically. In this group were the *Volksdeutsche*, Ukrainians, and the Baltic peoples. All of these POW's were to be released immediately after screening, provided their homes were under German occupation and they accepted the usual German conditions of not bearing arms again and of reporting to their local police and labor offices. The second general group of POW's consisted of Asiatic, Jewish, or German-speaking POW's. These POW's were to be kept in the immediate operational areas and used for any kind of work the

12 *NCA*, III, 840-841.
13 See the *Wi Stab Ost, Abt. Arbeit* report, on T-178, Roll 19, Frames 3674331-333. This report has in its enclosures a copy of the OKW and OKH agreement of August 23, 1941.

Army needed. The third group was the politically unreliable or suspicious elements; they were to be used in special details. This group was, for all practical purposes, eliminated by the SS under the Kommissar Order.[14] The fourth group of POW's was the officers and non-commissioned officers of the Red Army. The Germans felt that they were probably too indoctrinated to be used in the Reich, so they were to be removed from the operational areas and put to work behind the lines. The fifth group of POW's was, according to this agreement, held in prisons until later instructions were given. Presumably, they were to be sent into the Reich as workers.[15]

At about the same time that the Army was segregating the Russian POW's, Goering was preparing German industries for their use. Goering ordered that all French POW's not already assigned to the armament industry be immediately shifted to such industries, especially the aircraft industry.[16] Transfer of these French POW's was to be completed by October 1, 1941. Gaps resulting from this transfer were to be filled by Russians. The Russian POW's were to be used only in larger groups and in well-known difficult employment conditions such as mining. In the civilian field, the regional labor offices would have to determine the work projects from which French POW's could be withdrawn to be replaced by Soviet POW's. Goering ordered a canvass of all branches of the economy employing French POW's to determine where exchanges would be feasible. To reduce the resistance of individual employers to the exchange idea, Goering suggested that for every 100 French POW's exchanged, 120 Russians be given.[17]

[14] The Kommissar Order called for the liquidation of all Soviet political officers in the Red Army. For a complete account of this order, see Reitlinger's *House Built on Sand*, Chapter II.

[15] *Wi Stab Ost, Abt. Arbeit* report, on T-178, Roll 19, Frames 3674331-333.

[16] *IMT*, XXXI, 474.

[17] *Ibid.*, 475.

While Goering was preparing German industries for the Russian POW's, the Labor Ministry began its first cautious moves for the use of Russian civilian workers. At a conference held on September 24, 1941, representatives of the Labor Ministry, Munitions Ministry, German Labor Front, and SS discussed the possibility of using Russian workers in industry. The SS agent wanted to organize German plants so that each plant would have only one nationality of foreign worker. This arrangement would help the police in their security measures and confine the danger of foreign propaganda. The SS and the Labor Front also stressed the need of an intensive propaganda campaign aimed at the German workers in these plants to insure their cooperation.[18] The Labor and Munitions representatives pointed out the difficulties in assigning only one nationality to a plant, but both heartily endorsed the proposal for the propaganda campaign.

The Labor Ministry then set forth its proposals for the recruitment of Russian workers. At first the Labor Ministry wanted to confine recruitment to those areas of the Soviet Union that had been acquired by the Soviets since 1939, such as Poland and the Baltic countries. Once these areas had been exhausted, recruitment could be conducted for specially needed workers in the older parts of the Soviet Union, preferably the Ukraine. In general, to quote the representative of the Labor Ministry, Dr. Max Timm, "The Reich Minister of Labor does not intend to permit the recruitment to start to any great extent, but wants to collect experiences first. A too intensive recruitment would be out of the question in any case because of the numerous technical difficulties."[19] The "technical difficulties" included the lack of adequate rail transportation, the weather, and the police force in Russia.

At the beginning of November, after months of delay and

[18] See the notes of this September 24, 1941, conference, on T-77, Roll 384, Frame 1232443.
[19] *Minor Trials*, XIII, 965.

hesitation, *Der Fuehrer* finally approved a directive for the use of POW's in the Reich in various large enterprises, provided that POW's received "adequate nourishment."[20] Goering quickly sent instructions to all Reich agencies calling for the "maximum utilization of Russian manpower,"[21] ignoring the limitations originally suggested by the Labor Ministry.

This Goering directive reflected the changes in the German attitude after four and one-half months of fighting in the Soviet Union. Goering mentioned the need, in the Reich, for maintaining sufficient labor reserves, the removal of "the little-producing but much-eating workers from other states," and the desire to reduce the strain on German women. Goering's directive also frankly admitted the heavy demands on German manpower in the operational zones in Russia. Roads, airports, and railroads had to be repaired and built. There was also clean-up work to do and mine fields to clear; all had to be done by German construction personnel. Goering wanted to substitute Russians for the Germans because "the German skilled worker belongs in armament production, not shoveling and chipping stones; the Russian is there for that."[22]

In Germany's Eastern occupied zones, Goering ordered the Russians to be used in agriculture and mining. Within the Reich, the Russians were to be utilized according to requirements. Generally, the following order of priority was to be observed: (1) mining; (2) railroad maintenance (including repair shops and construction of vehicles); (3) war industries; (4) agriculture; (5) building industries; (6) large-scale shops (Goering mentioned shoe factories); and (7) special units for urgent, occasional and emergency work.[23] All employment of the Russians was to be done in groups of twenty or more, and in some fields, such as mining,

[20] *NCA*, vii, 337.   [21] *NCA*, iii, 844.
[22] *IMT*, xxxix, 498.   [23] *NCA*, iii, 836.

there were to be exclusive "Russian enterprises" consisting of Russian labor and German supervisors and guards.

The living conditions of the Russians in the Reich were to be extremely simple. Workers were to be housed in closed barracks completely removed from all other foreign workers and Germans. The guards for the Russians were to be instructed to take prompt and firm action in the event of any signs of insubordination. The clothes of the Russians were to consist of a uniform outfit, wooden shoes, and no underwear (Goering claimed that they did not know about underwear!). The Russians were to be "fed lightly and without serious inroads upon our food balance."[24] Herbert Backe, the German Food Controller, must have taken Goering's directive literally, for he ordered a daily ration of 2,540 calories for the Russians, most of which was Russian bread and *Freibankfleisch*.[25]

"Russian bread" was Backe's own concoction of 50 per cent rye husks, 20 per cent sugar beet chips, 20 per cent flour, and 10 per cent straw or leaf meal (*Strohmehl oder Laubmehl*). *Freibankfleisch* was meat rejected by the health authorities and then chemically processed to make it edible for humans. Horse meat was also suggested to Backe as a part of the Russian diet. (Germans ate both horse meat and *Freibankfleisch* during the war; they received a double ration of both for their regular meat coupons.)

The Goering directive stipulated that the Russian civilian workers in the Reich were to receive some pocket money and necessary food. The relatives of the workers should also receive financial help. However, the wages of the Russian workers were not to be based on the German standard. A social equalization tax, much like the special tax placed on the Polish workers, was introduced. The Nazi rationale for this special tax was that if the Russians received high wages in the Reich, this would prejudice the wage scale in the occu-

[24] *IMT*, xxxix, 500.   [25] *Ibid.*, 501.

pied areas of Russia. Besides, Goering was not averse to making a profit from the labor of foreigners. Goering mentioned that the cheaper wages for the eastern workers would reduce war costs and thereby lower the debt the German people would have to pay after victory had been won.[26] Hitler expressed the same view; he hoped that in ten years Germany would be able to free herself from the burden of the war without letting her purchasing power be shaken.[27] Both Goering and Hitler ignored one salient point: if good wages were paid to the eastern worker, they would be more productive, easier to recruit, and a source of excellent propaganda for the Germans within the Soviet Union.

The reasons the Nazis were unwilling to pay the eastern workers high wages were not economic, but rather racial and political. The Nazis regarded the eastern peoples as "a mass of born slaves, who feel the need of a master."[28] Hitler in particular regarded German rule over these peoples in nineteenth-century colonial terms. He was fond of comparing German rule in the East to British rule in India in the last century. The Germans, Hitler thought, would keep the eastern peoples in a primitive, unorganized, uninformed, and inferior position. Their destiny was to slave for the master race. In return, they would be supplied with "scarves, glass beads and everything that colonial peoples like."[29] No idea about the East was too fantastic for Hitler and his entourage. Nor were these absurdities mere after-dinner chatter of the Nazi leaders. The Nazis were busy in Russia translating

---

[26] *Hitler's Secret Conversations*, trans. by Norman Cameron and R. H. Stevens (New York: Farrar, Straus and Young, 1953), p. 46.
[27] *Ibid.*, pp. 26-27.   [28] *Ibid.*, p. 28.
[29] *Ibid.*, p. 29. Compare Hitler's comments made on the evening of July 22, 1942, in *Hitler's Secret Conversations*, with Bormann's letter to Rosenberg, dated July 23, 1942, on T-175, Roll 194, Frames 2734061-62. Bormann outlined to Rosenberg German policy toward the Russian people in the same words and expressions that Hitler had used the night before. Thus, through Bormann, Hitler's after-dinner chat was translated into active German policy.

their racial and political ideas into reality, and their efforts had important effects on the foreign labor program.

THE LOST RUSSIAN ARMY OF POW'S

While Goering and others planned for Russian labor and Hitler dreamed of Germany's new India, events in Russia moved ahead in an inexorable manner. By the end of October 1941, the encirclement tactics of the Germans had inflicted tremendous manpower losses on the Red Army. By the winter of 1941-1942, Germany had captured over three and one-half million Soviet POW's.[30] Never in the history of warfare had there been such a gigantic capture of soldiers. Indeed, the German preinvasion plans were completely inadequate for handling this huge body of POW's. Since Hitler had barred Russians from the Reich from July to November 1941, the camps constructed by the Army for Russian POW's stood empty and the food supply was correspondingly inadequate. Undoubtedly the German Army had tremendous difficulties in supplying this vast number with food and shelter, but there seems to have been a deliberate German attempt to decimate the ranks of the Soviet POW's by starvation and abuse.[31] Goering, who had predicted the deaths of millions of superfluous Russians in "The Green File," told Ciano that the Russian POW's, "after eating everything possible including the soles of their boots, have begun to eat

[30] Sources varied as to the exact number of Soviet POW's captured in the first half-year of fighting. Dallin, in *German Rule in Russia*, claimed 3,355,000. Dr. Mansfeld of the Reich Labor Ministry mentioned the figure 3,900,000 in a report published in *NCA*, Supplement A, 361.

[31] See Chapter xix in Dallin's *German Rule in Russia* and Chapter iii in Reitlinger's *House Built on Sand*. The Soviet government compiled accounts of the harsh treatment of Soviet POW's and published them in a book called *We Shall Not Forgive!* (Moscow: Foreign Languages Publishing House, 1942).

each other, and what is more serious, have also eaten a German sentry."[32]

Reports on this tragedy began flowing back to Berlin. Soldiers appealed to the traditional German sense of military honor to halt the deplorable situation. Armament inspectors wrote that shooting Jews and allowing POW's to die were antagonizing the native populations, thus making more difficult the job of the Germans in Russia.[33] Alfred Rosenberg told Hitler personally that over 2,500 Soviet POW's were dying daily in one army area alone.[34] The only rational solution was to allow these Russian POW's to come into the Reich to work. By the time Hitler had changed his mind and the Russians were actually transported or had walked to the Reich, incalculable damage had been done. Dr. Werner Mansfeld of the Reich Labor Ministry wrote, in February 1942, to the Munitions Ministry that the present difficulties would not have arisen if a decision had been made in time to allow generous employment of Russian POW's.[35]

Mansfeld explained that of the 3,900,000 Soviet POW's once available, only 1,100,000 were left.[36] Only about 400,000 Soviet POW's had been employed in the Reich by February. For Mansfeld, the employment of the remaining Russian POW's was "exclusively a question of transportation. It is insane to transport these laborers in open or closed unheated box cars, merely to unload corpses at the destination."[37]

Reports from individual German industrial plants confirmed Mansfeld's lugubrious report. The Warthe I. G. Far-

[32] *Ciano's Diplomatic Papers* (London: Odhams Press, 1948), pp. 264-265.
[33] *Monatsbericht Wi Stab Ost*, December 8, 1941, which appears on T-178, Roll 19, Frames 3674900-903; the entire report is on Frames 3674900-972.
[34] *IMT*, xxvii, 272.   [35] *NCA*, Supplement A, 362.
[36] *Minor Trials*, vi, 702.   [37] *NCA*, Supplement A, 362.

ben plant had 500 Russian POW's assigned for work in January, but only 185, or 37 per cent, were fit to work. A month later, only 158 Russians were able to work, 107 were dead, and 200 were sick.[38] The director of the Linke-Hofman Werke (Breslau) reported that the company doctor had ordered the Russian POW's to bed for eight days of rest because all had arrived in a "completely starved and exhausted condition."[39] The Hermann Goering plant at Regensburg found that the Russians were only able to produce from one-third to one-half as much as a German worker.[40]

The German Military Command recognized the serious effects of the harsh treatment of the Soviet POW's. In a report to OKW dated February 28, 1942, the German military command in Russia pointed out that the forced marches, diseases, and rough treatment were killing the Russian POW's by the thousands, and all of Germany's propaganda was negated by such actions. In the long run, the report continued, it was not only the German position in Russia that was being undermined, but also German industry, which needed the labor of the Russians.[41] OKW was unable to do much about some of these conditions since it did not control the SS and SD (*Sicherheitsdienst*). The liquidation of undesirables among the Russian POW's was done by special task forces of the SS and SD called *Einsatzgruppen*. OKW did, however, have control over the care of the POW's in army camps. The failure of many army officials to exercise greater care and concern resulted in their conviction before military tribunals after the war.

Although nothing could ever truly depict the suffering and death experienced by the Russian POW's, a German report of May 1944 does show the enormity of this tragedy (see Table VII). The folly of the German treatment of Soviet

[38] *Minor Trials*, VIII, 419.   [39] *Ibid.*, VI, 708.
[40] See report from Regensburg *Kreisobmann*, dated April 27, 1942, on T-81, Roll 65, Frames 77958-959.
[41] *NCA*, III, 129.

TABLE VII

THE FATE OF SOVIET PRISONERS OF WAR AS OF MAY 1, 1944

	In OKH Custody (in occupied USSR Territory)	in OKW Custody (in Germany and Poland)	Total
Number of Russian POW's	2,050,000	3,110,000	5,160,000
Recorded deaths in POW camps and compounds	845,000	1,136,000	1,981,000
Released to civilian or military status	535,000	283,000	818,000
Escapes	⎫	67,000	⎫
Exterminations	⎪	473,000	⎪
Not accounted for	⎬ 495,000		⎬ 1,308,000
Deaths and disappearance in transit	⎭	273,000	⎭
Surviving as POW's	175,000	878,000	1,053,000
POW's working	151,000	724,000	875,000

SOURCE: Alexander Dallin, *German Rule in Russia*, p. 427. Mr. Dallin based his chart on the German report of the *OKW/AWA* called "Nachweisungen des Verbleibs der sowjetischen Kr. Gef. nach dem Stand vom 1.5.1944."

POW's, judged from a purely economic view, quite apart from a humanitarian one, can hardly be overemphasized. At the same time that Germany was conducting recruitment drives in all of Europe, she was allowing millions of able-bodied Soviet POW's to die in camps in the East. Soviet propaganda quickly used this horrible example of cruelty to strengthen the fighting resistance of the Red Army and the Russian people.[42] As one writer pointed out, the treatment of

[42] Braeutigam, *Ueberblick*, p. 90. Braeutigam was Deputy Chief of the Political Department in the Eastern Ministry during 1941-

Russian POW's at the beginning of the war was the first major shock to many Russians who had expected better things from Germany.[43] The German treatment of POW's was but one of a series of actions that eventually eliminated every vestige of cooperation on the part of the peoples of the East.

FIRST EFFORTS AT CIVILIAN RECRUITMENT
IN RUSSIA

Ironically, while hundreds of thousands of Russian POW's perished in camps, the Germans started recruiting Russian civilians for work in the Reich. Since official approval for the recruitment of civilian workers was delayed until November 1941, and the winter was early and severe, very few Russian workers were transported to the Reich until the spring of 1942. In spite of the ghastly work of the SS, the mistreatment of POW's, and the terrible food situation in the occupied areas of Russia, the native population showed less hostility and opposition to the recruitment program than were expected.[44] In fact, there seemed to be a genuine interest in working in the Reich, which Otto Braeutigam attributed to the Russian love of wandering and a natural curiosity to see the much-scorned "capitalistic countries" personally.[45] A more probable explanation was that many Russians felt that, no matter how bad conditions in the Reich were, they could not be worse than in Russia. Instead of capitalizing on Russian willingness to work in the Reich, however, the Germans followed a course of action that made

---

1945. He currently is serving in the Eastern Section of the Bonn Foreign Office.

[43] Oleg Anisimov, *The German Occupation in Northern Russia During World War II* (New York: East European Fund, No. 56, 1954), p. 28. (Mimeographed series.)

[44] Dallin, *German Rule in Russia*, p. 56.

[45] Braeutigam, *Ueberblick*, p. 90.

even the pro-German elements in the Russian populace turn away in disgust.

Basically, the early German civilian labor policy in occupied Russia was a continuation of policies the Germans had used in Poland. The accent was on racial inferiority and the need for compulsion. First, compulsory labor laws were passed while German recruiters moved into the areas siphoning off all volunteers for the Reich.[46] By the time the flow of volunteers dried up, the German occupational authorities were in a position to apply force. The Economic Staff East reported that the initial drive for volunteers had gone smoothly. In Kharkov, for example, nearly 2,000 Russian workers signed to go to the Reich in the first five days of recruitment. By mid-January, Kharkov would be sending two trains a week to the Reich, with 1,000 workers per train.[47]

The first reports from the Reich indicated that the initial German fear of communist-trained workers was grossly exaggerated. The Russians were docile, yet skilled and eager workers. Even Hitler seemed impressed, for he told Reich Minister Fritz Todt that the major problem Germany faced was the scarcity of labor. The influx of Russian workers would allow the Reich to shift its own German and western foreign workers to other tasks. "It's better [*sic*] worthwhile to take the trouble of knocking the Russians into shape," Hitler said, "than to fetch Italians from the South, who will say good-bye after six weeks! A Russian is not so stupid, after all, that he can't work in a mine. In any case, we're completely geared for standardization."[48]

Although German recruitment of Russian civilian labor and utilization of Soviet POW's were slight until the spring of 1942, conditions within and outside the Reich made these

---

[46] *NCA*, Supplement A, 408-412.
[47] *Halbmonatsbericht Wi Stab Ost* report, dated December 31, 1941, on T-178, Roll 19, Frames 3675117-119.
[48] *Hitler's Secret Conversations*, p. 129.

efforts academic. Nazi Germany was on the verge of a revolution in her war economy that would completely alter the foreign labor program as well as the entire course of the war. Fortunately for Germany, but unfortunately for the rest of the world, a combination of accidents and the appointment of new leaders ignited this managerial revolution.

CHAPTER V

The Reorganization of the German War Economy

O N February 8, 1942, Reich Minister of Munitions Todt completed a personal report to Hitler. Todt left the headquarters of *Der Fuehrer* and drove to the airport at Rastenburg, East Prussia, where his aircraft was waiting to fly him to Berlin. Shortly after take-off, the plane suddenly failed and dropped to the ground with an explosion. There were no survivors.

The death of Todt was a serious loss to the German government. He had been an outstanding engineer and minister and had first won acclaim as the builder of the *Reichsautobahn*. Later, he built the Siegfried Line, or Westwall, opposing the French Maginot Line. In 1941, when Hitler created the new Ministry of Munitions, Todt was appointed its chief. In addition to being the Minister of Munitions, Todt held many other important posts in the Reich, including Head of the *Organisation Todt* (OT), the major construction unit for the German Army.

In choosing Todt's successor, Hitler made one of his best appointments—his 37-year-old private architect, Albert Speer. The son of a successful architect, Speer followed his father's occupation and studied architecture at the technical universities at Karlsruhe, Mannheim, and Munich. Speer graduated in 1928 as a *Diplom-Ingenieur*, and for the next four years he was an assistant instructor at the Technical University in Berlin. He joined the Nazi party in 1932. In 1933, Speer began his private practice in Berlin and Mannheim. The same year, he was commissioned by the Nazi party in Berlin to prepare for the May Day celebrations. In 1934, Speer first came into close personal contact with Hit-

8 7

ler, and after the death of Professor Paul Ludwig Troost in 1935, Speer became Hitler's private architect. Hitler, who fancied himself an architect, seemed to be impressed not only with Speer's technical abilities but also with his personal charm. The two men became close friends, which undoubtedly influenced Speer's meteoric rise in the German bureaucracy.[1] He was placed in charge of rebuilding the Reich Chancellery in Berlin and constructing the party's buildings at Nuremberg. In 1942, when he replaced Todt, Speer was not only made Reich Minister of Munitions, but also Head of the *Organisation Todt*; General Inspector of Roads, Water, and Power; General Inspector for the Reich's Capital; Plenipotentiary for Building Construction; and Head of the Technical Office of the Nazi party.

At the time of his appointment as Reich Minister of Munitions, Albert Speer was young, energetic, and gifted. His calm, balanced manner of thinking and writing had none of the vulgar arrogance that characterized many Nazi leaders. He had the art of surrounding himself with able men who repaid his faith with inspired work and great personal devotion. Most of the men that Speer appointed to his ministry were reflections of himself—technicians willing to work hard and usually very young. Speer was fond of remarking that "in my ministry, nobody is to be older than myself."[2]

Philosophically, Speer seemed to have the typical outlook of a modern-day technocrat. Although at first he was uninterested in politics or the countless political intrigues that surrounded Hitler, Speer, like all important officials in the Reich, was forced to engage in them. When he did so, it was usually for the purposes of protecting his associates or achieving a higher degree of production for Germany. Above all, Speer was a fanatic believer in efficiency, technology, and

[1] Werner Baumbach, *The Life and Death of the Luftwaffe* (New York: Coward-McCann, 1960), p. 190.

[2] Wagenfuehr, *Rise and Fall of the German Economy*, p. 18.

science. His reforms and the ideas behind them helped to shape the entire future course of the foreign labor program of Nazi Germany.

THE SPEER REFORMS

Unlike his predecessor Todt, Speer was dissatisfied with the condition of the German war economy. Speer was convinced that the economy had not been converted into a war economy on a sufficiently large scale.[3] Along with General Thomas, he advocated an armament policy of depth instead of mere breadth.[4] Germany needed to expand its production basis immediately by building new plants and ruthlessly weeding out inefficient or unnecessary plants. Above all, Germany needed a unified, powerful leadership in her economy. Speer intended to carry out such a program regardless of opposition.

Although Speer and others realized the need for radical changes in the economy, the official position of the ranking Nazi leaders remained unchanged. Not even the defeats suffered in the first winter in Russia could shake the predominant Nazi view that the war was nearly won. While German production had dropped slightly from the summer of 1940 to the winter of 1941, and stocks of materials had decreased at a tremendous rate, few Nazi leaders seriously questioned the intensity of the war effort.[5] When Speer suggested that new plants be built, he was told that such a plan was unprofitable, since new plants would be useless in the peacetime economy which was "within easy grasp."[6] Not even the appointment of Speer as Minister of Weapons and Ammunition in February 1942 could be interpreted as a decisive change in the Nazi concept of strategy, for his powers were

[3] *IMT*, xvi, 460.
[4] Thomas, *Studie der Wehrwirtschaft*, p. 533.
[5] USSBS, *The Effects of Strategic Bombing*, p. 24.
[6] Wagenfuehr, *Rise and Fall of the German Economy*, p. 16.

rigidly limited. Speer was not expected to assume complete control over the German war economy.

Initially, Speer lacked the necessary power and authority to alter the war economy. His ministry was one of many agencies connected with war production. Speer's job was that of an expediter of special programs and a coordinator for production of urgently required weapons and munitions. The basic direction of the armament industries and allocation of scarce materials was still in the hands of the traditional military offices of the various branches of the German armed forces and the Four Year Plan Office. The Economics Ministry also exercised control over many products directly needed for war production, such as textiles and basic materials. The Labor Ministry and the Four Year Plan Office were, of course, responsible for the allocation of labor for all war production. In short, no single office was charged with balancing Germany's resources with its demands for war production.

Moreover, the general organization of German business was not conducive to effective control of war production. The system was exceedingly complicated and demanded an unusual amount of cooperation in order to function properly. Basically, German business was organized along two lines, functional and territorial.[7] Functionally, all German industrial enterprises belonged to one of seven Reich Groups (*Reichsgruppen*), depending on the individual enterprise's activity. The seven Reich Groups were: Industry, Trade, Banking, Insurance, Power, Handicrafts, and Tourist Traffic. They were subdivided into Economic Groups (*Wirtschaftsgruppen*), which were in turn divided into subgroups

[7] The information on the organization of German business was taken from many sources, but the most important ones were Neumann, *Behemoth*; Eberhart Barth, *Wesen und Aufgaben der gewerblichen Wirtschaft* (Hamburg: Deutsche Verlag, 1939); and Robert A. Brady, *The Spirit and Structure of German Fascism* (New York: Macmillan Co., 1937).

or Trade Groups (*Fachgruppen*). Industry, for example, had thirty-one Economic Groups, each representing one special branch of industry. The Trade Groups were usually organized according to their production.

Territorially, German business was organized on three levels: local, regional, and national. At the local level, every German enterprise belonged to one of the one hundred Chambers of Industry and Commerce, or to one of the seventy Chambers of Handicrafts. At the regional level, there were forty-two Economic Chambers (*Gauwirtschaftskammern*) corresponding to the Nazi *Gau* organization. At the top of this pyramid stood the Reich Economic Chamber (*Reichswirtschaftskammer*). Membership in all territorial and functional groups was mandatory.

It is most difficult to determine how effective this organization of German business was in coordinating and encouraging higher war production. However, a study made after the war indicated that these trade organizations of German businesses all too often acted "as pressure groups and were strongly influenced by considerations of competitive advantages, postwar market prospects and monopolistic privileges."[8] Moreover, Funk's Economics Ministry, which was in charge of this vast array of trade organizations, seemed unwilling or unable to control the activities of these groups. Speer's agency found later in the war that this organization of business tended to protect the high-cost firms, encourage the production of unnecessary goods, hoard labor, and, in general, keep production output low. Rolf Wagenfuehr, an economist in Speer's ministry, frankly admitted that "German industrialists seem to have shown considerable ingenuity in keeping up the supply of unnecessary goods and with it their own profits; the fierce opposition of some Nazi regional authorities to any curtailment of the consumer goods

[8] USSBS, *The Effects of Strategic Bombing*, p. 24.

91

industry continued into 1943."[9] Unfortunately, the information on this topic is scant, yet everything points to the conclusion that the very organization of German business proved to be more of an impediment to the war economy than has been commonly assumed.[10]

Speer directed his first series of reforms at two sets of problems. First, he attempted to bring some order to the administrative muddle that characterized German war production before 1942; and second, he attacked the complacent attitude of many German leaders. His first opportunity to slash some of the undergrowth of overlapping jurisdictions and faulty administrative procedures came immediately after his appointment. Hitler asked Speer to investigate the chaos in steel distribution. In a series of reports to Hitler in March 1942, Speer pointed out that decisive measures were needed to solve the steel situation. The backlog of orders then amounted to from ten to fifteen million tons. Some German plants were forced to wait from twelve to eighteen months for delivery. At the same time, other plants had been able to hoard nearly a year's supply of steel.[11] Speer proposed to Hitler that an overall board with a subordinate organization be created to coordinate production planning with the allocation of raw materials.

Hitler's response to Speer was characteristically instinctive and negative. Immediately, he ordered a series of strict punishments for individuals or companies that gave false reports of their manpower or material requirements. Penalties for such actions included unlimited fines and death.[12]

[9] Wagenfuehr, *Rise and Fall of the German Economy*, p. 49.

[10] There exists no definitive work on this subject, but the works of Neumann, Klein, Wagenfuehr, and Thomas indicate that the organization of German business revealed serious difficulties in harnessing its capacity for war production.

[11] See reports from Speer to Hitler for March 1942, in the files of the USSBS.

[12] A full list of the penalties can be seen in Hitler's order of March 21, 1942, on T-77, Roll 234, Frames 975317-320.

However, Hitler did establish an overall board called the Central Planning Board (*Zentrale Planung*) under Goering's Four Year Plan Office. Placing the board under Goering was apparently a token measure, since only Hitler reviewed the board's decisions.[13] Possibly Hitler did not want to offend Goering, or perhaps he did not wish to show the outside world that the Reich's economy was in need of reorganization.

The *Zentrale Planung* consisted of Speer, Field Marshal Erhard Milch, who represented the *Luftwaffe*, and Paul Koerner, Chief Deputy of the Four Year Plan. Since Hitler had followed his usual inclination and refused to appoint a single director of the board, Speer quickly appointed himself. On occasion, other members of the government were invited to attend when decisions of the board affected their jurisdiction. The purposes of the board were to decide on priorities of new and future production plans; distribute raw materials, such as steel, coal, and other forms of energy; create new raw material plants; and plan, direct, and coordinate the requirements of the military and civilian economy in general, although this last purpose was not specifically assigned to the board.[14]

The detailed work for the *Zentrale Planung* was entrusted to a subordinate organization called the Planning Office (*Planungsamt*). The Planning Office was a permanent working group that actually was responsible for the overall planning of production and distribution. Its recommendations were given to *Zentrale Planung* and used as a basis for discussion. Normally the *Zentrale Planung* met only a few times each business quarter to establish the next quarter's quotas, to discuss urgent problems, and to formulate broad general decisions on matters affecting the entire economy. Speer

[13] Affidavit of Erhard Milch in *NCA*, viii, 653-656.
[14] *IMT*, xli, 413-414.

shrewdly had the Planning Office placed under his Ministry and headed by his Raw Materials Division Leader, Hans Kehrl. Thus, by directly assuming control over the Planning Office and thereby indirectly guiding the *Zentrale Planung*, Speer was able to take the first step toward virtual economic dictatorship of the German economy by 1943.

Speer's second general administrative reform was to bring the various armed forces' Armament Offices under his direction. In May 1942, the Military, Economic, and Armament Office (*Wi Rue Amt*) of the OKW under General Georg Thomas was transferred to the Speer ministry. Since the Army was the largest single user of German war production, Speer had, in effect, brought a considerable part of the total economy under his control. With this transfer, Speer also inherited the entire armament inspection system. The inspection system was responsible for insuring that the armament plants had the necessary labor, raw materials, and power to fulfill the Army's contracts and comply with the Army's standards. For Speer, the transfer of the armament inspection system of the Army meant that he could extend his control directly to the individual German plant. Later in the war, Speer managed to bring both the Air Force and Navy Armament Offices under his ministry, thus uniting the procurement and control of armaments.[15]

The administrative achievement of which Speer was proudest was his reorganization of German business. The conversion of German business to wartime uses made the old industrial, economic, and trade groups obsolete. Auto plants might be making tanks or airplane frames, while candy factories might be packaging parachutes. But the system did not consider wartime conversions, for plants were still organized into trade groups based on their prewar production. Speer, who had faith in the superior efficiency of private industry,

[15] Klein, *Germany's Economic Preparations*, pp. 156-157.

organized German business under the principle of self-imposed responsibility. Recruiting the best engineers, plant managers, and efficiency experts, Speer formed executive boards to act as liaison groups between industry and government.

The executive boards dealt entirely with the technical aspects of production. They sought to reorganize German production to correspond with wartime needs. There were two sets of executive boards, the central committees (*Hauptausschuesse*) and the rings committees (*Ringe*). The central committees were concerned with the technical production of finished products. For example, there was a special committee for Tiger tanks and another for artillery pieces. The rings produced intermediary or half-finished products such as electric motors, bearings, and cog wheels, and refined raw materials. There was, for example, a special ring for coal, another for steel. In the event that one factory was low in production or high in costs, the appropriate committee would investigate and recommend reorganizing or, in extreme cases, closing the plant. The special committees also served as collection points for new ideas and techniques. The committees would test, evaluate, and then pass these new techniques quickly to other plants involved in the production of similar goods. In short, the work of the committees was to rationalize the production in German armament factories.

Speer placed great faith in the young men he selected from industry. Throughout the war, he gave more responsibilities to his technical administrators. He granted them wide latitude in the executive boards, and he readily accepted their decisions. Speer also completely restaffed the old Armament Inspection Offices with these young men. All of Speer's writings during and after the war mentioned the mediocrity of the personnel in the old military organization compared with his technicians.

9 5

These organizations, consisting of officers and civil service officials, conducted purely theoretical deliberations on rearmament, and became so large that they managed only to keep each other busy. They committed what might be called mental incest, and when Germany's rearmament got actively under way, all the mistakes which later led to the surprisingly low level of armaments production were present in embryo. . . . The great administrative organizations of the Wehrmacht were incapable of exploiting the available capacity. Highly qualified personnel had found better pay in industry and were not called on for their cooperation.[16]

The keys to Speer's successes in production were the careful placement of technicians and the pragmatic approach to all problems; he had no basic principle of armament production. The main characteristic of Speer's armament program was the strategic placement of his personnel in the intermediate positions of authority; for example, they were placed in the Armament Inspection Offices, where they improvised solutions for all problems encountered by factories.[17] The scope of what constituted armament production was also broadened by Speer. Eventually the entire production of steel, chemicals, synthetic products, and products whose use could not be predicted at the time of manufacture fell under Speer's definition of armament production.

In summary, Speer's reforms were designed to correct the administrative problems that plagued the Nazi war economy in the early years of the war. Speer established the *Zentrale Planung* to control the distribution of raw materials and direct the total planning of the German war economy. The general decisions of the *Zentrale Planung* were effectively enforced by uniting the armament offices of the various military services under his ministry. Then Speer reorganized German

[16] *Ibid.*, pp. 158-159.   [17] *IMT*, xvi, 449.

business on the concept of self-imposed responsibility, and he appointed special technicians to oversee the change. These innovations in German administrative organization encouraged the rationalization of German production. The result of Speer's reforms was a striking increase in the production of weapons and munitions in the last years of the war.

OPPOSITION TO THE SPEER REFORMS

The Speer reforms which first emerged in the spring of 1942 were continued throughout the war. The more difficult the German war situation became, the harder Speer pressed, but the opposition was formidable.

Although the industrialists favored the idea of self-imposed responsibility, they disliked the minute regulations of Speer's ministry. Some of them were reluctant to exchange their trade secrets with other German plants. Some were afraid that the Speer measures would favor the large producers at the expense of the small ones. All were afraid that the concentration of power in the German economy might mean their economic ruin.[18]

The bureaucracy was also opposed to the Speer reforms, particularly Funk's ministry. Speer continually complained that the Economics Ministry was failing to curtail the production of goods using scarce materials, and it had not efficiently converted civilian industries to war production.[19] When Speer tried to curb these abuses himself, he met fierce opposition not only from the Economics Ministry but also from the Nazi Gauleiters. Both were interested in keeping the production of consumer goods high in Germany. In spite of many pious declarations by government and party officials about the need for a Spartan life, consumer production was not seriously reduced until 1943. As late as 1942, the con-

[18] *Goebbels Diaries*, pp. 84, 129.

[19] Klein, *Germany's Economic Preparations*, p. 162; and Thomas, *Studie der Wehrwirtschaft*, p. 533.

sumer expenditures were 66 billion marks—19 per cent below the 1939 peak, but still equal to the 1937 level.[20]

The most serious opposition to Speer came from the ranking Nazi leaders. Speer threatened their position by his attacks on their complacency and his uncompromising stand against the spectacular manifestations of their soft, expensive living.[21] There were traces of Speer's bourgeois background in his criticism of the overindulgence of many of the other Nazi leaders. Speer termed it "distinctly vulgar, typically *nouveau riche*," after the war.[22]

What the other Nazi leaders found most rankling, however, was Speer's close relationship with Hitler. *Der Fuehrer* had intimated a number of times in 1942-1943 that Speer was being considered, after Goering, as Hitler's successor.[23] As Speer himself remarked, "Relations between the various high leaders can be understood only if their aspirations are interpreted as a struggle for the succession to Adolf Hitler."[24] Both Goering and Robert Ley were especially disturbed when Speer was appointed Munitions Minister. Goering approved the appointment with the reservation that Speer was to be formally under his Four Year Plan.[25] Ley apparently wanted the Munitions Ministry for himself. When Speer was appointed, Ley wrote a series of articles attacking him. *Der Fuehrer* was so displeased by Ley's actions that he called him in and gave him what Goebbels termed "a tongue-lashing."[26] For one reason or another, almost all the top Nazi leaders wanted to undermine the position of the young architect.

Speer was able to complete many of his reforms in the face of such hardened opposition only because of Hitler's faith

[20] USSBS, *The Effects of Strategic Bombing*, p. 23.
[21] Speer interview, May 22, 1945, in the files of the USSBS, p. 1.
[22] *Ibid.*, p. 2.
[23] Speer interview, May 28, 1945, in the files of the USSBS, pp. 3-4.
[24] As quoted in Dallin's *German Rule in Russia*, p. 19.
[25] IMT, xvi, 455.   [26] *Goebbels Diaries*, p. 84.

in him during the first years of his appointment. Speer's notes found after the war revealed that he had direct and frequent contact with Hitler throughout 1942 and 1943. In conference after conference, Speer clarified his views to *Der Fuehrer* and, as often as not, Speer's viewpoints were accepted. This did not mean, however, that Speer found Hitler easy to work for. Hitler's ideas, methods, and interferences were a constant source of difficulty. The history of his intervention in detailed, technical aspects of the procurement of weapons and supplies for the *Wehrmacht* is too well known to bear repeating. However, these changes produced enormous amounts of work for Speer and his associates, for they contradicted the essence of Speer's reforms. Speer sought to establish a rational and standardized production system which would increase the quantity without affecting the quality of the armaments. Hitler and his immediate staff had no idea how difficult it was to retool, change, or shift production processes in order to accommodate last-minute minor alterations in design or detail.[27]

Moreover, the interference and opposition by Hitler, the Nazi party, the government bureaucracy, and the industrialists played just as decisive a role in the reorganization of the labor program as it did in the attempt to frustrate Speer's reforms.

THE NEW LABOR PROGRAM

From the fall of 1941 to the spring of 1942, German leaders were also engaged in reorganizing the entire labor program. The Russian war had placed an unexpected strain on the manpower of the Reich. German losses rose steadily and, with the failure of the blitzkrieg, German leaders were confronted with the problem of not merely replacing their losses but also enlarging the *Wehrmacht* considerably. In

[27] Klein, *Germany's Economic Preparations*, pp. 169-171.

effect, this placed a double strain on the civilian labor economy, because of the withdrawal of trained German workers and the need for increased armament production. Whole new armies had to be equipped, diminished stocks replenished, and, in the eyes of most German leaders, the level of the civilian economy maintained. All the errors of Germany's short-range, inadequate economic planning became painfully evident.

The most obvious solution to the critical labor shortage was to draft more women into industry. The administrative machinery already existed for this purpose; it was merely a question of using the power of the state to enforce the laws. Apparently the Reich labor officials and the Nazi party were against such drastic measures. In September 1941, the Labor Ministry estimated that women drafted into work would not be nearly as effective as voluntary labor.[28] The monthly reports from regional labor offices substantiated the opinion of the Labor Ministry. Judging by the tone of these reports, the Germans had many more difficulties with the German women who started working after the war began than with the foreign workers. These German women, the labor offices complained, were indifferent workers, had too much money, and consequently had a tendency to come and go as they pleased. When one official complained to the police authorities that they were not severe enough with women who stayed away from their work, he was told: "The local Gestapo has received orders from higher up to handle such cases with extreme circumspection as long as 'the little ladies of the upper-crust' (*Daemchen der oberen Zehntausend*) are not drafted for labor but spend their time in restaurants smoking expensive cigarettes and drinking the small amount of alcohol left in the country."[29]

[28] Stenographic notes of the Labor Ministry's conference of September 24, 1941, on T-77, Roll 384, Frames 1232441-448.

[29] Remsheid *Monatlicher Taetigkeitsbericht* for March 2, 1942, in the files of the USSBS.

100

But the real reason that the Labor Ministry was unwilling to draft women into industry stemmed from the opposition of Hitler and the Nazi party. *Der Fuehrer* continually told everyone connected with the labor problem that, judging from his World War I experiences, he considered it inadvisable to use German women in industry; there was a risk of doing great moral harm to women.[30] In addition, drafting women for work lowered the morale of the soldiers at the front.[31] For these political and psychological reasons, Hitler and the whole Nazi party opposed drafting women for war work until 1943. Franz Seldte, Labor Minister of Germany, in discussing Hitler's reasons after the war, thought that *Der Fuehrer* was anchored to old German lines of thought; a woman's place was in the home. Speer disagreed. He thought that Hitler and especially the Nazi Gauleiters wanted to keep German women out of war work in 1942 because they did not feel it was necessary.

The unconditional belief in victory—even with the Gauleiters—had something to do with it. They were too optimistic. Here our Reichspropaganda backfired. Nobody thought that we could lose the victory. The words of Churchill—"blood, sweat and tears" would have been the right slogan for us, too. Instead of that, we only had "Our victory is assured." Because of this mentality no Gauleiter wanted to make any personal sacrifices.[32]

General Thomas agreed with Speer. Thomas thought that the reasons for the Nazi opposition to women being drafted into war work was a combination of complacency, inept prop-

[30] Kleist, *Zwischen Hitler und Stalin*, p. 193.

[31] OKW report, *Erfahrungsbericht ueber die Entwicklung auf dem Gebiet der Personalbewirtschaftung in der Zeit vom Winterbeginn 1941/1942 bis zum Winterbeginn 1942/1943*, on T-77, Roll 440, Frame 1600367.

[32] Speer interview, May 31, 1945, in the files of the USSBS, p. 11.

aganda, and misunderstandings about the necessity of total war measures in the early years of the conflict.[33]

Speer's and Thomas' criticisms of Nazi reluctance to draft women were answered by the argument that Germany already had a method of supplying labor to industry—the foreign labor program. According to the Nazis this was the perfect solution. The labor was available and trained, and one did not have to extract sacrifices from the German people. All that was necessary was to apply more pressure in the occupied territories. Even the critical shortage of the winter of 1941-1942 could be solved, especially since *Der Fuehrer* promised victory in Russia after the summer campaign. Apparently this policy was the one the Nazi leaders decided to adopt.

At the end of January 1942, Dr. Werner Mansfeld, Director of Labor for Goering's Four Year Plan, sent to all occupied zone authorities an express letter discussing the possibility of extensive recruitment of foreign workers in the near future. Mansfeld advised the occupational authorities that, if possible, the labor program should be voluntary. However, should the results of the voluntary program prove to be unsatisfactory, the authorities should set up stand-by controls to apply more pressure. Mansfeld suggested four stages of controls. First, laws should be passed to prohibit workers from changing jobs and make it difficult for them to get new jobs in their own country. Second, unemployment relief should be lowered to provide a financial inducement to work in the Reich. Third, if workers still persisted in refusing such work, then unemployment rates should be lowered to a bare minimum or withdrawn entirely. Mansfeld even suggested removing ration cards for unemployed workers who refused to work in the Reich. The fourth and final stage was the use of force. Optimistically, Mansfeld thought the mere possi-

[33] Thomas, *Studie der Wehrwirtschaft*, pp. 172, 188, and 331-332.

bility of force would often be enough to fulfill labor quotas.[34]

In the occupied areas of Russia, the German authorities received instructions from the Economic Staff East, blunter in tone than Mansfeld's letter. The Economic Staff East told them that it was absolutely necessary to recruit Russian labor for the Reich. When voluntary methods were not enough, forceful measures must be taken. The precarious shortage of labor in the Reich demanded it.[35]

In addition to preparing the occupied territories for extensive recruitment, the Nazi leaders decided to overhaul the administrative program for both foreign and domestic labor. The recruitment and allocation of labor had become a bureaucratic muddle. The Army, Air Force, Goering's Four Year Plan Office, railroads, private companies, Reich Labor Office, and Reich Food Office were all recruiting and distributing labor with little regard for the others.[36] The situation was comparable to what Speer had found in the distribution of raw materials. The administrative program needed a central, powerful office under the direction of an influential man who could consolidate demands and recruit and distribute workers according to a priority system. Necessarily, this office would have to maintain close cooperation with Speer's production plans in the entire Reich.

In October of 1941, Martin Bormann, Hitler's ubiquitous private secretary, had already queried Hans Lammers, Chief of the Reich Chancellery, as to his opinion about establishing a central office for the utilization of foreign labor. Bormann apparently had written to Lammers that Hitler was contemplating such an office under Goering's Four Year Plan. Lammers told Bormann that the creation of another office in the

---

[34] *IMT*, xxvii, 53-55.

[35] Document Number 381-USSR, in the Nuremburg Trials Collection.

[36] *IMT*, xxxix, 501.

labor employment field would result in duplication of effort and further division of administration. Lammer suggested that the Reich Minister of Labor be made entirely responsible for foreign labor, since he already possessed a smooth-running machine which had the necessary experience in technical and legislative matters.[37]

In March 1942, when Hitler finally ruled on this administrative problem, his solution was a typical *Fuehrer* compromise. Instead of making either Goering or Seldte entirely responsible for foreign labor, Hitler established a new post called Plenipotentiary General for the Utilization of Labor (*Generalbevollmaechtiger fuer den Arbeitseinsatz*) under the jurisdiction of Goering's Four Year Plan, but composed of three sections of Seldte's Labor Ministry! Moreover, Hitler made the new post responsible for both foreign and domestic labor. Germany now had a Minister of Labor, a special Plenipotentiary of Labor, a Reich Labor Leader, and a Chief of the German Labor Front. It was organized chaos, but illustrated beautifully Hitler's technique of "divide and rule" for his civil servants. Hitler was intent on giving two or three men or agencies the same task without clearly defined powers and then letting them compete with one another. The ensuing struggle for power made a mockery of orderly administration but—and this was of real importance—no one official was able to gather in his hands enough power to threaten the position of *Der Fuehrer*. Hitler used this same system to control his generals,[38] his civilian advisors,[39] his economic leaders,

[37] *Minor Trials*, XIII, 969-970.

[38] Cf. Chester Wilmot, *The Struggle for Europe* (New York: Harper and Bros., 1952), pp. 83-90, 160-165, 190, 380-381, 417, and 435.

[39] Both Otto Meissner, *Staatssekretaer unter Ebert, Hindenburg, Hitler* (Hamburg: Hoffmann und Campe Verlag, 1950), and Otto Dietrich, *12 Jahre mit Hitler* (Muenchen: Isar Verlag, 1955), criticized Hitler's handling of his advisors in this manner.

and his party leaders. Adolf Hitler, who was so fond of ridiculing the Habsburgs, turned out to be more of a practitioner of their technique than they were. The vaunted *Fuehrer* principle was, in reality, a poor joke in Hitler's Germany.

Hitler's decision to appoint a special Plenipotentiary for all labor caused the usual political jockeying among the ranking Nazi leaders for the appointment. Robert Ley, who had failed to get the Munitions Ministry, now tried to be appointed chief of labor. Hitler told him that it would be a bad administrative practice to appoint the head of the organization that represented the workers to the job of directing labor allocation for the state.[40] No, Hitler told Ley, the new labor director had to be someone completely free of the present labor situation.

Albert Speer saw Hitler's decision to appoint a new labor director as a perfect opportunity to complete his reforms. Since Speer had already made his first moves to control economic planning, distribution, and production of the German war economy, he needed only the control of labor to perfect his system.[41] But Speer wanted someone who could also help him overcome the opposition in the party to his extensive war measures. A strong personality and a strong political figure were needed in the new post. To Speer, the major problem the new labor director would face was control of the many conflicting interests that had developed during the war in the political and state offices, in the internal administrative offices, and in the party and economic agencies. The biggest offenders were the Gauleiters, who, for territorial considerations, encouraged useless production and vehemently opposed the transfer of skilled workers from *Gau* to *Gau*. To correct this, Speer told Hitler that a *Gauleiter* should

[40] Speer's notes on his conference with Hitler, March 20, 1942, on T-73, Roll 192, Frame 405468.
[41] Speer interview, May 15, 1945, in the files of the USSBS, p. 4.

be chosen, especially since the Reich Labor Minister had little luck controlling the Gauleiters.[42] Speer had even suggested that *Gauleiter* Karl Hanke of Breslau be appointed. Goering and Hitler approved.[43]

However, Speer's hopes were not fulfilled. The appointment of a *Gauleiter* to the post necessitated the approval of Party Secretary Bormann. Apparently Bormann was able to convince Hitler that Fritz Sauckel, the *Gauleiter* of Thuringia and a close friend of Bormann, should be appointed instead. Two days after Hitler agreed to the appointment of Hanke, the official announcement was made of the Sauckel appointment.[44] Press releases of the announcement carried the story that Sauckel had been appointed at Speer's suggestion, but this came as a complete surprise to the Munitions Minister.

The appointment of Sauckel was viewed with pleasure by Goebbels who, like Speer, advocated more total war measures. Goebbels noted in his diary that Sauckel's "strong National Socialist hand will achieve miracles."[45] Goebbels thought that Sauckel would be able to secure easily an additional million German workers if he proceeded energetically.

The widely advertised decision by Hitler to create a supreme office for labor and the appointment of a *Gauleiter* to that post seemed to indicate the desire to dramatize the critical labor shortage. It also definitely marked a shift of administration from established governmental channels to the party. Hitler had always distrusted civil servants and when he was confronted with a difficult appointment he invariably selected an *Alter Kaempfer* (Old Warrior).

The decision to place Sauckel in the Four Year Plan was a token measure, much the same as in the case of Speer. Goering's chief deputy remarked after the war that it was strictly a cover for the outside world.[46] Goering's power was

[42] *NCA*, Supplement A, 907. [43] *IMT*, xvi, 478.
[44] *Reichsgesetzblatt*, 1942, Part i, 179.
[45] *Goebbels Diaries*, p. 150. [46] *Minor Trials*, xiii, 1106.

fading. Sauckel rarely bothered to contact Goering personally after his appointment, except to send him formal, periodical reports; Speer never even did this. Both men preferred to contact Hitler directly, and Hitler seemed to concern himself continually with labor allocation and recruitment and the general war production of the Reich.

In summary, the critical circumstances of Germany during the winter of 1941-1942 occasioned a series of long overdue reforms in the economy. To carry out these reforms Hitler selected two young, energetic men. Typically for this century, one of them was an avowed non-political technocrat and the other a fanatical party figure. Between the two, they were to create a managerial revolution in the German war economy. To Speer, it was a question of organizing the entire economy to achieve maximum production from the available men and materials. The ultimate objectives seemed clearly defined and the methods simple and direct. Speer would organize the planning, raw materials, and production; Sauckel would supply the labor.

To Sauckel, the ultimate objectives were less sharply defined. All too often, the need for maximum production and the racial and political goals of the Nazi party were not compatible. Speer and Sauckel clashed often over the goals of production and the methods of achieving them. These clashes had a profound effect on the entire foreign labor program of Nazi Germany.

The appointment of these two dissimilar men, in the spring of 1942, fundamentally altered the foreign labor program. Prior to that time, the program could be characterized as erratic in administration and execution, voluntary in nature, and, in general, peripheral to the central problem of Germany's war production. After that time, the foreign labor program became systematic in organization and execution, marked by compulsion, and of vital importance to Germany's economic survival.

CHAPTER VI

Sauckel Plans an Empire

FRITZ SAUCKEL, Hitler's new Plenipotentiary for Labor, was one of the rare Nazi leaders who stemmed from the working class. Sauckel was born in 1894, the only child of a postman. His birthplace was the tiny village of Hassfurt, near Schweinfurt, in the Main River area of Bavaria. His education was limited to four years of elementary and five years of secondary school. At the age of fifteen, Sauckel ran away from home to join the merchant marine. His first job was on a Norwegian sailing ship as a cabin boy at three marks a week. For the next five years, Sauckel worked as a seaman traveling around the world. When World War I began, he was on a German sailing ship heading for Australia. The ship was captured on the high seas by a French warship and taken to France as a prize.[1] Sauckel was interned by the French in a camp on the island of Ile-Longue near Brest. He remained there until September of 1919.[2]

When the war was over, Sauckel returned to Hassfurt. Since his small savings were made worthless by inflation, Sauckel immediately sought work. Too poor to take the examination for the mate's certificate, he worked as a machinist in the Fischer ball-bearing plant in Schweinfurt. It was there that Sauckel first became interested in politics. Although the area was predominantly leftist in political orientation, Sauckel was apparently repelled by socialism, especially the class conflict arguments. Instead, he joined right-wing political and racial groups.[3] In 1923, he became a member of the Nazi party, even though in the same year he married

[1] *IMT*, XIV, 602-604.
[2] Statement and interrogation of Carl Goetz, in the Nuremberg Trials Collection, National Archives.
[3] Neumann, *Behemoth*, p. 304.

the daughter of a strong trade unionist and Social Democrat.[4]

In 1927, when Dr. Arthur Dinter, *Gauleiter* of Thuringia, was removed from the Nazi party because he wanted to create a religious movement in it, Sauckel was appointed to the post. Sauckel entered the Thuringian legislature in 1929, and in 1932 he was appointed Minister of the Interior for Thuringia, one of the first Nazis to become a minister in a regional state. The next year, when Hitler swept into power, Sauckel was made Reich Governor for Thuringia (*Reichsstatthalter*) and a member of the Reichstag. Later, as was customary, he was given the honorary rank of Lieutenant General in the SS and SA.

Sauckel's private life appeared to be ordinary compared with some of the other ranking Nazi leaders. He was devoted to his wife and family of ten children, but before the Nazi seizure of power, he probably had difficulty in maintaining his family on his small salary as *Gauleiter* of 150 RM per month. After 1933, Sauckel's income increased considerably, especially when he became head of the Fritz Sauckel Foundation, a party-owned foundation which controlled the Herman Gustloff Werke.[5] The Gustloff Werke was named after a Nazi agent in Switzerland who was shot in 1934. It controlled six corporations and was one of the largest German munitions concerns.[6] In October 1944, on the occasion of Sauckel's fiftieth birthday, Hitler gave him a check for 250,000 RM in appreciation of his fine work for the Reich. Sauckel's regular governmental salary was about 30,000 RM per year.[7]

When the war broke out, Sauckel was eager for a better position or a military role. As he saw appointment after appointment go to his fellow Gauleiters, he became increasingly

[4] *IMT*, xiv, 604.

[5] Interview of Fritz Sauckel, Number 71, June 2, 1945, in the files of the USSBS.

[6] Neumann, *Behemoth*, p. 304.   [7] *IMT*, xiv, 616.

despondent. Sensitive to the point of desperation because he had no military service record and had not obtained a better post, Sauckel tried to smuggle himself on a submarine as an ordinary seaman. As soon as his identity was discovered, Admiral Doenitz ordered him returned to the Reich on the first homeward-bound ship.[8]

In 1941, Rosenberg suggested to Hitler that Sauckel be made Reich Commissioner for the Ukraine. Hitler rejected the proposal in favor of Koch. However, he did tell Rosenberg that he "esteemed Sauckel particularly highly, and wanted to keep him available for a better appointment."[9] Sauckel's chance finally came in the spring of 1942, when Hitler placed him in charge of the labor program.

Probably one of the most important reasons for Sauckel's selection was his blind obedience to Hitler and Nazi principles. Carl Goetz, a member of the July 20th conspiracy and a fellow prisoner of Sauckel in the First World War, reported that if Sauckel had known of his resistance activities, he would, in spite of their old friendship, "no doubt have handed me over to the Gestapo from which he endeavored to free me in November 1944," because of his faithfulness to Hitler.[10] Everything that Sauckel wrote and said, even after the war, indicated that he was thoroughly imbued with Nazi racial and political concepts.[11]

In short, Fritz Sauckel presented a three-faced image. There is the image of a hard-working, patriotic, devoted family man with limited education and average abilities[12]

---

[8] *Ibid.*, 610.

[9] Rosenberg, *Letzte Aufzeichnungen*, p. 278.

[10] Statement and interrogation of Carl Goetz.

[11] Cf. Sauckel's testimony, writings, and interrogations before the Nuremberg Court and the USSBS.

[12] Two American psychologists who examined the German leaders at the Nuremberg Trials have published their results. Both Douglas M. Kelley, *22 Cells in Nuremberg* (New York: Greenberg Publisher, 1947), and G. M. Gilbert, *Nuremberg Diary* (New York: Farrar,

who understood and appreciated the aspirations and needs of the working man because of his own experiences. There is the image of a typical, ambitious party functionary, eager for promotion and, once he received his big assignment, determined to succeed in order to enhance his position within the party. Finally there is the image of a fanatical doctrinaire of the Nazi philosophy, a man who entirely accepted Nazi racial gradations and the mystique of the charismatic leader.

FIRST PLANS FOR LABOR MOBILIZATION

Immediately after Sauckel was appointed Plenipotentiary for Labor (abbreviated as GBA), he went to see Hitler with his first plan. Sauckel reasoned that in the Reich there were from 23 to 24 million Germans who had not been fully integrated into the war economy. Furthermore, there were still many prisoners of war who had not been assigned to war industry. However, the availability of these POW's depended on Army authorities. With these people in mind, Sauckel drew up an ambitious program that included maximum utilization of POW's, thorough rationalization of German labor, and a *levée en masse* of German women and young people.[13]

Hitler listened to Sauckel's proposals but firmly rejected the timing of the program. *Der Fuehrer* emphasized the critical nature of the situation at that time and the urgent need for trained workers. In flamboyant language, Hitler described how many hundreds of German locomotives and almost all the mechanized armed units, tanks, planes, and mechanical weapons had become useless as a result of the abnormally hard winter. Hundreds of thousands of German

---

Straus and Cudahy, Inc., 1947), found Sauckel to be of average intelligence. Both psychologists found him insignificant and uninteresting, compared with some of the better-known German leaders on trial.

[13] *IMT*, xiv, 621.

soldiers had died or suffered terribly from the cold because their divisions lost their arms and supplies. Hitler explained that if the race with the enemy for new arms, new munitions, and new forces was not won, the Red Army would sweep across Europe as far as the English Channel by the next winter.[14]

In view of that, Hitler told Sauckel he could not wait for German women to become trained and experienced workers, nor could he wait for the rationalization of working methods along the Taylor and Ford lines. He needed trained workers immediately, and the place to obtain them was in the occupied areas. Hitler pointed out that in the West he had already released one-half of the French Army, most of the Belgian Army, and all of the Dutch Army. He could call them back into captivity and use them as labor if Sauckel had any difficulties recruiting civilians in those countries. However, Hitler preferred not to recall them at that moment, for he wanted to fashion through his collaboration program a grand alliance of a united Europe to fight against Bolshevism. Hitler thought that the East would be a better source of immediate labor for the Reich.[15]

When Sauckel brought up the question of international law regarding foreign workers, Hitler brushed it aside. In the West, *Der Fuehrer* explained, the recruitment would be carried out through the military commanders or, in the case of France, under the presidency of the German Ambassador in Paris, who would make the proper agreements with the French government. In the East, Hitler told Sauckel, since Russia had not signed the Geneva Convention, Germany did not feel bound by it. Besides, Hitler argued, Stalin had forceably recruited foreign workers from other countries for Russia, including three million Chinese workers. In regard to Poland, as in other such countries, it was a case of total

[14] *Ibid.*, 622.   [15] *Ibid.*, 622-623.

capitulation, and on these grounds Germany was justified in introducing German labor regulations.[16]

With Hitler's comments in mind, Sauckel altered his plan for mobilization, with the accent on foreign workers and POW's. Sauckel defined the aims of his plan as follows:

> . . . to use all the rich and tremendous sources, conquered and secured for us by our fighting Armed Forces under the leadership of Adolf Hitler, for the armament of the Armed Forces and also for the nutrition of the Homeland. The raw materials as well as the fertility of the conquered territories and their human labor power are to be used completely and conscientiously to the profit of Germany and her allies.[17]

To achieve this aim, Sauckel wanted all POW's actually in the Reich to be shifted immediately into vital armament or food industries. He also wanted their production increased to the highest possible level. However, Sauckel emphasized that an additional large quantity of foreign labor had to be found. The chief source of such labor was in the East. Consequently, Sauckel labeled it an immediate necessity to use Russian labor, even if it meant recruitment with force. From the West, Sauckel expected to draw about one-quarter of the total labor requirement.[18]

The key principle for Sauckel's plan was:

> All the men must be fed, sheltered and treated in such a way as to exploit them to the highest possible extent at the lowest conceivable degree of expenditure.[19]

Accordingly,

> All action making the stay and work in Germany difficult and unnecessarily unbearable for the foreign workers and exceeding the restrictions and hardships imposed by the

[16] *Ibid.*, 623. [17] *NCA*, III, 47.
[18] *Ibid.*, 52. [19] *Ibid.*, 57.

war must be avoided. We depend to a large extent on their good will and their production.

It is therefore only logical to make their stay and work in Germany as bearable as possible—without denying anything to ourselves.[20]

ADMINISTRATIVE ORGANIZATION

To accomplish his task, Sauckel was given broad general powers under the Four Year Plan but practically no formal organization. The original decree authorized Sauckel to make new laws or repeal old ones, subject only to the approval of Goering and Hitler. Sauckel was also able to issue instructions to the higher Reich authorities, the party offices, military commanders and chiefs of civil government in occupied areas, the *Reichsprotektor* in Bohemia-Moravia, and the Governor-General of Poland.[21] In contrast to his wide powers, Sauckel was to keep his administration to a bare minimum. Like Speer, he was to be more of an expediter for labor than the head of a distinct, separate economic administration. Basically, Sauckel was to utilize, with the help of a small staff of experts, the existing party, state, and economic agencies; he was to rely on their good will and cooperation to insure the quick and successful completion of his task.

Again, as in the case of Speer, Sauckel began building an administrative organization which eventually grew to the size of a ministry. In pursuance of Hitler's first decree, Goering abolished his labor offices in the Four Year Plan on March 27, 1942. The duties of recruitment and allocation of labor, the regulation of labor conditions, as well as most of the personnel of these offices, were taken over by Sauckel.[22] In addition to the Goering offices, Sauckel had Sections III, V, and many of the personnel from Section VI of the Reich

[20] *Ibid.*, 58.
[21] *Reichsarbeitsblatt*, 1942, Part i, 257.
[22] *Reichsgesetzblatt*, 1942, Part i, 129.

Labor Ministry placed at his disposal. Section III of the Labor Ministry had control over labor laws, labor legislation, labor production, factory inspection, social administration, and, most important of all, wage and economic policy. Section V was in charge of unemployment assistance and placement of both foreign and domestic workers in the Reich. Section VI, from which Sauckel drew key personnel, was the old Labor Ministry's European Office for Labor Supply. This office had formerly cooperated with other nations in the procurement of transient workers. Eventually, Sauckel's agency superseded the work of Section VI. In effect, Sauckel had stripped the Labor Ministry of most of its authority.[23]

In addition, the old labor system in the Reich was made subordinate to Sauckel's orders and directives, although not directly responsible to him. This system consisted of the Central Reich Employment Office (*Reichstelle fuer Arbeitsvermittlung*), the Regional Labor Offices (*Landesarbeitsaemter*), the Labor Offices (*Arbeitsaemter*), the Reich Labor Trustees, and the Special Labor Trustees.[24]

Since one of the main reasons for establishing the new labor office was to overcome the opposition of the Gauleiters, Sauckel decided to win their support by bringing them into his program. On April 6, 1942, Sauckel appointed the Gauleiters his special plenipotentiaries for manpower within their respective Gaus.[25] The Gauleiters were charged with the responsibility of establishing harmonious cooperation among all agencies of the state, party, armed forces, and the economy by creating common agreement on how best to obtain the highest efficiency in the field of manpower. To help them, Sauckel ordered the presidents of the regional labor offices and their staffs to be placed at the disposal of the

[23] *IMT*, xiv, 627.
[24] John H. E. Fried, *The Exploitation of Foreign Labour by Germany* (Montreal: International Labour Office, 1945), p. 26.
[25] *NCA*, vi, 83.

Gauleiters. The labor office personnel were to furnish information and technical advice. They were also ordered to carry
out the suggestions and orders of the Gauleiters in order to
improve manpower arrangements within their respective
Gaus.

In addition to making the Gauleiters the central authority
for labor allocation within their Gaus, Sauckel specifically
charged them with inspecting the treatment, handling, care,
and behavior of the foreign workers and the effects these
workers were having on the German population. Propaganda
for the foreign workers and propaganda aimed at German
acceptance of the foreign workers were to be directed by
Sauckel's office and Goebbels' ministry with the aid and assistance of the Gauleiters.[26]

Sauckel's decision to incorporate the regional labor offices
into the Nazi *Gau* structure was but one more step in a long-
term program of the Nazis. From 1933 to 1945, the Nazi
leaders sought, according to their totalitarian theory, to coordinate all public activities. This was the famous *Gleich-
schaltung* (synchronization) principle, which meant absolute
control from the top of all federal, state, provincial, and mu-
nicipal activities. The case of the regional labor offices illustrated this principle clearly. Before 1939, Germany had
thirteen regional (*Landes*) labor offices and two more branch
offices of the Reich Ministry of Labor acting as regional offices
in Austria and the Sudetenland. In March 1939, these offices
were made federal agencies. During the war, the number of
offices was increased first to twenty-six and then to forty-two
to make them coincide with the forty-two Nazi Gaus. This
reorganization was completed by 1943.[27]

In substance, Sauckel's directive of April 6 gave even

[26] *IMT*, xxxii, 200-201.
[27] Cf. Fried, *Exploitation of Foreign Labour*; and Neumann,
Behemoth.

116

more power and responsibility to the Gauleiters,[28] the very men Speer thought were the greatest detriment to the rational use of manpower. To Speer, it was a dangerous gamble to give the Gauleiters more power with the hope that they would be able to transcend their own regionalism. To Sauckel, the long-time *Gauleiter*, it was not a gamble at all but only the natural evolution of the Nazi state.

Apparently Sauckel's move of placing the labor offices under the supervision of the Gauleiters originated with Bormann. Speer reported after the war that Bormann made every effort to centralize all of the forces of the state and the party in the hands of the Gauleiters. The Gauleiters were made Reich defense commissioners, and by 1943 they had assumed responsibility for the entire war effort, except military operations and the Speer ministry.[29] Later in the war, when Germany was being invaded, the Gauleiters even encroached on the military jurisdiction by organizing the defense of their respective Gaus.

PLANS FOR RECRUITMENT OF FOREIGN LABOR

In general, the recruitment of foreign labor in the occupied, allied, friendly, or neutral states was carried out either by Sauckel's commissioners or by the competent German military or civil agencies for labor mobilization. In France and Italy, the competent civil agencies were the labor offices. In the occupied areas that had German civil governments, the officially approved labor offices were used. In the areas under military government, as was much of Russia, recruitment was the responsibility of the Army, with technical assistance by Sauckel's officials. In all areas, regardless of whether they were occupied or not, Sauckel deputized or

[28] *Verfuegungen, Anordnungen, Bekanntgaben* (Parteikanzlei, Muenchen: Verlag Franz Eher, 1942), Vol. ii, p. 509.
[29] *IMT*, xvi, 508.

117

appointed special agents to help direct recruitment of labor. Usually these agents were older men drawn from the Reich Labor Ministry.[30]

Other agencies, organizations, or persons were expressly forbidden to recruit foreign labor directly for the Reich unless they had Sauckel's written approval. Sauckel was also to determine the extent, nature, and methods other groups could use in recruiting labor. However, everyone related to recruitment was subordinated to Sauckel's agents or to the competent military or civil agencies.[31]

Before attempting any recruiting, complete information was to be given to the population through the press or other means of publicity, explaining the type of workers needed. The foreign workers were to be informed in detail at the time of recruitment about working conditions in the Reich. If possible, workers were to be told of their future place of work, the name of their employer, and the approximate amount of pay and deductions. In no case were the recruited persons to be given false or exaggerated promises. Foreign workers were also to be told of the possibilities for transferring their savings from the Reich to their families at home.

Sauckel wanted the recruiters to point out that living conditions were better in the Reich than in the rest of Europe. In this connection, however, recruiters were to warn foreign workers that they would be subject to limitations in housing, food, and other living conditions brought about by war just as they were at home.

The recruiting officials also were to examine the professional suitability and physical fitness of the foreign workers. Then, if the worker was accepted, a written contract or certificate of recruitment which contained the pay scale and important working conditions was to be drawn up.[32]

[30] *IMT*, xv, 6-7.   [31] *NCA*, v, 756.   [32] *Ibid.*, 759.

The foreign worker was to bring with him sufficient working clothes and shoes, since it was impossible to grant him ration stamps for such items in the Reich. The foreign worker had also to possess, on crossing the German border, validated papers either from his own government or from the proper German occupational authorities.

After recruitment, foreign workers were to be transported by rail to the Reich. In all areas except Italy and France, Sauckel's representatives supervised arrangements for the transport of foreign workers from the point of recruitment to the German frontier; in France and Italy, these powers were left in the hands of the local authorities. Sauckel's representatives and the comparable French and Italian authorities were also to be responsible for food, sanitation, and other needs of the workers until they reached the Reich.

Once the workers had arrived, they were to be cared for by the German Labor Front. Usually the workers were to be housed in a transient camp built by the Labor Front until their regular assignment to a factory was made. While in the transient camps, the foreign workers were to be decontaminated again and given another medical examination.[33]

As soon as the foreign workers were transported to their place of work, the individual factory was to assume responsibility for housing, feeding, and general care. Although the factories had the ultimate responsibility for the foreign workers, both the German Labor Front and Sauckel's organization, including the Gauleiters, had the power to inspect living conditions and correct any abuses in the system.

In summary, Sauckel's plans for the recruitment of foreign labor reflected his rational and rather tolerant views on the needs of the working man. While the plan stressed the urgency of bringing many workers into the Reich, it certainly urged that the recruitment of these workers be handled in a

[33] Pre-trial interrogations of Fritz Sauckel, October 8, 1945, in the Nuremberg Trials Collection, p. 4.

careful and critical way. Sauckel realized that it was absolutely necessary to treat these workers with respect and to
gain their confidence. If this could be done, the production
of the foreign workers would be insured, and the security
problems connected with their employment would be largely
solved.

Sauckel's plan was, however, extremely complicated. It
depended on the close cooperation of many different organizations without an adequate inspection system centralized
under Sauckel to insure that cooperation. The earlier plans
seemed also to ignore the effects of years of intensive racial
propaganda. It was one thing for Sauckel, in Berlin, to write
directives for the fair treatment of foreign workers and
another thing to have those directives carried out by some
ardent Nazi recruiter in the Ukraine, who was badgered
constantly by his superiors to fulfill his quota.

PLANS FOR ALLOCATING FOREIGN LABOR

Another problem that Sauckel faced in the spring of 1942
was the allocation of labor. After all, the recruitment of foreign labor had been carried out since the beginning of the
war, and although the system might be in need of overhaul-
ing, it still was functioning. The allocation system was not.
In brief, Sauckel found there was a group of primary agencies that controlled the employment of foreign and domestic
workers. This group was comprised of Speer's Ministry of
Weapons and Ammunition, the *Luftwaffe* Ministry, the ship-
yards for the Navy, Funk's Ministry of Economics, which
controlled the workers in most of the secondary war production and all of the consumer goods industries, the Ministry of
Food, the Mining Association, the Army's administration
system, public utilities, and public agencies like the East
Ministry, which were constantly drawing persons from the

Reich to work in the occupied territories.[34] All of the agencies were short of labor and all needed a certain number of skilled workers. The question for Sauckel was how to distribute the available labor. If he decided to allot an across-the-board percentage of workers to each user, invariably the users would inflate their demands. If Sauckel decided to give workers only to war production industries, he was open to criticism from the others on the grounds that their production was equally vital to the war economy. Besides, what percentage of workers should be given to the war production industries?

Speer had already given serious consideration to this problem and had reached the conclusion that Sauckel had to be under the direction of the *Zentrale Planung*. Through Sauckel, the *Zentrale Planung* could establish priorities for labor for the entire economy based on the immediate and future needs of Germany's war production. In effect, Sauckel would be the instrument for the drastic war measures that Speer wanted. By withholding labor from consumer and non-essential industries and giving labor only to the armament industries, Sauckel could enforce conversion of the economy to a total war basis.

But Sauckel saw his role in the allocation of labor differently than did Speer. Sauckel thought that he rather than the *Zentrale Planung* should be the final arbiter of the distribution of labor. He felt that Germany needed a labor czar who not only recruited labor but also trained, directed, and allocated that labor. Thus, Sauckel's reasoning was diametrically opposed to Speer's. Since Speer and Sauckel were both appointed at approximately the same time and neither man had a clear mandate from Hitler for his own plans, the stage was set for a series of continual conflicts.

[34] *Ibid.*, pp. 6-9.

SAUCKEL'S DEMANDS FOR BETTER WORKING CONDITIONS

In addition to controlling the allocation of labor in the Reich, Sauckel had other plans for his new agency. In his first meeting with the Reich Labor Ministry's officials, Sauckel told them he had accepted his new position with the understanding that all foreign workers, including the eastern workers, were to be fed adequately. Moreover, Sauckel wanted a drastic change in some of the living conditions for the eastern workers. The barbed wire fences around the camps of the voluntary eastern workers had to be removed and their basic wages had to be raised to at least one-half of the German worker's wages.[35] This program of Sauckel's was in opposition to the prevailing *Untermensch* philosophy propounded by many ranking Nazis and the SS. Besides conflicting with the *Untermensch* philosophy, Sauckel's intention to correct conditions for foreign workers brought him into jurisdictional conflicts with other Reich agencies, such as the Food Ministry and the police.

Apparently Sauckel made some progress in improving conditions at the time of his appointment. At a *Fuehrer*'s Conference held on March 22, 1942, Hitler finally agreed, after a long argument, that eastern workers were to be fed adequately. *Der Fuehrer* told Sauckel that he was to see Backe, the Food Minister, and arrange the details. At the same conference, Hitler was astonished to hear that Russian civilian workers were living behind barbed wire fences. When Speer and Sauckel told *Der Fuehrer* that it was one of his orders, Hitler remarked that he had never heard about it.[36]

Although Hitler had agreed in principle with Sauckel's

[35] *IMT*, xxxvi, 310-316.
[36] Speer's notes on *Fuehrer*'s Conference, March 22, 1942, on T-73, Roll 192, Frame 405474.

demands, it was difficult for Sauckel to get action from other Nazi leaders. Backe refused to consider an increase in food rations until he was able to insure an adequate food supply for the German population. Backe had, in the last days of March 1942, slashed the food rations for Germans, but still they were higher than the ration for the eastern workers. Yet Sauckel's insistence must have had some effect, for Goebbels noted in his diary on April 26, 1942:

> All Reich departments affected are now in favor of new regulations for the employment of labor from the East. In the long run we cannot solicit additional workers from the East if we treat them like animals within the Reich. They must, after all, receive enough food and clothing so that they will at least retain their capacity for work. Everybody is now in complete agreement about this.[37]

The question of removing the barbed wire fences and easing the security restrictions for the eastern workers was also difficult, but Sauckel managed to obtain some concessions. Regulations for eastern workers, based on Nazi racial considerations, had been established by Himmler in a decree on February 20, 1942, about a month before Sauckel was appointed. Himmler's decree stated that only workers living in the recruitment areas as of June 22, 1941, were to be employed in the Reich. Under no circumstances were Asiatic people to be recruited. Himmler also wanted the eastern workers to wear badges or symbols on their outer clothes. The eastern workers were to live in closed, guarded compounds, and they were to be strictly segregated from other foreign workers and Germans. The Gestapo was to be the only judicial authority for any offenses that involved eastern workers. The death penalty was to be invoked in many instances, including cases of sexual relations between easterners

[37] *Goebbels Diaries*, p. 186.

and Germans and cases of easterners spreading propaganda. Sentence to a concentration camp was advised for any minor offenses. The eastern workers were to be treated virtually as prisoners.[38]

Sauckel was disturbed by these conditions since they violated his basic principles about foreign workers. He brought the matter to the attention of Hitler and Bormann. Shortly afterward, Reinhardt Heydrich, head of the Security Police, invited Sauckel for a conference to discuss the matter. Heydrich frankly admitted that he thought Sauckel's program to bring millions of easterners into the Reich was fantastic. It meant more work for him, especially if Sauckel persisted in wanting the barbed wire removed from the eastern camps.[39] Sauckel persisted, and Heydrich agreed to modify some of the security regulations.

On April 9, Heydrich sent a circular to all police units and factories. The circular stated that the SD had agreed to reopen the questions of the security, feeding, and wages for eastern workers based on experiences collected to date. In agreement with Sauckel, the circular stated that it would appear "inadvisable strictly to segregate the workers from the pre-1939 Russian territory from the German civilian population, from foreign civilian workers, and from all other POW's, as otherwise the possibilities for using these workers would be too restricted."[40] The circular stated that the principle of segregation should still be applied but not if it interfered with working conditions. The restrictions on living conditions were also eased. The barbed wire was to be removed and Russian families were not to be separated in living quarters. As an added concession, Heydrich would allow the Russians to leave their quarters in groups as a reward for good work, provided the groups had adequate German supervision.[41]

[38] *IMT*, xxxi, 500-512; and *IMT*, xli, 214-216.
[39] *IMT*, xiv, 627.   [40] *Minor Trials*, ix, 879.   [41] *Ibid.*, 880.

With regard to wages, Sauckel had theoretical power to raise the wages of the foreign workers under Section III of the Labor Ministry, but Sauckel's actual power to change wages was strictly limited by the prevailing Nazi principles. Hitler told Sauckel that the order freezing all wages in the Reich (*Lohnstopgesetz*) was to be interpreted more as a principle than as a fixed law.[42] If possible, Hitler wanted Sauckel to stabilize wages throughout the Reich and Europe on the basis of the 1942 wage scale.[43] *Der Fuehrer* told him this would have two important effects. First, it would materially reduce the possibility of inflation in the Reich and thereby insure a strong home front. Hitler had mentioned again and again to Sauckel that the German people's confidence would be retained as long as wages and prices remained stable and the threat of inflation was not present. The post-World War I inflations had thus influenced Adolf Hitler. Second, Hitler felt that the artificial freezing of wages in Europe would create an incentive for foreigners to volunteer for work in the Reich. By 1942, Germany was the only country in Europe that had not suffered seriously from an inflationary trend.[44] For example, the German worker could buy much more with his wages in Germany than could the French worker in France.

Hitler's reasons might have been applicable in western Europe but not in the East, where Sauckel intended to recruit most of his workers. There, wages and living conditions were already below the subsistence level, and conditions for the eastern workers were hardly better in the Reich. In January of 1942, Goering had imposed a confiscatory tax on the earnings of eastern workers.[45] This tax was deducted by

[42] Pre-trial interrogations of Fritz Sauckel, October 5, 1945, pp. 1-3.
[43] *NCA*, Supplement A, 1445.
[44] Pre-trial interrogations of Fritz Sauckel, September 15, 1945, p. 3.
[45] *Reichsgesetzblatt*, 1942, Part i, 42.

the employer and paid to the Reich Treasury. The tax scale was arranged so that no eastern worker was able to receive more than 6.50 RM per week after deductions. The average was only 4.60 RM.

This special tax on eastern workers amounted to a double income for Germany. Eastern workers were hired at lower rates than other workers, and they contributed billions of marks to the Reich Treasury through their taxes. Nor was Hitler himself oblivious to this saving. In fact, the whole Nazi attitude of exploiting the eastern workers seems to have stemmed from Goering and Hitler. On May 4, 1942, Hitler in his usual exaggerated way made this frank acknowledgment about extracting profits from foreign workers:

> . . . integration of twenty million foreign workers at cheap rates into the German industrial system represents a saving which, again, is greatly in excess of the debts contracted by the State. A simple calculation, which curiously enough seems to have escaped the notice of the majority of our economic experts, will show the correctness of this contention; the foreign worker earns approximately a thousand marks a year, in comparison with the average earnings of two thousand marks by German workers. Work out what this comes to in toto, and you will see that the final gain is enormous.
>
> In the assessment of the national wealth I had to explain even to Funk, who, after all, is Economic Minister of the Reich, how the standard of living of the German people had been very considerably raised by the system of employing foreign labour which we had introduced. One has only to compare the cost of local labour with that of German labour abroad to see that this must be so.[46]

In June 1942, Sauckel finally succeeded in raising the earnings of eastern workers slightly. According to the new

[46] *Hitler's Secret Conversations*, p. 372.

regulations, there was no fixed ceiling on earnings for eastern workers.[47] Yet Sauckel admitted after the war that the average weekly earnings after deductions for an eastern worker under the June regulations was only 9.10 RM.[48]

Sauckel, like Speer, was to find that his planned reforms were to meet opposition from many governmental and party agencies. Sauckel's plans for reorganizing the labor economy were, in general, opportunistic, moderate, and rational. They aimed at securing higher production through careful recruitment and judicious handling of foreign workers. Like all Nazi plans, however, they were tainted with racialism, especially when the eastern peoples were involved. Yet, Sauckel realized that the German war production depended on the labor of foreigners, and every action that intimidated or hurt the foreign worker would result in an eventual loss for Germany.

Although Sauckel could plead for better conditions for the foreign workers, at times he too exhibited the prevailing mentality of the Germans. Gerald Reitlinger, in *The House Built on Sand*, aptly compared this mentality with the early Victorian governing class's view of the working people. The benefits of a higher civilization would be bestowed on the workers if they worked hard, were appreciative, and not too demanding. Long hours, insufficient pay, and a meager diet were viewed as wholesome in themselves, for they imparted the virtues that the governing class had long since ignored but still cherished.[49]

Apart from the mentality of Sauckel and others, the creation of a new agency in the labor economy had other implications. It was an outstanding example of the growing trend of assigning powerful political figures the job of solving technical problems. The accent on personalities probably dramatized the serious nature of problems that Germany

[47] *Reichsgesetzblatt*, 1942, Part i, 42.
[48] *IMT*, xv, 45-46.
[49] Reitlinger, *House Built on Sand*, pp. 257-258.

faced in the third year of war, but it also heightened the scramble for offices and power by these same personalities. The Bormanns, Sauckels, Goebbels, and Backes seized every opportunity in the labyrinth of offices, powers, and overlapping jurisdictions in the Third Reich to entrench their own positions and create their own empires. Moreover, as the foreign labor program of the Reich demonstrated, the implementation of policies was seriously compromised by this struggle for power among the Nazi underlings.

CHAPTER VII

Spreading the Net—The Four Sauckel Actions

FROM his appointment as GBA (Plenipotentiary for Labor) in March 1942 until the collapse of the Third Reich, Sauckel organized four major recruitment drives for foreign workers. In each of these drives, referred to by most German authorities as "Sauckel actions," an intensive effort was made not only by Sauckel but by governmental, party, and military agencies to recruit millions of foreign workers for the farms and factories of the Reich. The first drive began in April 1942 and lasted until August. The second drive, a continuation of the first, began in September 1942 and ended in January 1943. The third and fourth drives were yearly programs scheduled to run through 1943 and 1944. In each of these drives, quotas for the total number of new workers needed for the economy were given to Sauckel, who had the option of filling them with either foreign or domestic labor. The assumption was, in the spring of 1942, that most new labor would be foreign.

Problems were continually encountered in these recruitment drives that necessitated radical alterations in the foreign labor program. Sauckel's office and, indeed, much of the German governmental machinery had to be revised to cope with the fluid situation. Most of the difficulties were results of the deteriorating military position of Germany. As long as German arms seemed invincible, the populations in the recruiting areas were passive, dispirited, and unable to organize a defense against Sauckel's agents. Some responsible leaders in the occupied areas were urging moderation and cooperation with the German foreign labor program. The spirit of collaboration eased Sauckel's task. However, once it became apparent that the *Wehrmacht* could be stopped and

129

that a German victory was not inevitable, there was a swift transformation in the attitudes of the leaders and people in the occupied areas. At the same time, Germany, faced with an ever-growing labor shortage, began relying on more forceful measures for extracting labor from the occupied areas, thereby accelerating the hostility of the people in these areas.

Apart from the military situation, the German occupation policies played a role in alienating the people of the occupied areas and consequently increased the difficulties of the foreign labor program. The introduction of Nazi racial laws, the callous and ruthless exploitation of the native economies, and the German indifference in fashioning acceptable political goals for the occupied peoples combined to extinguish what little good will was left in the occupied areas. Paradoxically, while German policies in those areas were making the recruitment drives progressively more difficult, German treatment of foreign workers in the Reich showed improvement. From the appointment of Sauckel until the end of the war, as the Germans came to rely on foreign labor more and more, there was an increasingly visible tendency within the Reich to improve conditions for foreign workers. In particular, the eastern workers' status rose steadily from a place of marked inferiority to one of near-equality with western workers.

The foreign labor program was, then, throughout its existence a dynamic entity, evolving and changing with new problems and situations. The four major recruitment drives of Sauckel, in spite of their apparent similarities, illustrated clearly the changing patterns in the war and the attempts of the Germans to adapt their objectives and methods to them.

THE PROGRAM FROM APRIL TO
SEPTEMBER 1942

By the spring of 1942, it had become evident that German losses on the eastern front were much greater than originally anticipated. For the period from June 22, 1941, to February

20, 1942, the German losses in the east were 199,448 dead; 708,351 wounded; 44,342 missing; a total of 952,141.[1]

To replace Army losses and to keep pace with the scheduled increases for the Army and war industries, German officials estimated in February that about 625,000 workers were needed immediately. Sauckel, feeling that the required workers could be recruited faster abroad than at home, sent orders to the German agencies in the East to set up a mass recruiting program. Alfred Rosenberg, the Minister for the East, quickly established labor quotas for individual cities and emphasized that he wanted at least 247,000 skilled industrial workers among those drafted.[2]

By April, the original estimate was considered too low. At least one million foreigners were needed before the summer and possibly 600,000 more during the summer.[3] Part of the difficulty in establishing an accurate estimate at the time was due to the lack of coordination between army and civilian agencies. By late 1942, Speer's *Zentrale Planung* was in a position to establish quick, accurate projections of future labor requirements. After the war, Sauckel claimed that the objective of 1.6 million foreign workers was the basis for his first labor recruitment drive, even though he had deliberately slashed 200,000 from the formal requests.[4]

To achieve his quota, Sauckel thought that it would be necessary to recruit over one million workers from the East, the remainder from the West. The neutral and allied nations were to be used only for the recruitment of specialists.[5] In the East, Sauckel was prepared to use coercion in the recruit-

---

[1] *Goebbels Diaries*, p. 112. See also annual reports from *OKW WF St./Abt.L. (Heerespersonalamt)—Zusammenstellung ueber die personelle und materielle Ruestungslage der Wehrmacht*, in the files of the USSBS.

[2] *IMT*, xxvi, 161-165.   [3] *IMT*, xxxvi, 310-311.

[4] Interrogation of Fritz Sauckel, September 10, 1946, in the files of the Nuremberg Minor Trials Collection.

[5] *IMT*, xxv, 62.

ment drives if voluntary measures were not successful, even if it meant drafting young men fifteen years old. In the West, Sauckel was at first reluctant to use force.

Sauckel immediately began a round of conferences with other German agencies to determine the amount of labor he could recruit in the East. The Reich Labor Ministry informed Sauckel that, in their opinion, most of the Polish labor had been utilized. Furthermore, the Labor Ministry claimed that the forceable resettlement of Germans in former Polish lands was being carried out with police action, and this made it more difficult and dangerous to recruit Poles for work in the Reich. Sauckel countered the arguments of the Labor Ministry by pointing out that the area of the General-Government was densely populated and poor. The industry there was largely inoperative. In order to bring about a general economic improvement, it might be wise to send large numbers of Poles to work in the Reich.[6] Although the Labor Ministry was unconvinced by Sauckel's reasoning, orders were sent to Governor-General Frank to proceed energetically with the recruitment of Polish workers.

Next, Sauckel conferred with the Army. In general, Army officials agreed that it was necessary to recruit a million eastern workers in the shortest possible period of time. However, there were many difficulties involved with recruitment in the East, especially in Russia. The danger of infectious diseases, particularly spotted fever, demanded far-reaching sanitary preventive measures. For this purpose, *Wehrmacht* installations and medical officers were prepared to help Sauckel construct and operate hundreds of collecting camps, disinfection stations, and examination offices.[7]

The defective condition of communication and transporta-

[6] Pre-trial interrogations of Fritz Sauckel, September 15, 1945, in the files of the Nuremberg Trials Collection.
[7] *NCA*, Supplement A, 378.

132

tion facilities resulting from the great distances and severe weather involved made recruitment difficult. Also, there were the problems arising from the passive and open resistance and the mistrust of the population, which was abetted by clever Soviet propaganda. The Army was particularly worried about the effects of mass labor recruitments on the increased guerrilla activity. Finally, the Army was concerned with the effect Sauckel's drive would have on its own labor requirements in Russia.[8]

As a result, the Army suggested to Sauckel that he might be able to offset some of these difficulties by making work in the Reich more attractive for the eastern worker. This could be done by improving living conditions and wages, transferring wages to families, and, if politically feasible, promising the eastern worker that, once the war was over, workers who had volunteered for the Reich would be given land in Russia. The Army also pointedly suggested to Sauckel that in addition to recruiting foreign workers, he should make an effort to recruit more German women in industry through a propaganda campaign rather than through force, and that he should give German schoolchildren instruction in industrial work in the event his recruitment of foreign labor was not completely successful.[9] The Army's reactions to Sauckel's plans were hardly encouraging, and when Sauckel attended a staff conference at the East Ministry, he heard the same kind of suggestions.

Sauckel's attitude toward Rosenberg's ministry was entirely different from his attitude toward the Army. He was not talking to military men with fancy uniforms and impressive war records. He was talking to political men like himself and he felt on safer ground. In no uncertain terms, in an

[8] *Ibid.*, 379.

[9] OKW/Wi Rue Amt/Rue (IVa), *Besprechung im Reichsarbeitsministerium unter Leitung des Gauleiters Sauckel*, April 21, 1942, on T-77, Roll 153, Frames 889028-29.

hour-long address to the staff, Sauckel clearly placed himself on the side of the advocates of a tough policy for the occupied eastern territories. According to the instructions in Goering's "Green File," Sauckel declared that Soviet industries were not to be restored; this meant that a huge pool of labor would be available for the Reich. There should not be any particular difficulties in recruiting, transporting, and using millions of Russian workers. When members of the East Ministry stressed the need for better care and more attractive incentives for the eastern workers, Sauckel's reply was strictly in accordance with his Nazi beliefs:

> What you say might be good and proper, and if the people from the East want to come voluntarily, then let them. But I have neither the time nor desire to concern myself with the correct taste of Russian cooking or the spiritual life of peasants. I have received my mandate from Adolf Hitler and I will bring millions of eastern workers into Germany without considering whether they want to or not.[10]

Sauckel implemented his words a few days later when he ordered the labor office of Rosenberg to be incorporated into his own agency. The name of the office was changed significantly to the "Recruitment Commission" of the GBA (*Anwerbekommissionen des G.B.A.*)[11] Sauckel's order also reminded the East Ministry that the decision to recruit millions of Russians was a closed issue. To emphasize the point, he wrote that labor recruitment would have priority over everything else. Sauckel had also decided to double the number of agents he had in the East, and for this purpose he had already called two hundred more labor technicians to Berlin for a final briefing.[12]

Sauckel reported the results of his conferences to Hitler. In view of the lukewarm responses that he had received from

[10] Kleist, *Zwischen Hitler und Stalin*, p. 195.
[11] *IMT*, xxxix, 496-497.   [12] *Ibid.*, 494-496.

the Army and certain ministries, Sauckel asked for a re-affirmation of his program. *Der Fuehrer*, on April 4, agreed completely with Sauckel and pointed out that foreign workers were vitally needed, since it would not be wise to press German workers who were already living on short food rations.[13]

In May, still worried about the possibility of not recruiting enough labor in the East, Sauckel sought and received from Hitler an order to the military governments in occupied France, Belgium, and Holland to publish conscription laws at once. The laws had already been prepared according to directives sent out in January 1942 by Werner Mansfeld.[14] Hitler stated, furthermore, that under no circumstances were French POW's and conscripted labor to receive the same pay as voluntary workers. "It was not we but the French who declared war and they must therefore also bear the consequences."[15]

At the end of May, Sauckel made his first inspection tour of the East to determine personally how the recruitment drive was progressing. In general, Sauckel was assured of a good harvest which might help the food situation in the Reich, already aggravated by the presence of millions of foreign workers. The eastern areas were critically short of transportation and lacked German personnel for recruitment, but these problems could be overcome in time. What really worried Sauckel was the passive, sometimes hostile, attitude of German officials, especially those from the military. All too often, Sauckel complained, these Eastern officials wanted to use the native labor for military projects or to rebuild the economies of the area, without realizing how critically these workers were needed in the Reich. The local military com-

[13] Speer's notes on *Fuehrer*'s Conference, April 4, 1942, on T-73, Roll 192, Frame 405478.

[14] See Chapter V.

[15] Speer's notes on *Fuehrer*'s Conference, May 5, 1942, on T-73, Roll 192, Frame 405497.

manders were particularly opposed to the labor recruitment drive; they deemed it troublesome and dangerous. The military explained to Sauckel that they were unwilling to antagonize the local population further, because it would only mean an increase in partisan activity with a correspondingly heavy cost in German lives.

In addition to the difficulties with German authorities, Sauckel found that his recruitment drive did not produce as many skilled workers as had been planned. In retreating, the Soviets had taken as many with them as possible. Moreover, the German officials in the East had retained for their own use a large portion of skilled workers. Also, many had left the cities to go into the countryside to hide or to obtain better food rations. Another source that had been inadequately tapped in Sauckel's opinion was the POW's. He was disturbed by the slowness of the Army in screening out the skilled from their compounds. To accelerate the process, Sauckel ordered one thousand doctors from the Reich sent to POW camps to help the Army screen and recruit healthy Russian POW's for work in Germany.

The shortage of skilled workers among those recruited in the East meant that Sauckel had to find workers elsewhere and devise a plan to train the unskilled. Consequently, after his inspection trip, Sauckel decided it was necessary to increase recruitment in the West. Meanwhile, he would have the armament industries organize a massive training program for eastern workers.

One aspect of his first inspection trip to Russia was gratifying for Sauckel; even with all the difficulties involved, numerically the drive was progressing very well. By June 1, 1942, Sauckel estimated that he had already recruited 800,000 workers from the East, although admittedly a part of them had been seized by force.[16]

[16] The complete text of Sauckel's report on his inspection trip from May 26 to May 31, 1942, can be seen on T-77, Roll 234, Frames 975305-316.

No matter how fast Sauckel recruited foreign workers, Germany's appetite for new manpower seemed insatiable. Early in June, the OKW reported that the armament industries still needed 250,000 more workers, and that within three months they would need an additional 160,000 to keep pace with scheduled production plans.[17] The SS, through its private sources, estimated in the same month that there was still a need for two million workers in the Reich.[18] The Germans were on a treadmill; the faster they ran, the faster they had to run.

While Sauckel continued to press recruitment, the German officials in Berlin were beginning to hear ominous warnings from the East. The food situation was exceptionally precarious, and even Goebbels noted that "thousands and tens of thousands of people are dying of hunger without anybody even raising a finger."[19] Thousands of workers were deserting the cities in search of food, and even the occupation authorities were finding it hard to hire new labor. Many top Germans expected a violent reaction, but none was forthcoming. The recruitment drive moved calmly through the first half of the summer.

On July 27, Sauckel reported to Hitler and Goering that the original quota of 1.6 million workers had been exceeded. Since Sauckel had received his special appointment in March 1942, a total of 1,639,794 foreign workers had been obtained for the Reich. A detailed breakdown of the foreign workers as listed by Sauckel is shown in Table VIII.

In the same report to Hitler, Sauckel reviewed the total

---

[17] OKW/Wi Rue Amt/Rue IV (t/Zst), *Personalmeldung und Zusatzmeldung zur Personalmeldung—Stichtag 30.4.42.*, dated June 2, 1942, on T-77, Roll 216, Frame 952888.

[18] *IMT*, xxxix, 359-360.

[19] *Goebbels Diaries*, p. 115.

TABLE VIII

RESULTS OF THE FIRST SAUCKEL ACTION

A. FROM THE NEWLY OCCUPIED EASTERN TERRITORIES

	April	*May*	*June*	*July*	*Total*
Eastern workers	110,149	273,128	324,066	264,489	971,832
Galician district workers	20,525	17,496	9,013	61,118	108,152
Soviet POW's	43,074	53,600	38,335	86,000	221,009
Total	173,748	344,224	371,414	411,607	1,300,993

B. FROM OTHER COUNTRIES

	April	*May*	*June*	*July*	*Total*
Bohemia-Moravia	6,000	4,000	4,900	8,800	23,700
Poland	27,402	20,265	8,907	7,596	64,170
Wartheland	12,305	11,195	7,558	1,107	32,165
Belgium	8,000	8,000	6,200	7,900	30,100
France	7,000	7,000	5,500	11,800	31,300
Italy	14,250	28,534	8,842	4,100	55,726
Holland	5,905	12,895	8,100	4,400	31,300
Serbia	3,769	1,724	929	1,008	7,430
Croatia	1,057	2,045	4,093	4,400	11,595
Slovakia	13,324	335	1,406	200	15,265
Others	13,409	7,084	9,000	6,557	36,050
Total	112,421	103,077	65,435	57,868	338,801

A. Total of	1,300,993
B. Total of	338,801
Grand Total	1,639,794

SOURCE: *IMT*, XXVII, 116-117.

number of foreign workers and prisoners of war working in the Reich as of July 29, 1942:

(a) From the newly occupied eastern territories	1,148,000
(b) From other recruiting areas	2,400,000
(c) Prisoners of war	1,576,000
Total	5,124,000[20]

[20] *IMT*, XXVII, 121.

In the short period of Sauckel's appointment, the percentage of Russian labor had risen from 4 per cent to nearly 30 per cent of the total amount of foreign labor in the Reich.[21] In spite of difficulties, Sauckel had been able to complete his first recruitment drive with success. He received praise from all sides. When Goering held a conference for administrators of the occupied territories on August 6, he singled out Sauckel for special praise. Goering, in his usual baronial manner, had just scorned and ridiculed the administrators for failing to deliver more food and foreign labor to the Reich. Suddenly turning to Sauckel, he said:

> I must add one more thing. I don't have to praise Sauckel because he doesn't deem it necessary. But what he has accomplished in this short period of time—bringing workers from all of Europe into our factories with amazing speed—is really unique. I want to say with all my heart that if each of us would exert one-tenth the energy on our tasks that Sauckel has, then it would be rather easy for you to fulfill your required tasks.[22]

THE SECOND SAUCKEL ACTION

In August 1942, while the German Army continued its drive toward the Grozny oil fields, Hitler called another conference of his top-level economic advisors to discuss the problem of labor. Hitler, possibly realizing that the Red Army would not be completely defeated even if his Sixth Army were successful, decided that a further expansion in German war production was needed. Steel, coal, and fuel production had to be increased, and everything depended on

---

[21] See OKW/Wi Rue Amt/Rue IV (a), report dated January 1943, titled *Erfahrungsbericht ueber die Entwicklung auf dem Gebiet der Personalbewirtschaftung in der Zeit vom Winterbeginn 1941/1942 bis zum Winterbeginn 1942/1943*, on T-77, Roll 440, Frame 1600385.

[22] *IMT*, xxxix, 400-401.

1 3 9

the labor supply. When Hitler questioned Sauckel about the possibility of obtaining more foreign labor, he received the boastful reply that Sauckel could obtain another million Russian workers by the end of October if required. Confident that the problem could be solved, *Der Fuehrer* authorized Sauckel to take the necessary steps to bring another million foreign workers into the Reich. Hitler also agreed to any compulsory measures (*Zwangsmassnahmen*) in the East or West that Sauckel might consider necessary if the additional workers could not be recruited voluntarily.[23] Thus, in an almost casual manner, the second recruitment drive was launched as a continuation of the first.

Apparently impressed with the confidence that Sauckel had in his ability to recruit more foreign workers, Hitler asked him to complete another pet project. When Hitler appointed Sauckel, he mentioned that he wanted to lessen the burden of German women by bringing a half-million foreign female domestic workers into the Reich. On September 3, Hitler again repeated his demand. The domestic workers were to be voluntarily recruited in the Ukraine, and they were to be selected on the basis of a capability "of being Germanized." Himmler suggested that they have blond hair, blue eyes, and be of the "Germanic tribes" of the Ukraine.[24] The Ukrainian girls were to be considered eastern workers, but they were to receive German food rations. They were to be employed in better-class city and country households, preferably in families with many children and of strong National Socialist convictions.[25] To help Sauckel in recruiting them, Hitler approved of the illegal practice of members of the armed forces bringing female housekeepers into the Reich.

Backe, who had to supply the food for these new female

[23] Speer's notes on *Fuehrer*'s Conference, August 19, 1942, on T-73, Roll 192, Frames 405552-553.
[24] *IMT*, xxv, 84.   [25] *Ibid.*, 85.

workers, opposed the plan until the diet for Germans could be improved. Sauckel refused to discuss the matter with him, pointing out that it was a direct order from *Der Fuehrer*. Hitler's project came to nought, for Sauckel was able to recruit only 15,000 female housekeepers during the entire war.[26] Irrespective of the ultimate outcome of this project, it illustrates the mentality of Hitler. At a time when Germany was fighting most of the world and German industry was desperately short of labor, Hitler was, in the best tradition of Viennese courtliness, worrying about the additional burden the war had placed on the German *Hausfrau*.

At the end of September 1942, Hitler granted Sauckel new and broader powers over the recruitment of foreign labor. Now Sauckel had the authority to take all necessary measures for the recruitment and deployment of labor "according to his own judgment" in the Reich and all of its territories. Sauckel could appoint commissioners directly to military or civilian administrative agencies, and these commissioners were subordinate to him. The new powers also entitled Sauckel to issue directives to military and civil governments in the occupied territories.[27]

Armed with this new authority, Sauckel wrote to Rosenberg that labor recruitment in the East was to be given top priority and that a "ruthless commitment of all resources" was necessary to accomplish this objective.[28] Sauckel wanted Rosenberg to center recruitment in the areas that had been recently captured during the summer campaign, especially along the southern front. Accordingly, Sauckel gave Rosenberg a new quota of 225,000 workers from the Ukraine to be filled before the end of the year, and an additional 225,000 before May 1, 1943.[29]

[26] *IMT*, xv, 198.
[27] *Verfuegungen, Anordnungen, Bekanntgaben*, Vol. II, 1942, p. 510.
[28] *IMT*, xxv, 73.   [29] *NCA*, III, 60.

Just as Sauckel was applying pressure on the East Ministry to fill its labor quota, the employers of foreign labor in the Reich were demanding that Sauckel fulfill his promises, especially concerning skilled workers. Sauckel had attempted to alleviate this problem by a large-scale training program for foreign and German workers, but his efforts were still insignificant. During the first half of 1942, Sauckel's program had trained or retrained only 147,700 workers, of which 71,500 were foreigners.[30] Realizing that the program was inadequate, Sauckel tried a different approach. He sent orders to his representatives in the occupied territories to take more care in recruitment and comb the industries for more skilled workers. Sauckel's representatives were also to introduce modern German working methods in hopes of releasing additional skilled workers.[31] He was interpreting his powers more broadly than ever, since the industries in the occupied areas were under Speer's jurisdiction.

Sauckel's search for more skilled workers finally led him to the inevitable conclusion that if he could not find enough in the East, he would have to find them in the West or in the Reich itself. At the 21st meeting of the *Zentrale Planung*, Sauckel convinced the board that three recommendations were necessary to relieve the shortage of skilled workers. First, Sauckel's office should be allowed to handle POW's in the *Stalags*. This would facilitate a better utilization of the POW's skills. Second, the board should recommend to Hitler that he remove some of the stringent restrictions that the Army and Economic Staff East had placed on Sauckel's recruiters operating on the south side of the Don River in Russia. (These restrictions were intended to protect the oil industry and agriculture in the area.) Finally, Sauckel was

[30] Report from Sauckel's office, *Die Lage des Arbeitseinsatzes in der Ruestungswirtschaft im 2. Vierteljahr 1942*, dated July 29, 1942, on T-77, Roll 243, Frames 985890-899.
[31] *IMT*, XLI, 216-217.

to be allowed more discretion in combing skilled labor from the industries in France and the protectorate before applying new labor measures in the Reich.[32]

The search for skilled labor and Sauckel's energetic collection and use of additional powers to find labor enhanced his power position within the Reich. A clear recognition of Sauckel's new authority was the signing of an agreement by Sauckel and Speer in December 1942.[33] This agreement was one of many signed by the two men establishing a *modus operandi* between their two agencies. According to the agreement, Speer was to decide on all questions of priority for all labor assignments. Sauckel, in turn, was to locate workers and make them available to factories according to the requirements of the armament economy established by Speer.

To insure that the labor requests were valid and that workers were being utilized properly, joint investigation committees called *Bedarfspruefungskommission* were to be appointed. These committees were to include one representative of Speer's office and one of Sauckel's office. The committees were also to help in combing German factories for additional skilled workers. Heretofore, Speer alone had been responsible for combing German plants; now Sauckel had reached parity with Speer! From the role of labor recruiter, Sauckel had risen to codeterminer of what factories would receive labor, how much they would receive, and in what way they were to be used in the entire armament production of the Third Reich.

The confidence and power that Hitler had placed in Fritz Sauckel paid rich dividends. On December 23, 1942, Sauckel reported the successful completion of his second drive for one million additional workers. Sauckel boasted that, in the nine months since his appointment, he had

[32] Stenographic minutes of the 21st Conference of the Central Planning Board, October 30, 1942, in the files of the USSBS.
[33] *NCA*, Supplement A, 716.

brought 2,831,887 new workers into the Reich's war economy, an average of 340,000 workers per month.[34] Approximately 1,480,000 of these workers were from Russia alone. This rapid influx of foreign workers meant that, for the first year since 1939, the total number of workers employed in the Reich had increased instead of decreased by nearly one million workers. Sauckel stressed that before 1942 foreign workers represented only 26.5 per cent of the total number of new workers flowing into the Reich economy, while in 1942 foreign workers represented 80 per cent of the total number of new workers.[35] There were nearly six million foreign workers and POW's at work in the Reich by the end of 1942. This was no mean accomplishment.

THE LABOR PROGRAM FOR 1943

The year 1943 was a momentous one for the Third Reich. It began in the East with the staggering defeat of the German Sixth Army before Stalingrad and closed with the Red Army driving forward to Poland. In the South, Italy was turned into a battleground and the old government of Mussolini fell. In the West, the allied air war ground German cities into rubble. The year also marked the complete conversion of Germany into a total war economy. The concepts of total war as advocated earlier in the war by Thomas and Speer were finally accepted after the jolt of Stalingrad. Goebbels and Speer replaced Goering as the dominant voices in the German economy.

In January 1943, Sauckel, unaware of these future changes, was still thinking in terms of his brilliant successes of 1942. On January 13, Sauckel conferred with the French and German authorities in Paris about the labor quotas for the first quarter of the year. Sauckel wanted 150,000 skilled

---

[34] *IMT*, xxviii, 573.   [35] *Ibid.*, 580.

and 100,000 unskilled French workers by March 1943. Recruitment of another 50,000 skilled workers was scheduled for Holland, Belgium, and other occupied territories.[36] To fulfill these requirements Sauckel worked out a tentative agreement with the Paris officials to start calling French workers by age classes.

In the East, Sauckel was beginning to find that the flow of workers was diminishing. The main recruiting areas were becoming operational zones, and the weather was playing an important role in limiting operations. Still Sauckel prepared measures which would enable the Germans, on conservative calculation, to transfer from 150,000 to 200,000 eastern workers by the end of March.

For the first month and a half of the year, Sauckel had no definite quota for his 1943 drive. His agents were still recruiting workers to serve as replacements for workers with expired contracts or those lost through death, infirmity, and escape. On February 16, the *Zentrale Planung* established the quota for the first quarter of the year. The Board needed 400,000 new workers by the end of March. Sauckel estimated that these workers would be recruited as follows:[37]

Soviet Russia	200,000
Poland	40,000
France	60,000
Belgium	40,000
Holland	30,000
Slovakia	20,000
Bohemia-Moravia	10,000

A month later, when the weather was better in the East, Sauckel ordered a step-up in recruiting. Sauckel wrote Rosenberg that within the next four months he needed one million eastern workers. Starting the 15th of March, Rosenberg's quota was set at five thousand per day, and on April 1 the

[36] *Minor Trials*, II, 968.   [37] *NCA*, VIII, 180-181.

rate was to double.[38] A few days later, Sauckel authorized Rosenberg to use the SD in the labor recruiting, even if it meant large-scale raids; labor had to be procured.[39]

By April, Sauckel had established what he considered a reasonable estimate of the amount of foreign labor he could recruit in 1943. In his report to Hitler on April 15, summarizing his first year in office, Sauckel told Hitler that he expected to recruit 1,600,000 foreign workers in 1943. About 600,000 of these workers were to go to agriculture, the rest to industry. Sauckel thought that 1,000,000 would be recruited in Russia, 150,000 in Poland, and 450,000 in western Europe.[40] He added that in one year's time, from April 1, 1942, until March 31, 1943, he had recruited 3,638,056 new foreign workers.[41]

Although Sauckel had promised 1.6 million more foreign workers, his agents were encountering extraordinary resistance in the occupied countries toward further recruitment. In all areas, the Germans were compelled to register labor by age classes and to conscript them on this basis in the spring of 1943. Men often appeared for registration, but as soon as transportation was available they did not come back, so that the dispatch of labor to the Reich became a question of police enforcement.[42] In Poland, the recruitment drive led to open, violent battles. The head of Sauckel's agency in Warsaw was shot to death in his office on April 8, 1943.[43] Conditions were similar in other occupied areas, and Sauckel's field agents warned that recruitment, even if done with the best of intentions, would remain extremely difficult and dangerous unless additional police units were provided.

On June 3, Sauckel reported to Hitler the following results of his recruitment drive:

[38] *IMT*, xxv, 79-81.   [39] *IMT*, xxxii, 490.
[40] *NCA*, iii, 391.   [41] *Ibid.*, 392.
[42] *Minor Trials*, ii, 472.   [43] *Ibid.*, 473.

January, 120,085; February, 138,354; March, 257,382; April, 160,535; May, 170,155—TOTAL, 846,511.

In the same period Sauckel had been able to recruit 1,205,000 German workers to compensate for the lack of foreign workers. However, 800,000 of these Germans were women working part-time—that is, less than forty-eight hours a week.[44]

The foreign labor program slowed down after May 1943. A new system was devised by Speer to utilize labor in the native lands rather than bring them to the Reich. On his part, Sauckel deliberately recruited labor on a smaller scale in the West throughout the remainder of the year in order to give rest periods to the recruiting officials. In the East, the rapid advance of the Red Army eliminated any massive recruitment similar to that of 1942.

After the war, Sauckel claimed that he was required to furnish two million new workers for 1943. One million of these were foreign workers.[45] A document published during the war by Sauckel's office, however, indicated that the total number of civilian foreign workers in the Reich increased from 3,984,121 on December 31, 1942, to 5,411,801 on November 15, 1943, or by 1,427,680 workers. This same document listed the origin and sex of the foreign civilian workers in the Reich (see Table IX). Apparently Sauckel fell short of his original quota of 1,600,000.

THE 1944 PROGRAM

On January 4, 1944, a conference was held by *Der Fuehrer* to determine plans for the coming year's war production. Sauckel, Speer, Keitel, Milch, Backe, and Himmler attended the meeting. Hitler opened the conference by saying:

[44] *IMT*, xxvi, 13.   [45] *IMT*, xv, 53.

TABLE IX

NUMBER, ORIGIN, AND SEX OF CIVILIAN FOREIGN WORKERS
EMPLOYED IN THE REICH AS OF NOVEMBER 15, 1943

Origin	Men	Women	Total
Belgium	188,659	31,962	220,621
France	620,819	43,787	664,606
Italy	105,076	15,141	120,217
Croatia	49,361	19,653	69,014
Remainder of Yugoslavia	33,954	11,530	45,484
Holland	244,777	19,900	264,677
Hungary	19,685	7,571	27,256
Pre-1939 Russia	843,211	935,240	1,778,451
Baltic States	21,978	10,880	32,858
General-Government	709,181	342,746	1,051,927
Bohemia-Moravia	242,748	42,554	285,302
Areas placed under Reich's protection after 1939	375,490	183,982	559,472
Others	207,815	84,101	291,916
Total	3,662,754	1,749,047	5,411,801

SOURCE: *Die Ergebnisse der Auslaendererhebung vom 15. November 1943*, Sonderdruck aus dem statistischen Mitteilungsblatt, "Der Arbeitseinsatz im Grossdeutschen Reich," Herausgeber: Der Beauftragte fuer den Vierjahresplan/ Der Generalbevollmaechtigte fuer den Arbeitseinsatz, Nr. 1/1944.

I want a clear picture:

(1)   How many workers are required for the maintenance of the German War Economy?
(a) For the maintenance of present output?
(b) To increase its output?

(2)   How many workers can be obtained from occupied countries, or how many can still be gained in the Reich by suitable means?[46]

Sauckel told Hitler that in order to maintain the present level of production and cover the losses to the armed services

[46] *NCA*, III, 866.

he would have to recruit from two and a half to three million new workers in 1944. Speer estimated that he would need an additional 1,300,000 workers if it became possible to increase the production of iron ore. Hitler himself wanted 250,000 additional civilian workers for the air-raid protection system in the Reich. The total quota for new workers was thus placed at 4,050,000.[47]

In February, Sauckel estimated that the requirement for 4,050,000 additional workers could be met in the following way:

Native German labor	500,000
Italian labor	1,500,000
French labor	1,000,000
Belgian labor	250,000
Dutch labor	250,000
Eastern labor	600,000
All others	100,000
Approximately	4,200,000[48]

By March 1, Sauckel realized that his ambitious labor drive could not possibly be fulfilled. He told the *Zentrale Planung* that he could not guarantee the delivery of the additional workers because his whole program was being destroyed. The German military and civil officials in the occupied territories were refusing to support the recruitment drive because it only increased the resistance movements. To correct this, Sauckel wanted all German authorities to realize that continued recruitment of labor was indispensable to the war effort. He also wanted complete authority to comb out workers in the occupied areas, even if other German officials thought these workers were necessary for the war effort in their present occupations.

The *Zentrale Planung* agreed with Sauckel that more energetic action should be taken to recruit foreign workers, but they refused to grant him ultimate authority to draft

[47] *Ibid.*, 867-868.   [48] *Minor Trials*, II, 481.

workers from the occupied areas regardless of their value there. Speer's representative on the board especially opposed granting more power to Sauckel, arguing that as long as the Reich was subjected to heavy air raids, it was better to shift more war production to the occupied areas, where the Allies were reluctant to use massive bombing tactics.[49]

On July 7, 1944, Sauckel reported to Hitler the results of his recruitment drive. According to the original schedule, Sauckel should have recruited two million workers in the first two quarters, but because of increased difficulties only 1,482,000 workers were recruited. But the results were even more disastrous than Sauckel's figures indicated. Of the 1,482,000 new workers, only 537,400 were foreigners and 96,600 were POW's. The remaining 848,000 were Germans, most of whom were women and children working only part-time. The magnitude of Sauckel's failure in the first half of 1944 can be measured by comparing the results with his planned goals in the two principal recruiting areas of France and Italy. Instead of the planned one million from France, Sauckel got 33,000; instead of the one and a half million from Italy, he got only 37,000.[50] The foreign labor program was nearly bankrupt.

A special conference with all the top German agencies was held on July 11, to discuss an increase in foreign labor recruitment. At this meeting, new and far-reaching measures were suggested. The Army, now to be used in recruiting, was to clear partisan areas and send all captured labor in these areas to the Reich and, when retreating, to conduct mass-scale evacuation of cities and send that labor to the Reich. Many of the participants of the conference expressed doubts as to the wisdom of such measures. Speer pointed out that from 25 to 30 per cent of Germany's war production

[49] *IMT*, xxxviii, 147-160.
[50] Document RF-1507, 810F, in the files of the Nuremberg Trials Collection.

was in the occupied areas, and the proposed measure would almost certainly ruin this production. Instead Speer suggested that the executive authority in the occupied areas be given strict orders to recruit, but without using violent measures or mass raids. Field Marshal Kesselring, from Italy, and Otto Abetz, the German Ambassador in Paris, agreed with Speer; the recommendations of the Armament Minister were accepted.[51]

The moderate recommendations of the July 11 conference were apparently completely reversed because of the attempt on Hitler's life and the staggering series of defeats inflicted on the German Army. On July 24, Sauckel informed his labor recruiters that the Army and police were to seize labor wherever available.[52] The foreign labor program had entered its last violent and dying stage. The retreating Germans attempted to evacuate and seize labor where they could, but it was too late.

Although only a few German records were found for the period after July 1944, it appears that even these drastic measures of the retreating Germans obtained only 400,000 new foreign workers by the end of the year. Speer's statistical office estimated that there were 8,102,000 foreign civil workers and POW's at work in the Reich in December 1944,[53] which, incidentally, was the largest number of foreigners ever working in the Reich at one time. This was an increase of 449,000 more than in July 1944 and, added to the 537,000 foreign workers and 96,600 POW's that Sauckel reportedly recruited up to July, meant that approximately 1,083,000 new foreign workers were added to the Reich during the year 1944. This estimate would agree with

[51] Minor Trials, II, 428.

[52] Document RF-1507, 810F, in the files of the Nuremberg Trials Collection.

[53] Arbeitseinsatz (Arbeitsbuchinhaber) 21.3.45, nach G.B. Ruest./ Planungsamt/Statistische Leitstelle, on Microfilm Roll 2075 in the files of the USSBS.

Sauckel's report to Hitler on the 1944 program. On December 30, 1944, Sauckel reported that 3,313,000 workers were recruited in 1944, about 737,000 short of the original quota of 4,050,000. Of the 3,313,000 recruited workers, 1,024,000 were foreign civilian workers and 186,000 were POW's.[54] In the eastern territories and Poland the quotas were fulfilled, but in the West only one-tenth of the requirements were met. In spite of this, Sauckel said the results of the 1944 program were good. Later at the Nuremberg trials, Sauckel claimed that he had recruited about 900,000 new foreign workers in 1944.[55]

As Table X indicates, Sauckel was able to secure approximately 5,379,567 new foreign workers for the Reich in four major recruitment drives between 1942 and 1944. Although the acquisition of 5.3 million new foreign workers over a

TABLE X

SUMMARY OF SAUCKEL'S FOUR RECRUITMENT DRIVES FOR FOREIGN
LABOR FROM APRIL 1942 UNTIL 1945

Duration of Drive	Quota of Workers Needed	Foreign Workers Recruited
April to September 1942	1,600,000	1,639,794
September to December 1942	1,000,000	1,102,093
The 1943 drive	1,600,000	1,427,680
The 1944 drive	4,050,000	1,210,000
Totals	8,250,000	5,379,567

SOURCE: For the first three drives, *Die Ergebnisse der Auslaend-ererhebung vom 15, November 1943*; for the 1944 drive, Sauckel's report of December 30, 1944, to Hitler, on T-175, Roll 71, Frames 2588272-277.

[54] Sauckel's report to Hitler, dated December 30, 1944, on T-175, Roll 71, Frames 2588272-277.
[55] *IMT*, xv, 53.

period of thirty-three months was in itself an amazing feat, it did not include a number of additional foreign workers recruited as replacements for other foreign workers during the war. German labor records were always based on the number of foreign workers employed at a particular time. Sauckel's records were based on the increase of new foreign workers. Neither took into account the actual number recruited. The fluctuation caused by expiring contracts, deaths, injury, arrests, and escapes was tremendous. Sauckel estimated the fluctuation for 1944 was close to 2.0 million. This meant that the actual number of foreigners recruited was greater than the 8.1 million foreign workers that Speer's records indicated were at work in the Reich at the end of 1944.

Unfortunately, when the Russian prosecuting attorney at the Nuremberg trials attempted to establish the exact number of foreigners recruited during the war, his inquiries were judged irrelevant from a legal viewpoint by the court. However, Sauckel did admit vaguely that five million foreigners were recruited for the Reich before his appointment, and he had recruited another five million; this meant that a total of at least ten million foreigners were recruited.[56] The figure however, must be considered a conservative estimate. In a pre-trial interrogation, Sauckel hinted at the possibility that nearly 12.0 million foreign workers were recruited throughout the war, although at no time during the war were there more than 8.1 million foreigners actually employed in the Reich.[57] It is clear however, that by the end of 1944, at the peak of the employment of foreign workers, one out of every five workers employed in the Reich was a foreigner.

[56] *Ibid.*, 134-136.
[57] Pre-trial interrogation of Fritz Sauckel, October 5, 1945, in the files of the Nuremberg Trials Collection.

CHAPTER VIII

The Paradox of the Eastern Recruitment

THE method of recruiting eastern workers for the Reich varied greatly according to the area of recruitment, the German officials in charge of recruiting, and the time and conditions when the recruitment occurred. In general, however, the labor recruitment in the East involved establishing compulsory labor laws, drafting workers by age classes, and using force.

In the East, unlike elsewhere, force was prevalent in labor recruitment. There were many reasons for this: the East was in a constant state of flux, recruitment areas became military operational sectors time and time again, and the proximity of the battle lines stimulated partisan guerrilla activity with the usual consequence that the Germans became more severe in their methods. There was also a ready supply of German troops to enforce police measures against the native population. The fundamental difference in the attitude of the Germans toward the easterner compared with the westerner was an additional factor. Consciously or unconsciously, the Germans felt that they were dealing with racially inferior peoples.[1]

The German policy of employing force and violence against the *Untermensch* in the East was an extension of policies developed in Poland earlier; they were well established by the time Sauckel was appointed to direct the labor program. However, Sauckel was apparently prepared to make use of this harsh policy to further his own goals of recruiting millions of eastern workers despite the fact that voluntary recruitment drives had had limited successes. He

[1] *Das Dritte Reich und Europa*, Bericht ueber die Tagung des Instituts fuer Zeitgeschichte in Tutzing, May 1, 1956 (Munich: Institut fuer Zeitgeschichte, 1957), pp. 137-138.

told the Reich labor officials at his first meeting with them on April 15, 1942, that the eastern workers "would have to be handled so roughly by the German administration in the East that they would come to feel that they would prefer to go to Germany for work."[2]

Erich Koch, the Reich Commissar for the Ukraine, was completely in favor of such forceful recruiting measures, as was his commander of the Security Service Police, who stated in an order dated March 18, 1942:

> 3. The activity of the labor offices, especially of recruiting commissions, is to be supported to the greatest extent possible. It will not be possible always to refrain from using force. During a conference with the chief of the labor commitment staffs, an agreement was reached stating that wherever prisoners can be released, they should be put at the disposal of the commissioner of the labor office. When searching villages the whole population will be put at the disposal of the commissioner by force.
>
> 4. As a rule, no more children will be shot.[3]

Fortunately for the native populations in the East, the flow of voluntary workers was in excess of the German labor quotas until the midsummer of 1942. However, once the supply of volunteers stopped, the Germans began using force. The healthy, the ill, the young, and the old were gathered up and sent to the Reich. An interdepartmental report of the East Ministry dated September 30, 1942, complained that the drafting of eastern workers often occurred without the necessary examination of the capabilities of those concerned. From 5 to 10 per cent of the recruited workers transported to the Reich were either children or ill adults. The report further observed that in those places where no volunteers were obtained, coercive measures were used by

[2] *NCA*, vii, 1186.
[3] *NCA*, Supplement A, 732.

the police rather than recruiting workers pursuant to labor conscription laws.[4]

In another report dated October 7, from the Commandant of Kharkov, other abuses in recruiting were noted. The native Ukrainian militia was accused of dragging skilled workers from their beds for transportation to the Reich and justifying themselves by claiming that it was done in the name of the German Army. However, the report noted that "in reality the latter [the German Army] had conducted themselves almost throughout in a highly understanding manner toward the skilled workers and the Ukrainian population."[5]

In a secret memorandum by Otto Braeutigam, Deputy Chief of the Political Department in the East Ministry, the German recruitment methods were characterized as regular manhunts. Without consideration of health or age, Braeutigam wrote, the people were shipped to the Reich; immediately, more than one hundred thousand had to be sent back because of serious illnesses and other incapabilities for work. Moreover, complained Braeutigam, ". . . these methods were used only in the Soviet Union, and in no way remotely resembled this form [of recruitment] in enemy countries like Holland or Norway."[6] The recruiting methods had consequently increased the resistance power of the Red Army by making the struggle between Germany and Russia a fight for the preservation of human dignity. Braeutigam concluded that the recruiting methods and the lack of an appealing political and economic program for the easterners were making an effective, rational German rule in Russia impossible.[7]

Other German officials in the East complained that men and women were being beaten on the street and hauled away by labor recruiters to the Reich.[8] The situation was becoming so desperate that Rosenberg decided to complain publicly

[4] *Minor Trials*, II, 408. [5] *NCA*, III, 92.
[6] *Minor Trials*, II, 412. [7] *NCA*, III, 250-251.
[8] *IMT*, xxv, 344.

about labor recruitment in the East. In November, he attacked Sauckel in an address before officials of the German Labor Front, charging that Sauckel was bringing workers into the Reich under terrible conditions. Millions of easterners, Rosenberg said, now regarded Germany as another Siberia.[9]

The Army also began criticizing Sauckel's recruiting methods. A secret report from the Headquarters of the Army North stated that the area was in danger of a general popular uprising because of the food situation and recruitment drives. Solemnly, the Army warned that "if we continue our present attitude, it will be the combat soldier who will pay with his blood for this mistake."[10] The Army compared Sauckel's actions to a lost battle, but the full force of the Army's criticism was reserved for those of Sauckel's agents who were immediately involved with the recruitment. With lurid details, the Army described some of the horrors of recruitment:

> The executing agencies have committed errors which should have been avoided: de-lousing of Russian girls by men, taking nude photographs in forced positions, locking female doctors in cars in order to make them available to the transport leaders, transporting of shackled girls in nightshirts through Russian towns to the railroad, etc.[11]

As a result of such reports, Field Marshal Ewald von Kleist, Commander of Army Group B in the Ukraine and Caucasus, and General Erich Frederici, Commander of the Rear Area Army Group South, banned further labor recruitment in their areas. General Count von Schenckendorff had already forbidden labor recruitment in the area of White Russia under his command.[12]

[9] Reitlinger, *House Built on Sand*, p. 271.
[10] *NCA*, iii, 934.   [11] *Ibid.*, 945.
[12] Dallin, *German Rule in Russia*, p. 441.

To defend himself against such devastating criticism, Sauckel organized a mass meeting of labor officials in Weimar on January 6, 1943. Rosenberg, members of the Economic Staff East, and representatives of the Army were invited. Sauckel's address to the assembled group stressed the need for correct but firm handling of the eastern workers. He argued that a foreigner who worked in the Reich never had had his life or health so well protected. Skillfully, Sauckel presented the foreign labor program as an absolute necessity which aimed at helping the Reich by treating the foreign workers correctly.[13] The effect of his words was probably lost on his audience, in view of the fact that Sauckel also mentioned the possibility of drafting an additional one million eastern workers in 1943.

Apparently Sauckel convinced one high-ranking army commander, for General Kurt Zeitzler, Chief of the General Staff in Russia, issued a new labor duty law for the eastern areas. Zeitzler's law provided that everyone between the ages of fourteen and sixty-five was obligated to work according to his ability. The new law prohibited changing jobs and hiring new workers without permission from the labor offices and instituted a mandatory 54-hour work week.[14] The law was instrumental in pooling Russian laborers and thereby made it easier to recruit them for the Reich. Yet individual army commanders still refused to permit Sauckel's agents to recruit in their areas.

Finally, Sauckel was forced to use more direct measures. On March 10, he wrote to Hitler that he was having difficulties recruiting in Russia because army commanders forbade it for political reasons. Sauckel assured *Der Fuehrer* that the objections of the Army were meritless.[15] After a few days, the ban on the activities of Sauckel's recruiters in Russia was removed.

[13] *IMT*, xli, 225.   [14] *IMT*, xxxii, 481-485.
[15] *NCA*, iii, 389-390.

Sauckel's method of handling the objections from Rosenberg's ministry was different. He simply ignored the protests and, instead of working through the East Ministry, bypassed it and contacted the Reich Commissars directly.[16] There were three reasons why Sauckel could afford to ignore the East Ministry in such an open manner.

First, the political feud between Rosenberg and Koch had become so bitter by early 1943 that Sauckel realized he could use the situation to further his aims. Since most of the labor recruited in Russia came from Koch's Ukraine, Sauckel decided to accept a private agreement with Koch. Koch told Sauckel, "I am willing to supply them to you. How I do that is none of your business, and I don't want to be advised about it."[17] Koch apparently recruited for Sauckel with enthusiasm, in part out of sheer spite for Rosenberg. The more Rosenberg complained about the inhuman recruitment in the Ukraine, the more Koch enjoyed it.

The second reason that Sauckel could afford to ignore Rosenberg was more subtle. Sauckel the politician was close to the inner circle of Nazi leaders, and he could readily perceive that Rosenberg no longer enjoyed the confidence of that group. It had become fashionable to ignore Rosenberg.[18]

The third reason for Sauckel's behavior toward Rosenberg was that he no longer needed Rosenberg. According to Hitler's decree of March 4, 1943, Sauckel was granted formal, absolute control over the regional labor offices.[19] The original

[16] Braeutigam, *Ueberblick*, p. 93.

[17] Pre-trial interrogations of Fritz Sauckel, September 28, 1945, in the files of the Nuremberg Trials Collection.

[18] Cf. Reitlinger, *House Built on Sand*, pp. 200-212; Dallin, *German Rule in Russia*, pp. 160-162; Braeutigam, *Ueberblick*, pp. 32-33; and Kleist, *Zwischen Hitler und Stalin*, pp. 258-260.

[19] "Erlass des Fuehrers zur Durchfuehrung des Erlasses ueber einen Generalbevollmaechtigten fuer den Arbeitseinsatz, Maerz 4, 1943," in Friedrich Didier's *Handbuch fuer die Dienststellen des G.B.A. und die interessierten Reichsstellen im Grossdeutschen Reich und in den besetzten Gebieten* (Berlin: Verlag der DAF, 1944), p. 24.

grant of power at the time of Sauckel's appointment in March 1942 stipulated that the regional labor offices were bound by the directives and regulations of Sauckel, but that they were under the control of the Reich Labor Ministry. Hitler's new grant also allowed Sauckel to merge the labor trustee system (*Reichstreuhaender der Arbeit*) with the regional labor offices. Under Nazism, the duties of the labor trustees were to determine the wage and working conditions formerly settled by collective bargaining. The labor trustees also had the power to settle industrial disputes. Appeals against their rulings were impossible. Thus Sauckel was in a position to determine recruiting, wage, and working policies, not only within the Reich, but also in the occupied territories. Rosenberg had lost even nominal control over his own labor department. To emphasize this, Sauckel appointed one of his close friends from Thuringia to head the Main Labor Department in Rosenberg's East Ministry.[20]

Regardless of the methods that Sauckel employed, however, he was unable to muffle adverse criticism of recruiting techniques in the East. In the Ukraine, a special committee of pro-German native sympathizers reported to Rosenberg on February 23, 1943, about sixteen special instances of violence in labor recruitment, ranging from arrests to killings. Typical of these special incidents was the shooting of forty-five Ukrainians, including eighteen children between the ages of three and fifteen, on January 29, 1943, in the village of Sumyn in the district of Lublin.[21] The report also stated that the general nervousness in the Ukraine was enhanced by the increasingly frequent use of frightening methods for finding labor. The wild and ruthless manhunts carried out everywhere in towns and country, at night in homes, in streets, squares, stations, even in churches, had badly shaken the security of the inhabitants. Everybody was

[20] Braeutigam, *Ueberblick*, p. 31.
[21] *NCA*, iii, 64-65.

exposed to the danger of being seized anywhere and at any time by members of the police.[22]

In northern Russia and the former Baltic states, the recruitment was just as violent as in the Ukraine. In Latvia and Estonia, the recruiters were not permitted to sign up male workers because Himmler was already trying to recruit them for his *SS Waffen* divisions. In Lithuania and White Russia, however, Sauckel ordered the recruitment of all workers, regardless of sex, from the 19 to 24-year-old age groups. If the quotas were not met, they were to be filled from the 12 to 18-year-old age groups.[23]

In a secret report to Hans Riecke, Deputy General of the German Ministry of Agriculture, the Office of the General Commandant in Minsk claimed that "the recruitment of labor for the Reich, however necessary, had catastrophic effects. The recruitment measures in the last months and weeks were absolute manhunts, which have an irreparable political and economic effect."[24] Also, the quotas were unthinkably high; in White Ruthenia, for example, the report said Sauckel wanted 180,000 workers out of a total population of 2,400,000.[25] The entire agricultural program was in jeopardy because of Sauckel's recruitment drives.

At the end of June, Ernst Leyser, General Commissioner for the district of Zhitomir, located in central Russia, told Rosenberg that "actual conscription by force" was used in his district labor recruitment.[26] Sauckel had ordered the recruitment of the 1922 to 1925 age classes (approximately 18 to 21-year-old groups at that time), and in Leyser's opinion the limit for labor recruitment had been reached.[27] Regardless of the consequences, Sauckel had ordered Leyser to apply the severest measures in order to achieve the labor quotas.

[22] *NCA*, iii, 79-81.　　　　[23] *NCA*, iv, 969-970.
[24] *IMT*, xxxi, 466.　　　　[25] *IMT*, xxxi, 466-467.
[26] *NCA*, iii, 236.　　　　[27] *IMT*, xxv, 321.

By August, Sauckel, with quotas still unfilled, ordered the recruitment and transportation of the 1926 and 1927 age classes from the East. The drive was to be completed by September, and any suitable means of recruiting was authorized.[28] Even German agencies like OT (*Organisation Todt*) and the Army were to give up their workers in this age group without the possibility of replacing them.

THE FOREIGN LABOR PROGRAM AND GERMAN RULE

There was one other method of finding labor in the East —seizing people who were partisans or who helped the partisans. As early as October 1942, Goering had ordered the police and Army to seize all men and women in partisan areas who were capable of work and to send them to Sauckel's organization as POW's. Throughout 1943 and 1944, this method was increasingly used, although numerically the results were not significant. In the largest single operation against the partisans in central Russia, Project Cottbus, conducted in the early summer of 1943, only 3,512 people were turned over to the labor program, while at the same time nearly 5,000 others were shot to death on the suspicion that they were involved with partisan bands.[29] The SS report on Cottbus tersely remarked that the 5,000 dead could have just as easily been turned over as forced labor. In July 1943, Field Marshal Keitel specifically ordered the Army to turn over to Sauckel all prisoners from the age of sixteen to sixty-five captured in partisan fighting. These men were to be considered prisoners of war, and they were to work in coal mines in the Reich. Himmler suggested that women captured should also be forced to work in the Reich.[30]

By August of 1943, the *Wehrmacht* was beginning the retreat to the old frontiers of the Reich. The recruitment of

[28] *IMT*, xxxi, 478-480.   [29] *NCA*, viii, 206.
[30] *NCA*, iii, 543.

vast numbers of eastern workers was virtually impossible, since almost the entire occupied area of Russia was festered with partisans and rapidly becoming an operational area. The Army and the SS were replacing Sauckel as the chief recruiter. The recruitment became sporadic, violent, and without notable success. On March 1, 1944, Sauckel told the *Zentrale Planung* that only 262,000 foreign workers had been recruited since September 1943, and about 112,000 of these came from the East. He declared that the Army was accusing him of not taking enough easterners in the previous year because they now had joined partisan groups which the Army had to fight.

Sauckel was sensitive about the accusations that his recruiting had created the partisans, and he defended himself by arguing that unemployment was the major cause of them. To illustrate this point, Sauckel noted that in Kiev he had taken 100,000 workers, and there were no partisans, whereas in Minsk, where Sauckel recruited practically no labor, the partisans were so active that they managed to murder Wilhelm Kube, the General Commissioner of White Russia.[31]

In the few areas in the East that Germany controlled, an attempt was made to register additional age classes for work in the Reich in the spring of 1944. In Kauen, Lithuania, for example, when the Germans tried to register the age classes from 1919 to 1924, only 35 per cent of the people appeared. After numerous arrests and more political pressure, a second registration produced only 47 per cent. In desperation, the Germans had then to call all men from the 1912 to 1918 age classes, and all women from the 1914 to 1922 classes. Even then the Germans were able to send only 8,200 workers to the Reich. Their quota had been 30,000.[32]

By July 1944, the recruitment program in Russia was

[31] *NCA*, VIII, 152-153.   [32] *IMT*, XXV, 290-297.

bankrupt. At a conference in the Reich Chancellery on the 11th of July, Sauckel reported that only about three-fourths of the 560,000 foreigners recruited in the first half of the year came from the East. Many of these eastern workers were, in fact, *Volksdeutsche* and workers taken either from Vlassov's Army or from the German Army. At the same conference, Lieutenant General Walter von Warlimont reported that Hitler had issued orders to the Army to evacuate Russian cities as it retreated and turn the people over to the labor program. Sauckel was skeptical about such orders because, in his opinion, all too often the Army thought labor recruitment was "disreputable" and tried to protect civilians from the recruiters.[33]

The suggested use of the Army in recruitment at the July 11th conference was made meaningless by the military situation. Within a few days, the Russian armies completed the recapture of all of the prewar territories of the Soviet Union. There the labor program was finished.

In the General-Government, the recruitment methods employed by the Germans from Sauckel's appointment in 1942 until the end of the war can be summarized briefly as a miniature of what happened in the occupied Soviet areas. Age classes were called up, recruiting was often violent, and the resistance of the Polish people grew steadily. As in Russia, there were many conflicts over ultimate goals in the area. The liberal wing of the German authorities wanted to redevelop and increase the value of Polish economic resources, feeling that they could become an asset to the Reich. The more traditional Nazi approach was to exploit the General-Government for immediate gains without regard to long-term considerations. This latter view predominated until 1943, when the futility of such a policy became evident to everyone. Concessions were made to the Poles, but, as in the case of the Russians, they were too late and too few.

[33] *Minor Trials*, II, 428-431.

The major difference between the recruitment procedures in the General-Government and Russia was more of emphasis than technique. By the time Sauckel was appointed as labor chief, the reserves in the General-Government were already exhausted. Nearly one million Polish workers were in the Reich.[34] This represented a sizable proportion of the total Polish population. In 1943, the German labor quota for the General-Government was 150,000, and in 1944, 100,000. Both of these quotas were met by Hans Frank, the Governor General.[35]

Apart from the difficulties and results of the German labor recruitment in the General-Government and in the occupied Soviet areas, there remained the question of evaluating the total impact of recruitment on other problems. Were Sauckel's recruitment tactics the father of the partisan movement, as many Germans believed? Did the recruitment antagonize the native populations to the extent that it seriously undermined the entire structure of German rule in the East? Did the emphasis on recruitment predetermine the collapse of other German programs, such as agricultural and industrial utilization of the East?

The charge that Sauckel's recruitment methods encouraged the partisan movement in the East was a common one during the war. The military and civilian agencies were continually complaining that Sauckel's methods were sending thousands of workers into the woods. Otto Braeutigam and Peter Kleist, both important officials in the East Ministry during the war, emphasized that in spite of countless protests about recruitment, the program was continued until all of Russia was embroiled in the resistance campaign.[36]

[34] Frank's diary, entry for March 26, 1942, Document 2233-PS, in the files of the Nuremberg Trials Collection.

[35] *Ibid.*, entry for April 19, 1944.

[36] Braeutigam, *Ueberblick*, p. 92; and Kleist, *Zwischen Hitler und Stalin*, p. 196.

The American, Edgar Howell, who wrote a detailed study of the guerrilla war in Russia for the United States Army, agreed with this viewpoint. Indeed, Howell considered the recruitment program to be the chief factor in the partisan war.

> Granting the detrimental effect of the abortively handled land problem, the question of churches, and the general shortage of food in the occupied territories, the German labor program as instituted in the late winter of 1941-1942 probably contributed more to the ultimate frustration of the German war effort in the rear areas than any one other policy.[37]

The labor recruitment was accused of completely undermining German rule in the East. Hans Lammers' report to Himmler in April 1943 was typical. Lammers thought that the wrong methods had been chosen to achieve labor goals. Forceful recruitment had weakened the "people's willingness to work and the people's confidence to such a degree that it cannot be checked even with terror."[38] Hans Frank even claimed in June 1943 that labor recruitment not only crushed cooperation between eastern peoples and Germany, but insured excellent results of communistic propaganda.[39] Feliks Gross, in his book *The Polish Worker*, came to the same conclusion.[40] The consensus of other writers on this subject indicated that the labor recruitment in the East played a major role in thwarting German rule in that area.[41]

[37] Edgar M. Howell, *The Soviet Partisan Movement, 1941-1944*, Department of the Army Pamphlet 20-244, August 1956, p. 107. A later study, *Soviet Partisans in World War II*, ed. by John A. Armstrong (Madison: University of Wisconsin Press, 1964), confirms Howell's analysis.

[38] *NCA*, IV, 859.

[39] *IMT*, XXVI, 15-30.

[40] Gross, *The Polish Worker*, pp. 174-176.

[41] Cf. Dallin, *German Rule in Russia*; Reitlinger, *House Built on Sand*; Braeutigam, *Ueberblick*; and Ihor Kamenetsky, *Hitler's Occu-*

Supporting this conclusion was the increase in partisan activity, though one must approach this apparently obvious correlation with caution. All reports from German officials connected with labor recruitment agreed that until the summer of 1942 the Russian workers were volunteers. At the same time, the resistance movement had been organized and active since the early part of the year. In fact, the partisan movement in Russia, as elsewhere, became important and overtly aggressive only after it became clear that Nazi Germany could be defeated. An important prerequisite of any successful partisan movement had already been established before the forced labor recruitment started—namely, belief in the failing strength of the occupying power. The partisans were also responsible for some of the terror connected with the recruitment. Their activity brought down on the native peoples in the East the wrath of the fanatic SD and SS who, unlike the Army and East Ministry, cared nothing for cultivating mutual good will and confidence in the area.[42] The people in the occupied areas were caught between the terror of the Germans and the counterterror of the partisans. Other roots of partisan revolt were the massacre of minorities, the harsh handling of POW's, the inadequate food supply, and the lack of an appealing political and economic program for the Russian masses. Nevertheless, the labor recruitment was indisputably a contributing factor in creating the partisan movement. Possibly labor recruitment was the last and most dramatic gesture of German insincerity to the people of the occupied areas, the final bitter humiliation in a long series of humiliations.

The role that the labor recruitment played in the collapse of German agricultural and industrial plans in the East was also quite clear. As early as the winter of 1942-1943, a criti-

---

pation of the Ukraine (Milwaukee: Marquette University Press, 1956).

[42] Anisimov, *German Occupation in Northern Russia*, p. 29.

cal labor shortage had developed in the East. German economists were even suggesting importing labor into the Ukraine to increase production there.[43] Investigations after the war confirmed the opinion that agricultural production in occupied Russia was not as important to the German economy as was the agricultural production of Denmark and France.[44] The tendency of German agencies like Sauckel's to pursue mutually conflicting goals was summarized by Alexander Dallin when he wrote:

> At the very moment when some pressed for the utmost use of labour in Eastern agriculture, others forcibly transported farm hands to work in the Reich. While the Army sought to enroll Soviet prisoners as troops, German factories pressed for their use in industry. There was never any clear-cut decision on the priority of allocating men and resources, and there was an utter lack of understanding of the interrelation of economics and politics.[45]

Thus the manner in which labor was recruited in the East helped to destroy confidence in German rule, contributed to the creation of the partisans, and seriously interfered with other German plans. This was a heavy price to pay for the millions of workers shipped to the Reich.

SPECIAL CONDITIONS OF EASTERN WORKERS IN THE REICH

German recruitment difficulties in the East were further compounded by the treatment accorded eastern workers in

[43] Kuno Waltemath, "Deutschlands Aussichten der Versorgung mit osteuropaeischen Lebens- und Rohstoffen und zukuenftige Aufgaben im Welthandel," *Jahrbuecher fuer Nationaloekonomie und Statistik* (Jena: Verlag von Gustav Fischer, 1943), CLVII, 33.

[44] Karl Brandt *et al.*, *Management of Agriculture and Food in the German Occupied and Other Areas of Fortress Europe* (Stanford: Stanford University Press, 1953), Vol. II, p. 612.

[45] Dallin, *German Rule in Russia*, p. 664.

the Reich. Rumors about German abuses, mistreatment, and exploitation of eastern workers quickly swept throughout occupied Russia, aided by clever Soviet propaganda. Indeed, the Germans made a monstrous mistake in the initial way they handled the eastern workers.

When the eastern workers first arrived in the Reich, they were met with hostility and suspicion, and treated, as one German writer admitted, as Jews.[46] Like the Jew, the eastern worker wore a distinctive sign on his clothes, received smaller food rations, worked for practically nothing, and served as an object of racial ridicule and scorn. Often his poor clothes, gaunt features, and strange mannerisms seemed to reinforce the image of inferiority that Nazi propagandists had so assiduously cultivated in the minds of the German people. In short, he was subjected to literally thousands of minute legal and quasi-legal discriminations; he was always in a special category. One half of the 1,222-page book for employers of foreign workers dealt with special conditions for workers from the East.

However, the fact that racial resentment toward the easterner was not as deeply ingrained as that toward the Jew, coupled with the critical labor shortage, led officials to reconsider the role of the eastern worker. Slowly but steadily the easterners in the Reich achieved a degree of equality with other foreign workers and with the German worker. Changes in the treatment of eastern workers began in 1943. German officials became aware of the fact that better treatment of easterners would be useful in counteracting communist propaganda in the East. More important, however, was the gradual realization that the circumstances of the war dictated a

---

[46] Walter Herdeg, *Grundzuege der deutschen Besatzungsverwaltung in den west- und nordeuropaeische Laendern waehrend des 2. Weltkrieges* (Tuebingen: Studien des Instituts Besatzungsfragen zu den deutschen Besatzungen in 2. Weltkrieg, 1953), p. 117 (mimeographed).

better utilization of manpower regardless of dogmatic racial considerations. The German reforms passed after 1943 which aimed at improving the lot of the eastern worker were based, in reality, on the pragmatic assumption that those workers could be made more productive if treated more humanely.

The first reforms referred to the eastern workers' wages. As previously noted, the eastern worker originally received only wages for work done. He was not allowed extra pay or fringe benefits like the German worker. In addition to receiving lower wages, the eastern worker had to pay a confiscatory tax, the *Ostarbeiterabgabe*, which usually left him with from 7.0 to 22.5 per cent of his net earnings.[47] In June 1942, after the appointment of Sauckel, new regulations modified the wages of the eastern worker. He could receive incentive pay and extra wages for difficult or dangerous work; he was entitled to payment for hours lost because of bad weather, air raids, or illness incurred while working; and he was allowed to buy his work clothes at a lower price based on his lower wages.[48] However, by the beginning of 1943, the average eastern worker in industry was still only receiving about 3 RM per week after deductions.[49] In agriculture, the wages received were slightly less, averaging 2.10 RM per week but not more than 9 RM per month.[50] An official German Labor Front manual explained that such low

[47] *Ibid.*, pp. 117-118. The "slave labor" charges at the Nuremberg War Trials were substantiated by the abysmal wage scale for eastern workers. This was not the case, however, with the rest of the foreign workers.

[48] *Reichsgesetzblatt*, 1942, Part I, 419.

[49] Report from Regensburg *Kreisobmann*, dated July 24, 1942, on T-81, Roll 68, Frames 77947-948.

[50] Hans Kueppers and Rudolf Bannier, *Einsatzbedingungen der Ostarbeiter sowie der sowjetrussischen Kriegsgefangenen, Sonderveroeffentlichung des Reichsarbeitsblattes* (Berlin: January 1943), p. 45.

wages were due to the fact that the eastern workers were still considered "political enemies" of the Reich.[51]

New wage regulations for eastern workers were passed on April 5, 1943, and again on March 3, 1944. Under these new laws, the maximum amount the eastern worker could finally receive from his total earnings was 28 per cent.[52] However, on July 23, 1943, Sauckel issued an order which allowed the workers to receive a rebate of 20 per cent of their taxes after successfully accomplishing one year of work. After the second and third years of work, the rebate was to be 30 per cent and 50 per cent respectively.[53] The new regulations in 1944 also allowed the eastern worker pay for German holidays, the same pay as others for equal work, and the added right of vacation and leave. His taxes remained the same, but the easterner was given more social and health benefits.[54] With all these increases, according to Sauckel, the average weekly earnings of an eastern worker in 1944, after deductions and room and board, was 18 RM.[55]

Soviet POW's were paid even less for their work than Soviet civilian workers. As late as September 1944, the Speer ministry published a wage scale which showed clearly the difference in payment between Soviet and non-Soviet POW's. A statement was issued which noted that the increase in the

[51] *Der auslaendische Arbeiter in Deutschland, eine tabellarische Uebersicht* (Berlin: Arbeitswissenschaftliches Institut der Deutschen Arbeitsfront, 1943), p. 3.

[52] Herdeg, *Grundzuege der deutschen Besatzungsverwaltung*, p. 117.

[53] See the incomplete directive dealing with wages and other benefits for eastern workers, on T-71, Roll 78, Frames 580605-636. This specific reference is on Frame 580626.

[54] "Die Verordnung ueber die Einsatzbedingungen der Ostarbeiter vom 25 Maerz 1944," in *Amtliche Mitteilungen des Praesidenten des Gauarbeitsamtes und Reichstreuhaenders der Arbeit fuer die Westmark, 5 Mai 1944, Nummer 9*, in the files of the USSBS.

[55] *IMT*, xv, 45-46.

171

pay of POW's was accomplished through Sauckel's efforts. As Table XI indicates, the employment of POW's was

TABLE XI

DIFFERENCE BETWEEN SOVIET AND NON-SOVIET POW'S WAGES
IN RM
(weekly)

German Wage Scale	Non-Soviet POW's		Soviet POW's	
	Stalag's Share	*POW's Share*	*Stalag's Share*	*POW's Share*
0- 2.00	.50	.50	.75	.25
10-12.00	5.00	2.50	6.25	1.25
21-24.00	11.00	5.00	13.50	2.50
30-35.00	16.00	8.00	20.00	4.00
40-45.00	21.00	10.00	26.00	5.00
50-55.00	27.00	12.00	33.00	6.00
60-65.00	33.00	14.00	40.00	7.00

SOURCE: Letter from Speer's ministry, dated September 29, 1944, on T-73, Roll 97, Frames 3251043-46.

profitable both for the German employer and the German Army.

A second attempt to alter the status of the eastern worker was the change in his special identification badge. The badge, consisting of the German word *Ost*, had to be worn over the left breast of the worker, and had to be visible at all times. Himmler and his SS organization were apparently the instigators of this policy. Sauckel wanted to change the regulations after his appointment, but Bormann and Himmler refused. In 1943, the regulations dealing with the *Ost* badge were modified slightly. An incentive plan was devised that would allow eastern workers who had worked hard to replace their old badge with a smaller one to be worn on the left shoulder.[56] By April 1944, Himmler finally agreed to remove

[56] *Minor Trials*, IX, 900-901.

the badge. Regulations were published which allowed eastern workers to wear armlets denoting their nationality. Otto Braeutigam claimed that one of the reasons for this slow change of attitude about the badges was the opposition of the German Housewives' Association, *Reichsfrauenfuehrung*; they were jealous of the eastern women. The housewives argued that as long as eastern women wore badges, German men would be ashamed to be seen with them in public. Braeutigam maintained that German men were quite drawn by the charms of Russian women.[57]

Curiously, there were no special regulations dealing with personal discrimination against the eastern workers employed in France or Holland, as there were against those in Belgium. Apparently the military authorities in these countries refused to permit such discrimination. However, the economic discriminations against eastern workers were uniformly applied throughout the occupied western territories.[58]

Finally, besides improving legal conditions for the eastern workers, Sauckel's agency, the East Ministry, Speer's ministry, and the German Labor Front attempted to change the attitude of the Germans so that there would be more acceptance of the eastern worker. Sauckel's writings were filled with admonitions to his fellow citizens that they must appreciate the importance of foreign labor to the war economy. The Gauleiters were often singled out by Sauckel for severe criticism. A typical instance occurred in December 1942, when rumors had suggested that the coal supply would be inadequate. A number of Gauleiters reportedly had remarked that the "first to freeze will be Russians." Sauckel angrily told the Gauleiters that it was "crazy to think that these people aren't important—or rather to go through all the trouble

[57] Braeutigam, *Ueberblick*, p. 94.
[58] Herdeg, *Grundzuege der deutschen Besatzungsverwaltung*, pp. 115-117.

of bringing them to the Reich and then have them die or starve to death."[59]

Members of the East Ministry were also disturbed by the loose racial talk in the Reich. Rosenberg and Frank sincerely wanted to correct the position of the eastern workers in the Reich, if for no other reason than to make their own work easier. But some of the most effective propaganda advocating better treatment for the easterners came from Speer's ministry. Numerous books, pamphlets, and brochures were published emphasizing the ill-effects of the scorn that Germans held for eastern workers. One of the best examples of Speer's publications was a book issued in 1943, classified secret and entitled "The Placement of the Eastern Worker in the German Machine Industry."[60] It was meant to ease the problems of employers of workers from the East by presenting a series of reports from various companies on experiences with such workers. In non-technical language and with many illustrations, the book stressed the ability, desires, and interests of the eastern workers employed in the Reich. Unlike much of the obvious propaganda published in German newspapers or promotion materials, the book frankly discussed, for example, the abuses in recruitment of eastern workers and the effects on the workers.

The German Labor Front also prepared many publications to acquaint Germans with the eastern worker and his problems. These publications invariably soft-pedaled Nazi racial dogma by describing the workers in a sympathetic and fair manner. The dominant theme was always that the production of the eastern worker depended on the desirability of his sit-

[59] *IMT*, xxxii, 217-218.

[60] See *Einsatz von Ostarbeitern in der Deutschen Maschinenindustrie*, herausgegeben vom Hauptausschuss Machinen beim Reichsminister fuer Bewaffnung und Munition (Berlin and Essen: Buchverlag W. Girordet, 1943), on T-73, Roll 187, Frames 3400898-991.

uation and surroundings. One Labor Front book even remarked that, considering the circumstances of the workers, it was surprising that their production was so satisfactory.[61]

Paradoxically, while many German agencies were gradually exhibiting a concern for the welfare of eastern workers within the Reich, Sauckel's minions in Russia were resorting to increasingly brutal methods of handling and recruiting these same workers in their homelands. The effect of the concessions within the Reich were therefore largely nullified by the severity of German recruiting methods. Had the Germans treated the eastern workers fairly from the beginning, they might have been able to avoid some costly mistakes. This was especially applicable to the partisan problem; Sauckel recognized the fact when he cautioned his staff members: "It can not be allowed in our labor offices as has happened in some of the occupied areas that workers are so poorly handled that in the waiting rooms of these offices they are recruited for partisan activities."[62]

Despite warnings by Sauckel, the East Ministry, and the Army, Nazi leadership was too slow in realizing the connection between Germany's dependency on eastern workers to solve its labor problems and the granting of concessions to these workers. The delay between the realization of the importance of the eastern workers and the actual improvement of their lot can probably be traced to one of the fundamental flaws in any totalitarian society. The Nazis were victims of their own propaganda. Once the mold of the *Untermensch* concept was set, it was difficult to alter even though reason and military events indicated the need for a change. Tied as

[61] *Arbeitseinsatz der Ostarbeiter in Deutschland: Vorlaeufiger Bericht zur Untersuchung des Arbeitswissenschaftlichen Instituts ueber Arbeitseignung und Leistungsfaehigkeit der Ostarbeiter* (Berlin: Arbeitswissenschaftliches Institut der DAF, 1943), p. 22.

[62] Document RF 1517-816F, in the Nuremberg Trials Collection, p. 38.

the Nazis were to a dogmatic philosophy that could, for example, graduate food rations according to spurious racial characteristics, it was amazing that at least some German leaders could have managed what changes were accomplished, and there were changes. By the end of 1943, the eastern workers in the Reich had been granted parity with the other foreign workers. But it was too late.

CHAPTER IX

Recruitment in France: Classic Example
in the West

IN THE West, the labor recruitment program was voluntary until midsummer of 1942. The results of this program varied according to conditions in the individual countries. In Norway, the Germans were developing the port facilities, constructing new airfields, and extending the communication and transportation systems. Rather than recruiting labor in Norway for work abroad, the Germans were continually forced to send additional labor there. In Holland, Belgium, and France, conditions were the opposite. The general dislocation of the economy caused by the war and the sharp curtailment of production had produced widespread unemployment. The German military construction was not as demanding on the local labor supply in these countries as in Norway. Consequently, the Germans concentrated their recruiting in the West on the unemployed in these three countries.

Until 1942, the entire emphasis of the German labor recruitment policy was based on an exploitation of the immediate situation in order to insure the flow of labor into the Reich. As long as the labor quotas for the Reich could be met by unemployed workers, the labor recruitment policy did not conflict with other German aims. However, after the appointment of Speer, the Germans attempted to make better use of the production capabilities in the West. They began to contract for more raw materials and finished goods from the plants and mines of the western countries. Simultaneously, however, while the Germans sought greater production in the West, they found they needed more labor for their own industries at home. The pool of unemployed workers vanished quickly. German officials were now confronted with the dilemma of drafting an increasing number of workers for the Reich and, at the same time, stepping up production in the very countries where the workers were drafted. Obviously, if the Germans were to succeed in solving this problem, they had to develop a labor recruitment system in the West that was more sophisticated than that used in the East.

The German attempts to develop an efficient labor recruitment system in the West can best be illustrated by their program in France. France was the most important recruiting area not only because of the sheer size of her manpower reserves, but also because she had the largest number of skilled workers in occupied Europe. French skilled workers were desperately needed in the Reich to balance the influx of unskilled workers, usually women or younger men, from the East.

LABOR RECRUITMENT IN FRANCE DURING 1942

Conditions in France in the spring of 1942 seemed ideal for Sauckel. Although France already had over a million POW's at work in the Reich, there was still unemployment in the country and many French workers were working less than forty hours a week. At the time of his appointment, Sauckel had convinced Hitler that compulsory labor laws in France were needed to create an adequate pool of workers for the Reich.

Moreover, both the French and German executive authorities seemed ideally suited for Sauckel's plans. In Marshal Pétain and Pierre Laval, Germany had leaders who enjoyed some confidence among the French people and who could be expected to support Germany's professed aim of destroying communism. It must be remembered that although the Pétain government controlled only Vichy France, it negotiated with the Germans as if it were the legitimate government for all of

France. In General Karl Heinrich von Stuelpnagel, who had replaced his cousin, Otto von Stuelpnagel, as military commander in France in February 1942, Germany had not only an excellent military man but also an astute student of economics and politics.[1] General von Stuelpnagel was expected to realize the importance of further labor recruitment for the Reich. Despite these circumstances, however, Sauckel found that harnessing France to the German war chariot was no easy task.

As early as January 14, 1942, Elmar Michel, the chief of the German Economic Services in Paris, was demanding that the French government publicly encourage the departure of French workers to Germany. In March, despite the continual urging of Michel and Sauckel, the Vichy government decided that it should remain absolutely neutral. The Germans were furious at the French attitude, and undoubtedly this was one of the reasons why they pressed for a reorganization of the Vichy government. Finally, in April, Laval returned to power as Prime Minister, and the Germans expected a change in the official attitude of Vichy. They were not disappointed. In May and June, Laval started to reorganize French industries with the accent on greater productivity and longer hours of work. For example, the prohibition against working more than forty hours a week was removed. The measures by Laval were a direct reversal of earlier French policies that attempted to curb unemployment by lowering the work week and encouraging the maximum employment of labor. Laval was artificially creating a labor pool for the German recruiters.[2]

On June 10, Laval's Labor Minister sent a confidential note to French labor officials and prefects asking them to help establish recruiting offices for the Germans. The note stressed the need for active collaboration with the Sauckel

---

[1] *France During Occupation*, III, 1629.
[2] *International Labour Review*, XLIV, 430-432.

organization. More importantly, the French labor offices were to give the Germans, in strict confidence, a list of skilled workers in their areas, noting the workers' specialties and addresses.[3] Apparently Laval thought that this was the most he could do without gaining some concessions from the Germans.

From Sauckel's point of view, the results of Laval's measures were inadequate. Sauckel had originally estimated that he would need at least 250,000 workers by the end of July, of which 150,000 were to be skilled. This was an enormous quota for France in light of the fact that only 150,000 French workers had volunteered for work in the Reich from June 1940 until May 1942.[4] When Sauckel realized that the current rate of recruitment in France would not meet his quota, he went to Paris personally to impress upon Laval the urgency of the situation.

In the early part of June 1942, Sauckel had several conferences with the French leaders. Otto Abetz, German ambassador in Paris, presided over these meetings.[5] Sauckel bluntly told the French that they could have the choice of either stimulating the departure of volunteer workers or accepting a draft imposed by the German authorities. The draftees would be drawn from among the 400,000 repatriated French prisoners of war. Moreover, Sauckel further intimated that if the French did not produce the workers, he would see that they were denied vital shipments of coal, other combustibles, and lubricants. This would upset their economic machinery and swell the ranks of the unemployed, whom he would immediately draft for the Reich.[6]

Laval was stunned and angrily told Sauckel: "If you apply

[3] Aron, *The Vichy Regime*, p. 381.

[4] *The Diary of Pierre Laval*, ed. by Josée Laval (New York: Charles Scribner's Sons, 1948), p. 111.

[5] *IMT*, v, 484.

[6] Statement of Paul Marion, Secretary of State for Information, *France During Occupation*, iii, 1347-1348.

your ordinance to France, I will resign. The armistice convention forbids you to do in France what you are doing in Poland and other places."[7] Sauckel asked Laval what he wanted, and it was then that Laval linked the question of workers for Germany with the return of French POW's from the Reich. Laval suggested that as compensation for the departure of workers the French should receive an equal number of liberated prisoners.[8] Sauckel told Laval that this was impossible. Laval answered that the French government would not give even the slightest degree of support to the German plan to draft workers unless the German government were at least ready to admit, in principle, that the French ought to receive compensation in the form of liberated French POW's.[9]

Laval was so insistent that Sauckel telephoned Hitler, and on the following day he promised Laval that if 150,000 skilled industrial workers would leave for Germany, 50,000 French agricultural workers would be liberated from the POW camps and returned to France.[10] Sauckel explained: "We cannot possibly admit an exchange on an equal basis, because these French prisoners are already working in Germany and, in addition to losing control of them, we shall lose the benefit of their work."[11]

This system of exchanging POW's for French civilian workers at the ratio of one to three which Laval and Sauckel agreed upon in June 1942 was called the *Relève*. The released POW's were to include healthy workers as well as sick or disabled ones. The French civilian exchanges were to work in Germany on a contract basis; the contract was to average nine months. Later arrangements were made for what was called "transformation." This provided that French POW's in the Reich were given the same contracts and status as

[7] *Ibid.*, 1348.   [8] *IMT*, xv, 49-50.
[9] *Laval's Diary*, p. 112.   [10] *IMT*, v, 484.
[11] *Laval's Diary*, p. 113.

French civilian workers. In effect, the French POW's signed a contract in which they gave up all their rights as prisoners of war under the Geneva Convention in order to be converted or transformed into civilian workers in Germany.[12]

Laval, apparently satisfied with the *Relève*, publicly supported the German recruitment in France. In a speech on June 23, Laval encouraged French workers to volunteer for work in the Reich, claiming that it was their patriotic duty to help release their fellow countrymen who had fought for them and were now in German POW camps.[13] When the first train load of POW's arrived in France on August 11, Laval was there to greet it.

The rest of France did not apparently share Laval's enthusiasm for the *Relève* system; only 31,300 French workers were recruited from April to July of 1942.[14] Sauckel was so displeased with the results that he accused the French government of bad faith in recruiting workers and decided to institute a system of compulsory labor applicable to all men and women in the occupied areas.[15]

The decision of Sauckel was communicated to the French in a circular of August 22, 1942, which the Germans wanted published in all newspapers in the occupied areas. Laval succeeded in obtaining a delay of a few days pending new negotiations. On the 29th of August, Elmar Michel informed M. Jean Bichelonne, Minister of Production, that the voluntary system had proved to be a failure and would have to be abandoned in favor of a more reliable method. Michel then outlined the new system. First, the French government would have to pass laws freezing French workers in their place of employment and make the hiring of new workers in France dependent on the approval of labor authorities. Second, all French labor offices would have to submit an obliga-

[12] *IMT*, xv, 49-51.
[13] Aron, *The Vichy Regime*, p. 365.
[14] *IMT*, xxvii, 117.   [15] *IMT*, v, 484-485.

tory report of all unemployed or part-time employed workers to the Germans. Third, the French would have to publish ordinances which would mobilize workers for the Reich. Michel suggested taking a census and passing a compulsory labor law for everyone between the ages of eighteen and fifty-five.[16] Finally, the French would have to pass ordinances which would make mandatory the training of skilled workers by every industrial firm in France.[17]

On September 4, 1942, Laval passed his own law, which followed the general lines of the German demands with slight modifications. The law obligated men between the ages of eighteen and fifty and unmarried women between twenty-one and thirty-five to work, if necessary, away from their homes. The law also prohibited termination of work without permission of the French labor offices. Those who worked less than thirty hours a week had to report this to their local magistrate's office. Decrees of the 19th and 22nd of September provided regulations for enforcing the law and registering idle workers.[18]

Laval's law of September 4 was milder than a similar law imposed by German military authorities in Belgium and the two northern departments of France. The military government's law required a minimum of forty-eight work hours per week and all workers had to have German-style work books, which meant, in effect, an accurate census of all workers.[19] Sauckel's office had also ordered that all work contracts signed by persons out of the North-France-Belgium military district were to be considered as extending for an unlimited period.[20]

---

[16] Aron, *The Vichy Regime*, pp. 388-389.

[17] *France During Occupation*, I, 55.

[18] *International Labour Review*, XLVII, 503-505; and *France During Occupation*, I, 55.

[19] *Bulletin des Ordonnances du Commandant Militaire*, October 7, 1942, pp. 1060-1063, in the files of the USSBS.

[20] Sauckel's order, dated September 10, 1942, on T-77, Roll 377, Frames 1223318-319.

By the end of 1942, Sauckel had recruited only 240,386 French workers, of whom 137,400 were skilled.[21] This was about 10,000 short of the original quota for France. These results were hardly gratifying to Sauckel and other German leaders, who now began believing that the failure in France was caused by lack of "good will" on the part of the Vichy government.

THE CRUCIAL YEAR IN FRANCE—1943

After a conference with Hitler on January 4, Speer telephoned Sauckel and told him that *Der Fuehrer* was displeased with the French economic support. Under no circumstances, Hitler argued, was France to be allowed to bear a lighter burden than Germany, especially since Germany was forced to offer the cream of her manpower for the war. Sharper measures would have to be taken in France to force her to contribute her fair share, even if it meant the seizure of French workers.[22] Armed with Hitler's decision, Sauckel went to Paris to negotiate for further French labor.

The first day in Paris, Sauckel conferred with the German authorities. He told them that another 250,000 French workers were to be recruited by the 15th of March. At least 150,000 of these new workers had to be skilled. Sauckel estimated that France still had about 450,000 skilled workers; freeing one-third of them for work in the Reich could be accomplished by allotting two unskilled workers to French factories for every skilled worker that they gave up. To help in the selection of these skilled workers, Sauckel wanted twenty special combing commissions created, with one representative from the GBA, one from Speer's ministry, and one from the French government. As a concession to the French, Sauckel was prepared to continue the *Relève* system and

---

[21] *France During Occupation*, i, 66.

[22] Speer's notes on *Fuehrer's* Conference, January 4 and 5, 1943, in the files of the USSBS.

allow the members of the immediate families of POW's working in the Reich to visit them for two weeks.[23]

On January 12, Sauckel presented his new demands to Laval and his ministers. Laval immediately objected and claimed that the last recruitment drive had seriously disrupted the French economy. Besides, Laval argued, France had no money, colonies, or other resources and nearly a million French POW's already were working in the Reich. To expect any more from France was asking the impossible unless the Germans were willing to make political concessions. Laval protested:

I am doing everything in order to facilitate the German victory; however, I must declare that the German policy is making more severe demands upon me almost every day, without these demands being placed within the bounds of a uniform policy. *Gauleiter* Sauckel can tell German workers that they are working for Germany. I cannot say that the Frenchmen are working for France.[24]

Sauckel refused to discuss the matter, claiming that only Hitler had the power to grant political concessions to the French. Yet, each time Sauckel returned to the details about labor recruitment, Laval obstinately demanded political concessions. When Sauckel blamed the French leaders for failures in recruitment, Laval answered that it was because they could not move without German authority. The French leaders needed more freedom in operating. Only if the Germans would grant concessions, Laval argued, could he be sure of securing the necessary labor. The political concessions that Laval wanted were the return of the two northern departments and the removal of the "useless bureaucracy at the

[23] Report by Sauckel, dated January 11, 1943, on T-71, Roll 5, Frames 398130-150.
[24] Document RF 1509-809F, in the Nuremberg Trials Collection, p. 1.

demarcation line." Without these it would be impossible to pass the draft law that was necessary to secure another quarter of a million workers. The necessary "favorable climate" of opinion had to be created in France.

Stubbornly Sauckel refused to discuss the demands of Laval, and only after veiled threats and the promise that he would relay Laval's demands for concessions to Hitler did Sauckel manage to win Laval's approval for his new labor program. Sauckel had Laval in a difficult position and he knew it. In spite of his vocal opposition, Laval had to accede to the new demands or run the risk of having France ruled like Belgium. The German rule in Belgium had been particularly severe, and French leaders quickly realized the implications of a similar German rule in France.

In Sauckel's report to Hitler on his negotiations with Laval,[25] he accused the French of "dragging their feet" and trying to gain political concessions at a time when the war situation in Russia and North Africa was not favorable to the Germans. Sauckel also felt that the Laval government was shrewdly trying to prepare for every eventuality, should Germany lose the war, by finding a historical justification for any cooperative measures with the Germans. Sauckel mentioned the possibility of dismissing Laval and replacing him with someone more pliable.

During the month of February, compulsory labor was established in France by two decrees. The first, on February 2, prescribed a general census of all French males born between January 1, 1912, and January 1, 1923. The accompanying circular to the census decree lamely explained that "this census is particularly intended to make certain that the need for laborers to go to Germany, and to work on engineering projects undertaken in France by the occupation authorities, or in French factories is not met only by taking men who

[25] Sauckel's report to Hitler on his inspection trip to Paris, January 10-16, 1943, on T-71, Roll 5, Frames 398129-169.

are already doing work useful to the country."[26] The census had just begun when the second decree of February 16 appeared, establishing the STO (*Service du Travail Obligatoire*). The STO introduced two years of compulsory labor for all young men born in the years 1920, 1921, and 1922. Agricultural workers were in a special category and usually exempt.[27]

The German and French authorities had hoped that these laws would fulfill Sauckel's quota of 250,000. German labor officials in Paris were so confused about the new laws that in the first few days they sent their own men to order the inducted workers directly to the Reich without waiting for the French to process them.[28]

These compulsory labor laws, although passed by the French government, were really forced on the French by Sauckel. This fact was confirmed by Sauckel when, on February 16, he told the *Zentrale Planung*:

> My collaborators and I having succeeded, after difficult discussions, in persuading Laval to introduce the law of compulsory labor in France, this law has now been so successfully extended, thanks to our pressure, that by yesterday [*sic*] three French age-groups had already been called up. So we are now legally qualified to recruit in France, with the assistance of the French government, workers of three age-groups whom we shall be able to employ henceforth in French factories, but among whom we shall also be able to choose some for our needs in the Reich.[29]

Sauckel and Laval had also agreed upon a continuation of the *Relève*. Under this system another 50,000 POW's were to be exchanged for 150,000 civilian workers. In addition,

[26] *France During Occupation*, I, 58.
[27] *IMT*, v, 486; and Aron, *The Vichy Regime*, p. 445.
[28] *France During Occupation*, I, 59.
[29] *IMT*, v, 487.

the "transformation" of other French POW's in Germany was started. These POW's were to be given adequate salaries and the right of a two-weeks leave in France.[30] The transformed workers were to be counted in the labor quota of 250,000.

During these labor drafts, the French administration intervened only to prevent the most flagrant injustices in the choice of individuals. Most of the drafting took place in factories, and there was a public outcry because in many cases older men were drafted while younger ones were spared. In response to this outcry, it was decided to recruit the 1940 and 1941 military age classes and the last third of the class of 1939, with the exception of agricultural workers.[31]

By the end of March, the quota of 250,000 French workers was reached. Nearly 156,000 of these workers were skilled.[32] Approximately 80,000 of the 250,000 were drawn from the younger men of the three classes called up under the French draft.[33] The first recruitment drive of 1943 had been so successful that Sauckel returned to Paris on April 9 and asked the French authorities to furnish him another 250,000 men. Sauckel wanted 120,000 of these workers recruited in May, and the remainder in June.[34] Coupled with the new quotas, he demanded a radical policy of closing inefficient or non-essential plants in France and, where possible, thoroughly converting non-armament plants to armament production.[35]

The French officials protested against Sauckel's new demands by arguing that the census of the three French classes earlier in the year revealed that only 245,000 of the total of 715,000 were available, and 88,000 of them already had been recruited by the middle of April. Sauckel countered their arguments by claiming that there was a mass con-

[30] IMT, xv, 51.
[31] Laval's Diary, p. 117.
[32] IMT, xxvi, 11-12.
[33] Laval's Diary, p. 117.
[34] IMT, v, 489.
[35] NCA, Supplement A, 383.

spiracy to falsify the number of Frenchmen available. Many of the French workers had not registered, and many others had false employment cards or forged certificates of exemptions.[36] If the French did not obtain enough men from the three age classes already registered, Sauckel suggested that they call up other classes.

During May 1943, instead of the planned 120,000, only 21,000 French workers departed for the Reich. In a note written on June 1, Sauckel complained about the poor results. The French services, Sauckel wrote, could not obtain the necessary workers because of faulty organizational structure and a decided lack of enthusiasm. He therefore ordered the German labor organization in France to inspect, instruct, and supervise the recruitment. Military commanders were also given instructions to help with recruitment by every possible means.[37] Two days after Sauckel's note, the French began mobilizing the military class of 1942. All exemptions provided by the law of February 16 for special hardship cases, such as specialists and agricultural workers, were withdrawn, and the young men of the 1942 class were tracked down. The responses to this measure were inevitable. There was an exodus of young men from the cities; some joined the French resistance movement. The German minister, Hans Richard Hemmen, wrote from Paris: "There is no doubt that the name 'Sauckel' sounds today pretty bad to French ears. The mere announcement in the press of an impending visit of the *Gauleiter* is sufficient for one to see for days hundreds of young people hurrying to the various Paris stations with their little suitcases."[38]

Sauckel's rougher tactics, however, seemed to pay dividends. In June, nearly 80,000 French workers were recruited and 36,000 more in July, but then the supply halted suddenly.[39] The French leaders thought they had at last

[36] *France During Occupation*, i, 61.   [37] *Ibid.*, 61-62.
[38] *NCA*, Supplement A, 403.   [39] *France During Occupation*, i, 62.

found a more effective method of stopping Sauckel. That method was Gallic simplicity itself. The French would play Sauckel against another equally powerful German official, Albert Speer. Sauckel's increasing demands for labor were continually coupled with the additional demands for more labor for German authorities in France and for an increase in production within France. Sauckel recruited labor not only for the Reich, but also for German needs outside the Reich. Jean Bichelonne, the French Minister of Industrial Production, had noted as early as April that there was a direct loss in production in France after every Sauckel action. Sauckel himself had noted this in his report to Hitler in April.[40]

Bichelonne wanted, however, to prove to the Germans that it would be to their advantage to develop a system of protecting those factories working on German armament products from Sauckel's recruiters. The Germans had refrained from drafting certain workers in agriculture, mining, railroads, and a few critical industrial plants that had important war contracts. Bichelonne wanted the classification broadened to include most of the industrial concerns in France that produced raw or half-finished materials which might eventually be used in war production. Bichelonne was especially eager to initiate his plan after Sauckel's organization began to ignore the French labor service in June.

With this idea in mind, the French began to cultivate Elmar Michel, the Chief of German Economic Services in France, and General Studt, Speer's representative. On July 15, by order of the Chief of Government, Bichelonne submitted to Michel "constructive proposals for increasing the amount of work done in French factories for the benefit of the European war economy."[41] Michel was favorably impressed with the proposals, for he realized the difficulties in

[40] *IMT*, xxvi, 11.
[41] Statement of Roger Gaillochet, Chief of the Private Secretariat of the Bichelonne Ministry, *France During Occupation*, i, 47-48.

further recruitment in France. On the 26th of July, Bichelonne informed General von Stuelpnagel that he wished to talk over his proposals with Speer personally, and he wanted the General to organize a meeting.

Although Bichelonne claimed after the war that he originated the idea of protected plants in the occupied zone, the idea had occurred simultaneously to German officials in the occupied areas and to members of Speer's ministry. Apparently everyone realized by the middle of 1943 that in order to recruit from a steadily diminishing amount of labor in the occupied areas, a disproportionate amount of German pressure and force would have to be applied. A better solution would be to use that labor in war production within the occupied areas. Such a procedure would minimize the difficulties in recruitment and lessen the dangers of the ever-increasing air raids on the Reich. (Speer argued that the Allies would be reluctant to use massive bombing tactics on cities in the occupied areas.)

Results of the negotiations for protected plants in France were so favorable that Laval decided, at the end of July, to risk halting further recruitment. Sauckel immediately went to Paris to protest this action and make new demands for labor. On August 6, a dramatic meeting occurred between Laval and Sauckel. The *Gauleiter* reiterated his old demands by insisting that there were still plenty of laborers in France and accusing the French administration of not being able to recruit them. In his usual way, Sauckel threatened and cajoled Laval. In the past, Laval finally had yielded; this time he did not.[42] Instead, he stalled for time, believing that the tide was running against Sauckel.[43]

Sauckel returned to Berlin empty-handed. Since the French were unwilling to make any more new moves, Sauckel decided to act alone. On the 14th of August, Sauckel

[42] *Ibid.*, 49-50.   [43] *Ibid.*, III, 1142.

sent instructions to the Gauleiters to establish a sponsorship system between German *Gau* labor offices and French department labor offices. Each German *Gau* labor office was to take over and sponsor two French departments and provide them with a commission of specialists who were to organize the French offices more efficiently. The German labor officials were specially instructed to build an organization which would combat the "evident passive resistance" of the lower and higher orders of the French bureaucracy.[44]

Another purpose of this arrangement was to eliminate the unsolved problems between the French government, departments, industrialists, and factories on one hand, and the administrative offices in Germany on the other. This did not mean necessarily that the workers from a particular department would work in the *Gau* which sponsored their department. The sponsorship idea was to help spread favorable propaganda about working conditions in the Reich, settle complaints and, in general, clear away any mistrust that had arisen.[45] Even the French later admitted at Nuremberg that the German reorganization had beneficial effects;[46] at the time, though, the French saw the move as another attempt of the Germans to supersede their own labor organization.

At a meeting of the German labor organization on August 26 in Paris, Sauckel frankly admitted that in his opinion the French executive authority was no longer of any use. Difficult as might be the task of confiscating (*Beschlagnahme*) men rather than property, Sauckel warned, it must be done.[47] However, Sauckel realized how perilous the situation had become. The lower echelons of the French governmental administration were systematically opposing further recruitment and the Church was openly preaching against it. Even

[44] *IMT*, xxvii, 114.   [45] *IMT*, xv, 80.

[46] *Ibid.*, 78.

[47] Document RF 1517-816F, in the Nuremberg Trials Collection, p. 30.

more ominous was the increased activity of the *Maquis* and
Sauckel wondered aloud what effect additional pressure
might have on the *Maquis'* growth.[48]

In spite of Sauckel's frenzied activity to reorganize the
recruitment in France, before the French could reach an
agreement with Speer on protected plants, the time ran out.
On September 15 and 16, at an armament conference for
all occupied areas, Speer accepted, in principle, the plan to
set up protected plants (*Schutzbetriebe, Speerbetriebe*), or
S-plants. At first, Speer wanted plants to be classified as
S-plants only if their work was from 75 to 80 per cent on
German orders. Bichelonne and others managed to broaden
this classification to include any plant that was a part of some
definite production program. The classification of individual
plants was to be determined by a joint French-German
committee.[49]

By October, nearly 10,000 French concerns were classified as S-plants and protected from recruitment. The
French even managed to exempt workers from the labor
draft whose names had been already called but who had
found work in protected factories. In spite of Sauckel's protests about the S-plants, which he derisively dubbed the
"legal *Maquis*," the agreement covering such plants was continued and even enlarged. As a result, further intensive labor
recruitment in France was suspended reluctantly by Sauckel
until the beginning of 1944.

The ultimate success or failure of Sauckel's program in
France in 1943 could, in a sense, be measured by the actual
number of French workers allocated to work in Germany.
The Bichelonne ministry reported a total of 456,000 workers
recruited in France in 1943. In addition, nearly 197,000
French POW's in the Reich were transformed into free ci-

[48] *Ibid.*, p. 38.
[49] *France During Occupation*, i, 49; and *Minor Trials*, xii, 1128-
1129.

vilian workers, making the grand total about 653,000 for 1943.[50] Sauckel's original quota for France in 1943 was 470,000 workers, although Sauckel had, in August, mentioned the possibility of recruiting another 500,000 French workers from August 1943 to March 1944. Neither Sauckel nor Laval seriously attempted to recruit this additional half-million French workers in 1943.[51] Regardless of tentative plans, Sauckel was highly successful in his recruitment plans in France in 1943. Although his overall quota for 1943 was not fulfilled, he was able to surpass his quotas in the West. This illustrated again the basic shift in German recruitment during 1943 from the East to the West.

The importance of France as a recruiting area can be seen in Table XII. By the autumn of 1943, the largest group of foreign males working in the Reich were French. Among the foreign female workers in Germany, the French women formed the third largest group. Their number was, however, considerably smaller than those of the Soviet and Polish groups.

THE FINAL PHASE: 1944

Throughout the last few months of 1943, Sauckel continually agitated for a change in the S-plant system in France. However, Speer already had discussed the program in detail with Hitler, and finally, at a conference on December 16, Hitler agreed to hold a full-scale conference on January 4 to settle the issue once and for all.[52] At the January meeting, Hitler agreed with Speer instead of Sauckel that the S-plants in France should be continued.[53] Speer immediately wired his representative in France, General Studt, that Hitler

[50] *France During Occupation*, i, 66.
[51] *Laval's Diary*, p. 118.
[52] Speer's notes on *Fuehrer's* Conference, December 16 and 17, 1943, on T-73, Roll 192, Frames 405715-716.
[53] *NCA*, iii, 867.

TABLE XII

DISTRIBUTION OF FOREIGN WORKERS IN THE REICH ACCORDING
TO SEX AND ORIGIN
(in thousands)

	Civilian Men	POW's	Total Men	% of Total Men	Total Women	% of Total Women
France	605	739	1344	26.3	44	2.6
Soviet Union	817	496	1313	25.8	899	52.4
Poland	1094	29	1123	22.0	527	30.7
Belgium	195	53	248	4.9	33	1.9
Bohemia-Moravia	244	—	244	4.8	42	2.5
Holland	236	—	236	4.6	20	1.2
Serbia	34	94	128	2.5	11	0.7
Italy	103	—	103	2.0	14	0.8
Others	303	54	357	7.1	124	7.2
Total[a]	3631	1465	5096	100.0	1714	100.0

[a] Figures rounded off.
SOURCE: This chart was submitted by the French government at
the Nuremberg Trials and can be seen in NCA, Supplement A, p. 874.
Although no exact date in the autumn of 1943 was given for the
information, it would appear that the figures cited were compiled
earlier than Sauckel's figures for November 15 which were used as
a basis for Table IX in Chapter VII. A comparison of Tables IX and
XII indicates general agreement. The slightly higher figures of Table
IX are due probably to a later accounting date.

had ordered Sauckel to be more careful in recruiting in the
western areas, and the labor in the S-plants was to be protected from Sauckel.[54] Speer thought the issue was settled,
but apparently Sauckel did not. On the 5th of January,
Sauckel wrote a long report to Lammers repeating all his
arguments against the S-plants; he ended with a plea for
more support for his program. Sauckel especially wanted the

[54] IMT, XLI, 416.

S-plants curtailed in France, since he had been given the task of recruiting one million workers in France during 1944.[55]

Sauckel also carried his fight against the S-plants to other party leaders. At a meeting in Weimar, he gave a speech before the Gauleiters, pleading his case again and ending with a manifesto for more production. The German newspapers which carried the speech minimized the S-plant controversy but played up Sauckel as the official who should naturally issue a manifesto for greater production within the Reich. Speer was furious and sent a blistering letter to Hitler stating that Sauckel should be subordinate to him and not the opposite. Specifically, Speer wanted Hitler to establish the old relationship of Sauckel working for Speer and to stop Sauckel from using his position as a *Gauleiter* as a platform for propagandizing his labor ideas. Speer also wanted Hitler to inform Sauckel that any such future speeches and impromptu manifestoes must be approved by Speer.[56]

While Sauckel was attempting to influence German leaders to change the S-plant system in France, he was reorganizing his recruitment to fit the decisions of the January 4th Conference. On January 14, Sauckel and the German officials in France signed a protocol outlining future plans for recruitment. The agreement called for the establishment of a French recruiting organization of from two to three thousand men and a French protection force for the labor recruiters. Both were to be selected by Sauckel's agency in cooperation with the SS, Army, and police. The protocol also envisioned the establishment of a compulsory labor law for all males between the ages of sixteen and sixty and women between eighteen and forty-five. The law would prescribe a legal work week of forty-eight hours and would carry severe penalties for infractions, including the death sentence.[57]

[55] *IMT*, xxvii, 107.
[56] Speer's letter to Hitler, January 24, 1944, on T-73, Roll 19, Frames 1336951-964.
[57] Document RF 1512-813F, in the Nuremberg Trials Collection.

On the 19th, Sauckel presented this program to Laval with new labor quotas. Sauckel also wanted to limit the role of the French in the combing commissions which determined what workers were to be sent to the Reich. The French accepted the demands of Sauckel but insisted on maintaining their rights in the combing commissions. After the war, Laval and Bichelonne claimed that the combing commissions offered the best opportunity to use Fabian tactics against the German recruitment policies. The commissions, which had branches in even the smallest French towns, quickly exhausted the supply of German specialists. Hence the French gradually gained control of these commissions through appointments.[58]

Regardless of French actions, Sauckel ordered the military commanders in the West to start organizing a native protective corps for the labor recruiters. This protective corps in France, euphemistically called "The Committee for Social Peace," was to number five thousand and was to be selected by Sauckel's agency but placed under the immediate jurisdiction of the military and police. The protective corps was to be armed.[59]

Later in February, Sauckel also organized a special corps of French recruiters who were to inform the SD of propaganda, rumors, and reports against the German recruiting system, and, most important, conduct personal recruiting of French workers on a bounty system. Each recruiter was to receive a fixed salary ranging from 60 RM to 100 RM per month and a bounty for every worker recruited. For an unskilled worker, the recruiter received 5 RM; for a skilled worker, 10 RM; and for a first-class specialist, 20 RM. After recruiting ten workers per month in any class, the recruiter

[58] *Laval's Diary*, p. 120; and Statements of Emile Boyez, Secretary-General of the Ministry of Labor, *France During Occupation*, III, 1235.

[59] Document RF 1815-827F, in the Nuremberg Trials Collection.

received an additional 5 RM per worker for the second ten workers, until a maximum rate of 30 RM for unskilled, 40 RM for skilled, and 50 RM for specialist workers was reached. Payment of the bounty was delayed until the worker passed the German frontier.[60]

Besides organizing his own private group of recruiters, Sauckel forced the French to pass a new compulsory labor law on February 1, 1944. The new law extended the scope of the first labor law of September 4, 1942. Under the February 1944 law, all men between the ages of sixteen and sixty and all women between the ages of eighteen and forty-five were subject to compulsory labor.[61]

The results of these measures appalled Sauckel. Less than 30,000 French workers were recruited in the first two months of the year, which was less than the number of workers who were returned to France in the same period. In desperation, Sauckel ordered the drafting of workers from S-plants. On the 11th of March, Speer sent a letter deploring Sauckel's latest action as a direct violation of Hitler's order.[62] Instead of answering Speer, Sauckel sent a letter to *Der Fuehrer* explaining that the S-plants had placed his program in jeopardy. In France alone, Sauckel claimed, there were 14,400 S-plants with 1,440,000 workers. Another 4,070,000 French workers in agriculture, mining, transportation, and those working for the military were exempt. Sauckel's agents were refused permission even to canvass these exempt workers. If Hitler wanted his labor quotas filled, Sauckel insisted that his agents be allowed a free hand in France.[63]

Again Speer was able to convince Hitler of the need for S-plants at a conference on April 9. Hitler notified Sauckel

[60] *Ibid.*, letter to Military Commanders in the West, dated February 19, 1944.
[61] *IMT*, xv, 494.   [62] *IMT*, xli, 442-443.
[63] *NCA*, vi, 760-761.

accordingly, although he did promise Sauckel that the Speer ministry would conduct a thorough combing of French plants to release more labor.[64] Sauckel had suffered another defeat at the hands of Speer.

Refused permission to draft from S-plants, Sauckel had one more recourse, to apply more pressure on Laval's government and the Army. In April, Sauckel asked Field Marshal von Rundstedt to use the Army in recruiting. The Field Marshal wrote to Sauckel that his troops could only support the recruitment in case of actions against the partisans.[65] Left to his own resources, Sauckel then decided to negotiate with Laval for further draft calls by age classes. As usual, Laval cleverly dragged out the negotiations with Sauckel. April and May passed and only a few thousand French workers were recruited. Sauckel's patience reached the breaking point in the first week in June. On the 6th of June, Sauckel telegraphed Abetz and complained bitterly about Laval, who promised to do everything and did nothing. Sauckel ordered Abetz to tell Laval that if his signature were not on a decree calling up the 1944 military age class for labor duty by ten o'clock the next day, German soldiers would recruit them without French permission. Sauckel would wait no longer, nor would he listen to more technical reasons for not drafting them. Either Abetz had Laval's signature, or he was to report a "nein."[66]

The same day that Sauckel wired Abetz, Allied troops landed in Normandy, and recruitment of labor in France became subordinated to military actions. It was not until July 8 that Field Marshal Keitel instructed the Commander in the West to continue recruiting labor behind the lines if it did

[64] *IMT*, xxxviii, 362.

[65] Document RF 1514-815F, letter from von Rundstedt to Sauckel, dated April 18, 1944, in the Nuremberg Trials Collection.

[66] Document RF 1513-822F, telegram from Sauckel to Abetz, dated June 6, 1944, in the Nuremberg Trials Collection.

not lead to disruptions.[67] On the 25th of July, Field Marshal von Kluge rescinded Keitel's earlier orders and allowed recruitment anywhere in France except in the immediate combat areas, providing that the people there showed a willingness to support the Germans.[68] For all practical purposes, effective, organized recruitment in France ceased. From January 1 to May 31, Sauckel had managed to recruit only 34,244 French workers.[69] That was a far cry from the one million he had promised *Der Fuehrer*.

SUMMARY AND CONCLUSIONS

From April 1942 to August 1944, Sauckel was able to recruit nearly 730,630 French workers in his various recruitment drives. His method was simple: he coupled compulsory labor laws to extract idle labor with systematic combings of the non-essential industries to release labor into the larger pool of the unemployed. By continually combing industries and raising the work week, this program produced greater concentration in French industry and released additional labor which was drafted for the Reich.

Apart from the General-Government and the occupied Russian areas, the methods used in the other occupied countries followed the pattern used in France. Compulsory labor laws were introduced in Norway, Denmark, Slovakia, and Croatia in the same manner as in France. In Belgium, Holland, Greece, and Serbia, the compulsory labor laws were implemented by ordinances of the military occupational government. In those areas marked for eventual assimilation into the Reich, such as Luxemburg, Wartheland, Alsace-Lorraine, and the Protectorate, the regular German labor administra-

---

[67] Document RF 1516-814F, telegram from Field Marshal Keitel to Commander in the West, July 8, 1944, in the Nuremberg Trials Collection.

[68] *Minor Trials*, ii, 542-543.

[69] *France During Occupation*, i, 66.

tion was organized and operated as if these areas were already a part of the Reich.

It was notable, however, that in the West the Germans made far more use of the existing governments in formulating and enforcing their labor demands than in the East. There were scattered cases of violence in the West, notably in 1944, but use of violence was the exception rather than the rule, compared with German methods in the East. Some of the German restraint in the West was dictated by military and racial considerations. The Germans had to construct numerous military installations, and they sought better utilization of the industrial potential of these areas than they did in the East. Then too, Himmler, the guardian of racial doctrines, believed that the people in the West were racially superior to those in the East and therefore could be recruited as troops for his *SS-Waffen* divisions.

German recruitment methods were, of course, entirely different in the neutral countries and in the countries allied with the Reich. In these countries, the German Foreign Office negotiated formal agreements for the recruitment of labor. The contributions of the neutrals were insignificant and that of Germany's allies dropped sharply after the invasion of the Soviet Union. The long and exhausting Russian war heavily taxed the manpower economies of Germany's allies so that little labor was left for work in the Reich. Italy illustrated this clearly. In October 1941, Italy had 271,667 workers in the Reich, but by November 1943 the number had decreased to 120,217.[70] The rest of Germany's allies showed similar decreases. Italy, however, played an unusual role in the foreign labor program in 1944. After the Badoglio regime concluded an armistice with the Western Allies in September 1943, the Germans began to intern much of the Italian Army for work in the Reich. Italy became an occupied

[70] Compare Table IV, p. 57, with Table IX, p. 148.

201

area, and the Germans recruited ruthlessly in the country. By the end of 1944, the Germans were able to place at work in the Reich about 400,000 Italian POW's and 227,000 Italian civilians.[71] As Goebbels callously remarked, "This Italian debacle has proven good business for us, both in seizing their weapons and taking over their manpower."[72]

The case of France, however, best illustrated the strengths and weaknesses of German methods in the occupied areas. By attempting to cooperate with the existing government in France, the Germans were able to avoid much of the violence and needless bloodshed that they encountered elsewhere. The more moderate methods also yielded better results. Until late 1943, in spite of countless attempts of the Vichy government to delay and hinder recruitment, the Germans were able to fill their labor quotas. Yet in 1944, when the Germans resorted to force and violence, they were singularly unsuccessful.

The difficulties that the Germans had with the Laval government were also typical of the problems they encountered with collaborating governments in the recruitment of labor for the Reich.[73] Regardless of Laval's many statements about helping the Germans, he opposed with limited effectiveness German attempts to recruit labor in France. Helmut Knochen, Chief of the General Staff of the SS in Paris, thought that Sauckel was Laval's No. 1 enemy.[74] Besides Knochen, many other German leaders expressed grudging admiration of Laval's tactics in dealing with Sauckel. When plans for S-plants were suggested, Laval and his fellow French officials were quick to exploit them as a method of

[71] *NCA*, v, 257.

[72] *Goebbels Diaries*, p. 480.

[73] For an excellent discussion of the great burden the labor program placed on German rule in Holland, see Werner Warmbrunn's *The Dutch Under German Occupation, 1940-1945* (Stanford: Stanford University Press, 1963).

[74] *France During Occupation*, iii, 1639-1640.

keeping French workers in France and of insuring that the Germans would not seek to ruin or export French machinery.

Yet despite the obvious ability of Laval's government to modify, direct, and protect French interests against Sauckel, it must be recognized that another German, Albert Speer, probably did more to help France and the other occupied areas than anyone else. The French might suggest alternatives, such as the establishment of S-plants, but Speer had the power to enforce them. It must be granted that Speer's ultimate objective was to strengthen the German war economy, yet he, unlike Sauckel, was able to realize that this could best be accomplished by using other methods. In a sense, Sauckel and his foreign labor recruitment in France had reached a point where Germany's own self-interests were placed in jeopardy by continued recruiting. It was to Speer's credit that he recognized this.

CHAPTER X

The Sauckel-Speer Controversy

ROM his appointment in the spring of 1942, until the
collapse of the Third Reich in 1945, Sauckel was continually faced with the problem of interference by other German agencies. The Foreign Office, Goebbels' ministry, the
SS under Himmler, the Army, the industrialists, Ley's DAF,
the Nazi party, and Hitler himself tried to affect the foreign
labor program. But all of these were overshadowed by the
continual struggle that Sauckel waged with Speer and his
ministry. It began over a technical disagreement but broadened, during the course of the war, into a major dispute
which ultimately involved the leading personalities, fundamental economic policies, and devious party politics of the
Nazi state.

Trouble between Speer and Sauckel began shortly after
the appointment of Sauckel to the position of Special Plenipotentiary for Labor in March 1942. Speer had supported
the idea of appointing a *Gauleiter* to this position because he
thought this would be the best way to overcome the resistance of the Nazi party to his reforms and bring under his
control the labor resources of Germany.[1] Speer was of the
opinion that the only rational method of directing the German war economy was to combine the control of labor, raw
materials, and capital under one supreme agency. This
agency would also be responsible for the planning, directing,
and executing of all production in the Reich. By securing
the appointment of a prominent *Gauleiter* who would be
sympathetic to his own ideas about reorganizing the war
economy, Speer hoped not only to secure additional workers
for his armament programs but, more importantly, to control

[1] Interview Number 11 of Albert Speer, May 15, 1945, in the
files of USSBS, p. 7.

and redistribute the native German workers in a more efficient manner. Thus, by controlling and then slowly withholding the supply of new labor to consumer industries, Speer thought he could eliminate unnecessary production and place Germany on a better wartime basis.

Speer's plans went awry from the start. Instead of his own nominee, *Gauleiter* Karl Hanke, Fritz Sauckel was appointed as GBA at the suggestion of Martin Bormann. Even more perplexing to Speer were the terms of Sauckel's new office. The jurisdiction and responsibilities of each of the men were not definitely designated. Sauckel was placed under Goering's Four Year Plan, and not under Speer directly.[2] Sauckel himself viewed his new position as entirely independent of Speer's direction. To Sauckel, Speer's agency was but one of nine that had to be supplied with labor.[3] Sauckel also considered his new position as more political than merely economic. He had been appointed because of his position in the Nazi party and his strong Nazi convictions. Now, as a *Gauleiter*, he naturally looked to the party for guidance and considered every task—be it economic, social, or military— a political one.

As far as Sauckel was concerned, it was equally important for him to arouse the German workers to new heights of endeavor under National Socialism as well as supply new labor forces for German production. Goebbels and Sauckel both quickly recognized the importance of the political implications of the new position, but Speer did not.[4] If anything, Speer wanted a new GBA to help him overcome the opposition of the party and reduce the amount of political influence within the German economy. He was to find out that the appointment of *Gauleiter* Sauckel as GBA was to increase rather than diminish political influence.

[2] *IMT*, xvi, 478.   [3] *IMT*, xiv, 627.
[4] *Goebbels Diaries*, p. 150.

The first clash between Speer and Sauckel arose over the technical question of dividing the newly recruited workers among the various German economic agencies. Speer wanted most of the new workers and practically all of the skilled ones channeled into his armament programs. To do this, according to Sauckel, Speer tried to "jealously supervise the situation, to see I wasn't tempted to place too many workers in agriculture."[5] Sauckel even claimed that at first Speer ordered him not to supply any additional workers to the *Luftwaffe* factories because he felt that they already had more than enough labor.[6] Sauckel considered this an encroachment on his position, especially since Speer, at that time, did not have the responsibility for air force production. After the war, Speer stated: ". . . labor input belonged to me, and also the question of manpower supply, while Sauckel represented the standpoint that not only manpower supply was his business, but also the question of how that manpower should be used."[7]

Because of Sauckel's party connections, his personal contacts with Hitler, and the vagueness of his jurisdiction, he managed to remain independent of Speer for the first six months of his appointment. However, by late summer of 1942, Speer had thought of another method to bring Sauckel under his direction; he intended to use the *Zentrale Planung*. The latter had already begun to take the first steps in establishing a new steel allocation system, and it was natural for Speer to attempt to extend the board's authority to the labor allocation system as well. By August, a priority system of armament programs was finally established for the utilization of manpower in order to insure that the most important production plants would receive immediate attention in re-

[5] Pre-trial interrogations of Fritz Sauckel, October 5, 1945, in the files of the Nuremberg Trials Collection, p. 18.

[6] *Ibid.*, September 19, 1945, p. 9.

[7] Interview Number 11 of Albert Speer, May 15, 1945, pp. 7-8.

spect to labor needs.[8] The only difficulty was in forcing Sauckel to adhere to the decisions and priority system of the *Zentrale Planung*.

At that time, the *Zentrale Planung* did not enjoy the confidence of most of the Reich leaders, nor did it have the authority that it acquired later in the war. Although as an integral part of his defense at Nuremberg Sauckel stoutly maintained that the decisions of the *Zentrale Planung* were binding on him,[9] all of the members of the board and their associates claimed that Sauckel never accepted the principle of the board's supremacy over labor allocation.[10] The statement of Hans Kehrl, head of the Raw Materials Division of the Armaments Ministry, at Nuremberg was typical. According to Kehrl, Sauckel consistently refused to recognize the authority of the *Zentrale Planung* or of Speer in regard to labor, although Sauckel intended to accept the opinion of the board regarding the allocation of some labor needs. Indeed, Sauckel felt that he might be guided but not bound by the decisions of the board.[11]

As long as Sauckel remained free of the *Zentrale Planung* control, Speer's reform program of curtailing unnecessary production by choking off the labor supply remained ineffective. That Sauckel could and did remain free of the board, Speer could only later attribute to political influence. As Speer remarked after the war:

[8] Thomas, *Studie der Wehrwirtschaft*, p. 538.

[9] *IMT*, xv, 53.

[10] For opinions of various ranking economic leaders about Sauckel's attitude toward the *Zentrale Planung*, see the statements of Walter Schieber, head of armament supply in the Speer ministry, in *IMT*, xli, 453; Walter Rohland, head of steel production in the Speer ministry, in *IMT*, xli, 496; Fritz Schmelter, head of labor allocation in the Speer ministry, *Minor Trials*, ii, 568; *Memorandum on Organization/Speer* prepared by Dr. Gerhard Fraenk, in the USSBS files; Dr. Theodor Hupfauer, Chief of the Central Office of the DAF, *IMT*, xli, 477; and Field Marshal Erhard Milch, *Minor Trials*, ii, 763.

[11] *IMT*, xli, 445.

My goal was to get control of labor input. Sauckel succeeded because of his powers to remain independent. He did not usually bow to Central Planning. That was at the time, however, more a question of power politics, rather than an objective one, since Sauckel, as a *Gauleiter*, was at the top with Bormann. Thus the thing was not settled on a purely rational basis.[12]

The problem of the board's control over Sauckel was not, however, as crucial in August 1942 as it was later in the war. The first year of German occupation of Russia had brought in a steady stream of new workers to cover most of the immediate requirements of Speer.[13] For the first time in the war, many German armament plants were installing second and third working shifts, made possible by the diligence of Sauckel in gathering millions of new workers from Russia and western Europe.[14]

By the end of 1942, Sauckel had successfully completed two gigantic recruiting programs which tremendously improved his position vis-à-vis Speer's. As has been noted, in September 1942, Hitler had granted Sauckel increased authority over labor recruiters in the occupied areas, and in December Sauckel was given the responsibility, with Speer, to comb German factories for additional labor. Sauckel quickly recognized the political value of his recruitment drives by intimating, in his reports to Hitler, that further increases in his power would be matched by even greater successes.[15]

Speer was already beginning to be skeptical of Sauckel's numerical successes and motives, for Speer found that there was a considerable difference between Sauckel's records and his own. According to Sauckel, nearly two million new work-

[12] Interview Number 11 of Albert Speer, May 17, 1945, p. 7.
[13] Interview Number 11 of Albert Speer, May 15, 1945, p. 9.
[14] Thomas, *Studie der Wehrwirtschaft*, p. 533.
[15] *IMT*, xxviii, 580-581.

ers had been placed in the war economy between the spring of 1942 and the end of that year, whereas the statistics compiled by Speer's ministry from individual factory reports indicated that only a few hundred thousand workers had been placed in armament plants during the same period of time.[16] Speer could not understand the basis for Sauckel's figures, and he and the other members of the *Zentrale Planung* began to suspect that the wide discrepancy in figures was caused more by design than by accident.[17] However, they could not prove this.

At the end of 1942, the first phase of the Speer-Sauckel dispute closed with a stalemate. Sauckel adamantly refused to accept the supremacy of the Speer-dominated *Zentrale Planung* over labor allocation, and Speer became increasingly suspicious of Sauckel's alleged successes in labor recruitment. Any good will that had originally existed between the two men had long since evaporated. What was once a technical disagreement between two leading economic administrators was growing into a fundamental struggle between conflicting philosophies and personalities.

DISAGREEMENT OVER TOTAL MOBILIZATION

The defeat of the German Sixth Army before Stalingrad in January 1943 had a tremendous impact on all levels of the German economy. Almost at once, the minor difficulties of 1942 became major problems. The new heavy drafts for the Army were coupled with an incessant demand for more and more production. Yet the magnitude of this disaster was not clear to all of the top-ranking Nazi leaders. To Speer and Goebbels, Stalingrad meant that Germany had to accept the idea of total war. Ruthless measures had to be passed immediately eliminating everything that was not absolutely essential to the war effort. Consumer production had to be cut to a bare minimum. German domestic help and especially

[16] *Minor Trials*, VI, 795.   [17] *Minor Trials*, II, 657.

women had to be drafted. German leadership had to be streamlined, and clear-cut authority and responsibilities had to be installed.

To Sauckel, Bormann, and Goering, mesmerized by their own confidence in the final victory of Nazism, Stalingrad was just an excuse that the advocates of total war were using to undermine their established positions. Hitler's reaction to the defeat was typical of his thinking. Instead of accepting Speer's and Goebbels' concept of thorough reforms in the German economy, he emphasized the need for more political leadership. In February, Hitler appointed a Committee of Three to take charge of the tasks of total defense and total reorganization of the economy. The Committee was composed of three of Hitler's inner circle: Lammers, Keitel, and Bormann. None of the three possessed, in Speer's opinion, any technical knowledge of the German economy.[18] Goebbels and Speer wanted a supreme council for the defense of the Reich, headed by either Goebbels or Goering instead of the Committee of Three.[19] The choice of Goering seemed, at first glance, unusual, but apparently Goebbels was convinced that at the time Goering could be won over to the idea of total war. Besides, Goering was too important to Goebbels and Speer as a "first-rate factor of authority"[20] not to be used. Goebbels and Speer were also counting on Goering's well-known dislike of the "Wise Men from the East," as the *Reichsmarshal* had dubbed the Committee of Three.[21]

Aware of the efforts of Speer and Goebbels, Sauckel became alarmed. He rightly believed that the Speer-Goebbels combination aimed at destroying his independent position. Early in the year, Speer had received permission from Hitler to determine completely the amount of labor needed by his individual armament factories. Sauckel and his *Gau* labor offices were not allowed to contact individual plants directly

[18] *IMT*, xvi, 478-480.   [19] *Goebbels Diaries*, p. 260.
[20] *Ibid.*, p. 264.   [21] *Ibid.*, pp. 264-265.

about their labor needs without the permission of Speer's armament inspectors.[22] Henceforth, all labor requirements were to be compiled by Speer's office alone, instead of by joint committees composed of one representative from Speer and one from Sauckel. Under this new system, Speer's chief labor official, Fritz Schmelter, would collect the labor requirements from the armament factories monthly and then pass them to Sauckel. Usually the requirements would stipulate the sex and training of the workers that were needed.[23] Sauckel then had to determine how he could meet these demands, in the light of his knowledge of the rate of recruitment. The actual allocation of the workers to the factories was made by the armament inspectors on one side and the *Gau* labor offices on the other.[24]

Sauckel was completely opposed to Speer's new system for personal and technical reasons. Personally, Sauckel thought that Speer's request to Hitler for permission to determine labor for the armament factories without consulting anyone else was another illustration of Speer's reckless "artistic and intuitive nature."[25] Undoubtedly, Sauckel was piqued that Speer was held in such great favor by Hitler. Technically, Sauckel opposed the new Speer system because he thought Speer's armament plants already possessed too many workers.[26] Sauckel wanted to be able to comb the armament plants himself, lest these plants deliberately inflate their requirements to the detriment of the non-armament plants.

Typically preoccupied with politics, Sauckel also opposed the new system on party grounds, or at least that was what

---

[22] Pre-trial interrogations of Fritz Sauckel, September 20, 1945, pp. 1-2.

[23] *IMT*, XLI, 455.   [24] *IMT*, XLI, 465-466.

[25] Pre-trial interrogations of Fritz Sauckel, September 28, 1945, p. 4.

[26] Pre-trial interrogations of Fritz Sauckel, September 24, 1945, p. 10.

he told Speer. The *Gau* labor offices, Sauckel argued, were obligated in the Nazi state to protect workers in the independent agencies and their professional positions. Since there was a distinct possibility that many workers would have to be shifted from their old occupations to meet the needs of the armament plants, Sauckel wanted to refer the entire issue to either *Der Fuehrer* or the party.[27]

Speer would hear nothing of Sauckel's proposal. In fact, according to Sauckel, Speer took a very strong position against the party mainly because he did not want any party control over his department.[28] As far as Sauckel was concerned, his difference of opinion with Speer was now becoming political rather than technical.[29]

Behind Sauckel's stubborn opposition to Speer was the firm conviction that the total war measures proposed by the Speer-Goebbels group were impractical and unnecessary. Drafting German women and eliminating consumer goods production were, in Sauckel's opinion along with that of most of the other Gauleiters, too drastic. Besides, the manpower crisis could be met and was in fact being met by the foreign labor program. As Sauckel explained to the 33rd Session of the *Zentrale Planung*, on February 16, 1943, there still existed large supplies of workers in France, Poland, and Czechoslovakia. Indeed, argued Sauckel, Germany should rely on further recruitment of foreigners, since any limitation would mean longer hours and harder work for German women and youths.[30]

Speer, on the other hand, was not at all satisfied with the foreign labor program. Early in 1943, Hitler and Goering had demanded an increase in steel production from 2.6 million tons per month to 3.2 million tons. Speer told them that this was impossible because he was unable to produce the

[27] Pre-trial interrogations of Fritz Sauckel, September 20, 1945, p. 3.

[28] *Ibid.*, pp. 3-4. [29] *Ibid.*, p. 7. [30] *NCA*, VIII, 182.

necessary additional coal owing to the manpower shortage. When Speer and Milch tried to convince Goering that the necessary manpower could be obtained only by shifting more German workers into mining, Goering told them that Sauckel's figures indicated the workers were there. Allegedly, Sauckel had fulfilled all of the requirements of the mining industries with foreign workers. According to Milch, however, Sauckel was deliberately forging his manpower figures to "impress Hitler with his own efficiency in his ability to fulfill all the demands of Hitler in the sphere of labor."[31] There was nothing left for Speer and Milch to do but attack Sauckel directly.

Backed by Goebbels, Milch and Speer accused Sauckel of being too bureaucratic, too weak to carry out orders, and too insistent on exerting his personal influence on the German economy and labor offices.[32] On February 23, they again demanded that Sauckel be placed under the jurisdiction of *Zentrale Planung*, which would then assume control over labor assignments.[33] However, Hitler did not share these views. Instead, on March 15, *Der Fuehrer* issued a decree giving Sauckel complete authority over the departments of the Ministry of Labor which had been originally placed at Sauckel's disposal. In effect, the new decree more firmly entrenched Sauckel's position in the economy. Goebbels recognized immediately the major mistake Hitler had made and pointed out clearly a cardinal fault in the Nazi administration when he fumed in his diary:

> Here we have another case of a ministry being hollowed out bit by bit without the head being removed. That is a very dangerous procedure which in the long run is quite harmful to authority. We are living in a form of state in

[31] *Minor Trials*, II, 658.
[32] Pre-trial interrogations of Fritz Sauckel, September 21, 1945, pp. 2-3.
[33] *Minor Trials*, II, 763.

which jurisdictions are not clearly defined. From this fact stem most quarrels among leading personalities and in the departments. In my opinion it would be best if Sauckel or, better still, Ley were put in the place of Seldte. That isn't done, however; Seldte is left at his post but is gradually undermined. The same thing is true of many other departments. As a result German domestic policy completely lacks direction.[34]

That Hitler still had confidence in Sauckel can be explained by two factors. First, Sauckel enjoyed the support of the Nazi party and its First Secretary, Martin Bormann, and second, the results of the foreign labor recruitment during the first months of 1943 seemed to indicate that Sauckel was well along toward repeating his earlier successes of 1942.[35]

Speer did manage to score one notable victory over Sauckel in the spring of 1943; that dealt with the increased utilization of German women in industry. He finally convinced Hitler to agree that Sauckel should recruit at least 800,000 German women to work on a part-time basis in industry, even if they would only work half a day.[36] But all the attempts of Speer to force the rest of his reform program on Sauckel failed.

Meanwhile, Speer and his associates who had originally supported the recruitment of foreign labor were beginning to understand better some of the other implications of Sauckel's program. Speer realized that as long as Sauckel and the rest of the Nazi party were convinced that the manpower problem could be solved by recruiting foreigners, his long-range program of internal reforms was in jeopardy. In general, Speer discerned four ways in which the foreign labor

[34] *Goebbels Diaries*, p. 301.
[35] Pre-trial interrogations of Fritz Sauckel, September 20, 1945, p. 2.
[36] *IMT*, XLI, 460.

program was adversely affecting not only his own plans, but also those of the entire German economy.[37]

First, as long as many Germans believed that the labor shortage could be solved by recruiting foreign labor, there was a widespread feeling that the level of peacetime production and activity could be maintained to the fullest extent. Since, in Speer's opinion, this was an impossibility for Germany, the foreign labor program was, in fact, lulling the nation into a false sense of security. Second, many German plants, aware of the massive foreign labor program, were deliberately inflating their labor requirements to an extraordinary degree. Some of the inflation was not, of course, premeditated but was the normal result of the constantly changing programs and the nature of the armaments produced. In general, however, under the pressure of higher quotas and new products, plants had a natural tendency to want to insure their production by inflating their labor demands.[38]

The third adverse effect of the foreign labor program was directly related to the second one; it slighted one of Speer's most cherished aims—that of fully utilizing German labor, particularly women. Speer's emphasis on rationalization of German industry through the introduction of more efficient techniques, along with his incessant demands for a more realistic attitude toward the war by the leadership element in Germany, were being defeated by the continual reliance on the foreign labor program.[39] The program had become a crutch. Speer reasoned that if the economy were independent of this crutch, it would soon find better ways of operating. Speer hoped that the same thing might happen in labor management as was happening in the field of raw materials. German scientists and engineers were finding hundreds of ingenious methods of substituting readily available materials

[37] *IMT*, XLI, 486.   [38] *Minor Trials*, XIII, 1123-1124.
[39] *IMT*, XLI, 466-467.

for rarer ones once they were deprived of the latter. But as long as the German manager had the foreign labor program to lean on, the first answer he would have for more production would always be "more men."

Lastly, Speer was aware that the addition of millions of foreign workers in the Reich meant the slow deterioration of the German food supply. Hans Kehrl echoed Speer's objections when he said: "In my opinion there was no increase in working capacity because every new worker had to be fed, which happened at the expense of the workers who were already there. That decreased their output. Therefore, it was merely a self-delusion that this would increase the output."[40]

It was not that Speer and his associates wanted to discontinue the foreign labor program; they wanted to change its emphasis. Speer wanted his basic reforms enacted in conjunction with foreign labor instead of simply being replaced by the foreign labor program.[41] On April 12, Speer and Milch presented their ideas to Sauckel. A serious clash occurred. Sauckel had somewhat of an advantage, for Speer and Milch were not completely prepared with facts and figures and Sauckel was. Thus, in Goebbels' words, Sauckel "won the race by default."[42]

Regardless of who won this latest clash, the arguments of Speer and Milch must have had some effect on Sauckel. A few days later, on the occasion of Hitler's birthday, Sauckel issued a pompous, bombastic manifesto which incorporated many criticisms of Speer and Milch. Sauckel called for the complete utilization of German and foreign labor, plus the drafting of more women into industry. He emphasized the need for more political indoctrination and better technical preparation for German workers. Contrary to Speer, Sauckel also promoted the idea of "every German a foreman."[43] Nor did Sauckel forget his critics in his manifesto, for he called

---

[40] *Minor Trials*, XIII, 1124.   [41] *IMT*, XLI, 486.
[42] *Goebbels Diaries*, p. 327.   [43] *IMT*, XLI, 233.

for the cessation of "class struggle" among officials in the Reich.[44] Sauckel's manifesto ended with one parting shot at Speer and his other critics; Sauckel concluded, ". . . the time for theoretical consideration and discussion of the labor program and its methods is finally over. Further reservations are pointless."[45]

Speer and Goebbels were furious about Sauckel's manifesto. Goebbels, in particular, decided that something had to be done about the sage from Weimar. He wrote in his diary:

> For our next meeting I am going to arm myself with material to hit back at Sauckel. Speer informed me about a so-called manifesto that Sauckel addressed to his organization within the Reich and the occupied areas. This manifesto is written in a pompous, terribly overladen, baroque style. It smells from afar and gives me a pain. Sauckel is suffering from paranoia. When he signs the manifesto with the words "Written on the Fuehrer's Birthday in a Plane Above Russia," that has the smell of the corniest Weimar style. It is high time that his wings be clipped.[46]

But it was neither Goebbels nor Speer who clipped Sauckel's wings; it was the deterioration of the war front. In the summer of 1943, the vaunted German summer offensive stalled after two weeks, and a massive Russian counter-offensive began that snatched the initiative away from the Germans. In the South, the Western Allies continued their offensive in Italy. At the same time, the air war over Europe continued unabated, and night after night German towns felt the ever-increasing might of Allied power. Every square foot of ground recovered by the Red Army, every Italian village occupied by the Allies, and every bomb raid over Fortress Europa that slowed production or diverted workers to reconstruction work magnified Germany's manpower short-

[44] *IMT*, XLI, 229.   [45] *IMT*, XLI, 239.
[46] *Goebbels Diaries*, pp. 341-342.

age. The stream of foreign workers was reduced to a trickle; it was only with the internment of most of the Italian Army in September that Sauckel was able to meet his quotas for the last three-quarters of the year.

The deteriorating war front, the rising wave of opposition in the occupied territories, and the growing chaos caused by the air war goaded Speer to a point of frenzied activity. In early September, Speer began to organize the S-plants in the occupied zone. He also worked out a general plan to shift all consumer goods production to the occupied areas, especially France. This would, in turn, release German factories and manpower which then could be incorporated into the armament program. Since Speer's plan would reduce the number of foreigners that were to be recruited for the Reich, he hoped that the plan would have the additional benefits of reducing the growth of the *Maquis* in France, easing the German food supply, and obtaining better production results.[47]

Speer told Goebbels that these measures of braking civilian production in the Reich would release approximately 800,000 workers to the munitions industries and another 300,000 to the *Wehrmacht* within a couple of months. In addition, he reported to Goebbels, "Sauckel will pull 500,000 men out of civilian production, so that we shall actually see the entire German civilian production come to a standstill in a few months."[48]

Early in November, at a meeting of Reichsleiters and Gauleiters in Munich, Speer detailed his new plan and emphasized that its success depended on the political leadership of the party. He stressed three points: the need for total mobilization, including women; the transfer of civilian production to the occupied areas; and the need for more foreign labor. He qualified the last point by saying that the food

[47] Interview Number 11 of Albert Speer, May 15, 1945, pp. 9-10.
[48] *Goebbels Diaries*, p. 488.

problem made it mandatory that there be complete utilization of German labor before more foreign workers were brought into the Reich.[49]

Speer then took his program to Hitler personally. With *Der Fuehrer*, he was especially critical of the inflated size of the civil and party administration and of the still large production of civilian goods. Speer also attacked the laxity and corruption of party leaders, even those of the highest echelon, whom he charged with Byzantinism and with setting a poor example for the German worker. Hitler refused to comment on the criticism about the party leaders. As far as the rest of Speer's program was concerned, Hitler rejected the suggestion concerning the increase of women workers on the grounds of his personal feelings. Nor did *Der Fuehrer*, who was compulsively suspicious of the ability of civil servants, think much of Speer's idea of drafting them for production work; students would be better in his opinion.[50]

The next day, Hitler received a delegation of Gauleiters, including Sauckel. This group presented views which were apparently diametrically opposed to Speer's. Although there are no records available on what transpired, Walter Rohland, head of steel production in the Reich, had this opinion about the Gauleiters' reasons for opposing Speer's measures:

> As a result of the brilliant course of events in the early years of the war, none of the Gauleiters believed in the necessity of total war measures. They especially did not believe that such measures were necessary as far as labor allocation or the curtailment of consumer goods were concerned. The Gauleiters greeted every new measure of Speer's Ministry and the other business leaders with mistrust, and they were openly scornful of the judgment and abilities of these experienced economic leaders. It went so far that the demands of the Speer Ministry for any addi-

[49] *IMT*, XLI, 487.   [50] *IMT*, XLI, 487-488.

THE SAUCKEL-SPEER CONTROVERSY

tional manpower were no longer taken seriously. Some of the Gauleiters intimated that many industrialists were hoarding skilled labor for their own gains and thereby sabotaging the army's need for men. Moreover, all of them felt that the alleged manpower shortage was greatly exaggerated. They, acting from personal egoistic motives of ambition and the desire for more power, declined every new measure and did nothing for the general good of the country if they thought it would reflect unfavorably on themselves.

In this respect they were supported at that time by Bormann and Adolf Hitler himself.

The standpoint of the Gauleiters was fundamentally that the total war measures that Speer demanded would weaken the resistance of the people.[51]

Granting the obvious fact that Rohland was decidedly pro-Speer, his opinion about the reasoning of the Gauleiters coincided with the testimony of Sauckel at Nuremberg. Sauckel thought that Speer had been strongly influenced by "those gentlemen of heavy industry, the great industrialists," for his plan seemed to neglect deliberately the interest of the smaller enterprises.[52] As far as Sauckel was concerned, Speer always wanted a superabundance of labor.[53] Despite Sauckel's best efforts, Speer always was complaining that he needed more workers, yet Sauckel knew many of Speer's workers were not doing a thing.[54] Speer's idea, in November 1943, to cut out all civilian goods was characterized by Sauckel as "crazy."[55]

[51] *IMT*, XLI, 488-489.
[52] Pre-trial interrogations of Fritz Sauckel, September 20, 1945, p. 7.
[53] *Ibid.*, p. 8.
[54] Pre-trial interrogations of Fritz Sauckel, September 24, 1945, p. 10.
[55] Pre-trial interrogations of Fritz Sauckel, September 18, 1945, p. 14.

In fact, Sauckel knew of many small concerns that continued to produce civilian goods for a long time after November 1943, with only a third or a half of their labor force. Moreover, Sauckel surreptitiously continued to supply these concerns with additional labor! When Speer tried to reproach Sauckel for sending workers to unimportant factories, the *Gauleiter* claimed that he was independent and did not have to follow Speer's opinions. He bluntly told Walter Schmelter, Speer's Labor Allocation head, "Nobody but Hitler can give orders to me."[56]

The Sauckel-Speer dispute over general mobilization and the S-plant program also began to affect Speer's personal influence on Hitler. Erhard Milch noticed that until the middle of 1943, Hitler had invariably supported his Munitions Minister's programs. After that date, however, there was a notable cooling in the relationship. *Der Fuehrer* grew more impatient and critical of Speer, and by the end of 1943 the reproaches he directed at Speer became, in Milch's words, insufferable. Milch claimed that this change in Hitler's attitude was caused by the continual conflict between Speer and Sauckel.[57]

Finally, other members of the Nazi hierarchy attempted to intervene in the Speer-Sauckel dispute. Goering was ordered to investigate Speer's charges that Sauckel was delivering only a fraction of the laborers that he claimed he was giving the armament plants. However, Goering could not determine conclusively if Sauckel was padding the records.[58] Sauckel's own defense, at the time, was that a considerable number of workers were being stolen from his transports by Speer or someone else. Sometimes Sauckel thought that even his own *Gau* labor offices were stopping

[56] Interview with Fritz Schmelter, May 26, 1945, in the files of the USSBS, p. 2.
[57] *Minor Trials*, II, 657-658.
[58] *NCA*, Supplement A, 1128.

trains and taking off workers.[59] Besides, as Sauckel correctly pointed out, the problem of accounting for so many millions of workers at one time was tremendous. There was a constant fluctuation in his labor statistics caused by the transfer of workers to new programs, the drafting of workers, the displacement of workers by air raids, the expiration of contracts, and the normal changes resulting from death and illness.[60]

Robert Ley, the head of the German Labor Front, also attempted to moderate the Sauckel-Speer dispute.[61] Despite Speer's attacks on Ley's sumptuous manner of living, Ley was a member of the Goebbels-Speer groups that insisted on the immediate enactment of total war measures.[62] However, Ley tended to agree with Sauckel about pushing the foreign labor program at all cost. Realistically viewing the war fronts, Ley expressed the opinion that Speer's S-plant program and shift of consumer production to the occupied areas was "more elegant," but Sauckel's was more "far-sighted," for the simple reason that if the occupied areas were lost to Germany she still had at least the labor from these areas.[63] Then, too, Ley was much more sensitive to the attitudes of the Nazi party than was Speer, and so he naturally tended to side with Sauckel and the Gauleiters.

The intervention of Goering and Ley apparently had some effects on Sauckel and Speer, for late in 1943 the two economic leaders came to a partial reconciliation over the question of labor requirements for the armament plants. Sauckel and Speer agreed to a new "red slip" procedure (*Rotzettel-*

[59] Pre-trial interrogations of Fritz Sauckel, September 24, 1945, p. 5.
[60] Pre-trial interrogations of Fritz Sauckel, September 20, 1945, pp. 3-5.
[61] Interview Number 11 of Albert Speer, May 18, 1945, pp. 12-13.
[62] *Goebbels Diaries*, pp. 268, 277.
[63] Interview Number 57 of Robert Ley, June 27, 1945, in the files of the USSBS, p. 2.

verfahren) which was aimed at reducing the number of their disputes over labor requirements. According to this plan, Sauckel was to negotiate directly with Speer to determine the number of new workers needed per month. Once a definite figure was agreed upon, an equal number of red tickets was printed each month and given to Speer's ministry. The ministry would then apportion these tickets among its various armament plants. The plants would submit the red tickets to their local *Gau* labor offices, which were required to honor these demands before granting labor to any other factories.[64] Speer's office could also request red ticket workers in special categories—for example, welders, machinists, crane operators. However, Sauckel's offices were not definitely bound to supply the requested specialists.[65] The red slip procedure affected only from 10 to 20 per cent of the total manpower requirements for the entire Reich.[66] Later in 1944, it was augmented by a priority system (*Dringlichkeitsstufen*) which formally divided the requests for workers by place and type of work.[67]

The red slip procedure, along with the many other agreements between Sauckel and Speer, could succeed only in an atmosphere of mutual confidence. But at the time Speer and Sauckel were working out their red slip plan, they were already at loggerheads over the S-plants in the occupied areas.

1944: THE FINAL CLASH

January 1944 opened with a victory of Speer over Sauckel on the issue of the S-plants. Hitler had, on January 4, given his approval of the Speer plan, although Sauckel continued protesting to *Der Fuehrer* that the S-plants meant the ruin of his recruitment in the occupied areas. At the same time,

[64] Speer Defense Document 51-36, an interview of Fritz Schmelter, in the files of the Nuremberg Trials Collection, p. 123.
[65] *IMT*, XLI, 460.
[66] Interview Number 11 of Albert Speer, May 15, 1945, p. 7.
[67] *Minor Trials*, II, 455.

Sauckel was busy strengthening his connections with the other Gauleiters. Early in the year, Sauckel placed the control of the *Gau* labor offices under the local Gauleiters, thus severing the last connection between the labor offices and the old Reich Labor Ministry.[68]

Meanwhile, the red slip procedure had already started to break down. At the February meeting of the *Zentrale Planung*, Speer's ministry reported that although they would need 544,000 men in the first quarter of the year, Sauckel had promised to supply 27,000 red slip workers in January and had delivered only 13,500.[69] Sauckel's representative at the meeting answered these charges by claiming that by reading the mail of foreign workers, they found many of the workers were idle in factories that were demanding even more workers.[70] Not content with the explanations of the GBA, the *Zentrale Planung* requested that Sauckel be present at the next meeting.

On March 1, Sauckel appeared before the *Zentrale Planung* and explained that as long as there were S-plants in the major recruiting areas, he could not meet the demands for new labor in the Reich. His program in the West was smashed and recruitment in the East was almost nil. In Sauckel's own words, "There is no longer a genuine German direction of labor."[71] Sauckel blamed the army, occupation authorities, and the Speer ministry for the destruction of his program. In the ensuing argument between Sauckel and Speer's representatives (Speer was ill at the time), it was pointed out that although only from 14 to 20 per cent of the

[68] *IMT*, XLI, 486.

[69] *Stenographische Niederschrift der 53. Besprechung der Zentralen Planung betreffend Arbeitseinsatz am 16 Februar 1944, 10 Uhr im Reichsluftfahrtministerium*, in the files of the USSBS, p. 10.

[70] *Ibid.*, pp. 54, 62.

[71] *Stenographische Niederschrift der 54. Besprechung der Zentralen Planung betreffend Arbeitseinsatz am 1 Maerz 1944, 2 Uhr im Reichsluftfahrtministerium*, in the files of the USSBS, p. 149.

workers in France or Italy were involved in the S-plants, Sauckel recruited no more than 11,000 from these countries.[72] Sauckel was unable to answer this charge.

On March 28, 1944, Walter Schmelter, a Speer associate, again confronted the *Zentrale Planung* with the difficulties the armament ministry was having with Sauckel's red slip program. According to Sauckel's own released figures, between 300,000 and 400,000 new workers had been recruited in the first three months of the year, but "not even a miserable 66,000 red tickets could be honored."[73] By way of illustrating the faulty labor distribution, Schmelter claimed that in 1943 the total number of female domestic servants in Germany had risen by 200,000, while the total number for the armament industry had increased only by 600 in the same period.[74]

Sauckel's only answer to such bludgeoning criticism was that he needed complete power over all the manpower in the Reich. Since Speer would never agree to an extension of his powers, Sauckel decided to go over Speer's head and appeal to Field Marshal Keitel for control of the 6,000,000 army of deferred workers in the Reich, two million of whom were under Speer's ministry. Goebbels, however, effectively blocked this new maneuver by insisting that the vast reserves in the German officialdom and the half-million scrubwomen be drafted first.[75]

Faced with Goebbels' ultimatum, Sauckel ordered the drafting of civil officials and women. To facilitate this unpopular measure, Sauckel made the Gauleiters responsible for the new draft.[76] Thus Sauckel hoped to eliminate the possibility of any favoritism being shown on the part of the

---

[72] *Ibid.*, p. 158.   [73] *Minor Trials*, ii, 548.
[74] *Minor Trials*, ii, 549.
[75] Pre-trial interrogations of Fritz Sauckel, September 21, 1945, p. 6.
[76] *IMT*, xli, 486.

regular Reich labor officials toward their fellow civil servants. The party, and only the party, could be trusted with the
final mobilization of German labor. This implicit faith, so
typical of Sauckel, completely ignored the traditional aversion of the Nazis, and especially the Gauleiters, to passing
measures unpopular with the German people.

In addition to his orders for drafting more Germans for
work, Sauckel also ordered a step-up in the recruitment of
foreign labor, but time had run out. The invasion of France,
the summer offensive of the Red Army, and the constantly
increasing air war made it impossible for Sauckel to recruit
the number of workers needed by Germany. With the failure
of his recruitment drives, Sauckel's prestige within the Reich
dropped rapidly. In July, Goebbels was appointed as Plenipotentiary for Total War (*Reichsbeauftragter fuer den
totalen Kriegseinsatz*), a position that Sauckel had desired.[77]
Goebbels, who had backed Speer and fought against Sauckel
ever since the *Gauleiter* was appointed, was now given complete control over distributing, mobilizing, and drafting all
German labor. Sauckel was beaten. Even his personal contact
with Hitler was broken, for Goebbels refused to allow
Sauckel to speak with his *Fuehrer*.[78] In the closing months
of the war, Goebbels ruthlessly passed his total war measures
without even bothering to ask Sauckel's advice. Fritz Sauckel
faded from the ranks of leadership, and when the war ended
he was what he had been when the war began, only the
Gauleiter of Thuringia.

Although the appointment of Goebbels as Plenipotentiary
for Total War marked the end of the importance of Sauckel,
the Speer-Sauckel dispute still had more ironic twist. Immediately after Goebbels' appointment, Speer wanted Hitler to divide the Reich into seven or eight armament com-

[77] Pre-trial interrogations of Fritz Sauckel, September 21, 1945,
p. 10.
[78] *Ibid.*, p. 11.

mands directly under Speer. These commands, staffed by Speer's business leaders, would have complete control over labor offices, plants, and the entire party structure, including the Gauleiters, insofar as they were connected with economic production. The police and the SS were not to be allowed to arrest or remove anyone from his position without the consent of the armament commands. Speer felt that this was absolutely necessary in order to obtain the last ounce of production in the Reich. It must have given Sauckel a peculiar pleasure when Bormann and even Goebbels violently opposed these suggestions of Speer, claiming that Speer's ministry was a collection of reactionary business leaders who were *parteifremd*, or hostile to the party.[79] Bormann, in particular, resented any interference between himself and the Gauleiters. He distrusted the Speer organization as being too nonpolitical.[80] Also Bormann, as well as Sauckel and the older members of the party, resented Speer as a late party member who had obvious influence with Hitler.[81]

Regardless of their motives, Bormann and Goebbels managed to block Speer's new plans and force a number of Speer's closest associates out of office. In particular, Walter Schieber, Speer's Chief of Armament Supplies, was forced to resign because of Bormann's attacks. After the war, Speer claimed that the party panicked in the fall of 1944 and sought to place blame for the impending defeat on Speer and the industrial leaders. Speer frankly thought that much of the intrigue of Bormann and Goebbels against him and his associates originated at the *Gauleiter* level, where Sauckel was one of his most active opponents. Besides accusing Speer and

[79] *IMT*, XLI, 395, 482.

[80] *IMT*, XLI, 480, 481.

[81] Speer Defense Document 46-80, in the files of the Nuremberg Trials Collection, pp. 186-187; and *The Bormann Letters: The Private Correspondence Between Martin Bormann and His Wife from January 1943 to April 1945*, ed. by H. R. Trevor-Roper (London: Weidenfelt and Nicolson, 1954), pp. 103-104.

his collaborators repeatedly of disloyalty, the Gauleiters were also muttering threats about "another July 20 in industry."[82] To head off overt action by the Gauleiters, Speer replaced a number of his high officials with staunch party men, and finally, on September 20, Speer sent a letter to Hitler stating his position and offering to resign his post.[83] Hitler refused to accept his resignation, and even later, when Speer did not follow Hitler's last instructions on the scorched-earth policy for the Reich, *Der Fuehrer* refused to dismiss or punish his young architect and friend.

The Speer-Sauckel dispute ended only with the collapse of the Reich. Neither man won a conclusive victory. After the war, Speer admitted that ". . . the question of labor input was the only completely unsolved problem of administration in the house which I had built."[84] Sauckel could only claim that Speer, along with the rest of his countrymen, never recognized the importance of his labor allocation system during the war.[85]

The Speer-Sauckel dispute can be explained, in part, as a personality conflict which pitted the young, unconventional technocrat against the older, orthodox party doctrinaire. The dispute was also caused, in part, by the very nature of improvised wartime agencies. Every country involved in World War II found that its agencies had engaged in extensive infighting. Germany was hardly an exception to this rule.

However, the Speer-Sauckel dispute was also an inevitable product of an authoritarian system lacking sharp lines of authority and overly dependent on personal influence. Given the massive concentration of power in the hands of *Der Fuehrer* and the prevailing philosophy of the Nazi party as

[82] Interview with Albert Speer, May 28, 1945, in the files of the USSBS, p. 8.
[83] *IMT*, xli, 394-401.
[84] Interview Number 11 of Albert Speer, May 15, 1945, p. 7.
[85] *IMT*, xv, 12.

typified by the Gauleiters, it was only natural that minor technical disputes soon grew into fundamental clashes which affected the entire state. Without a rational, pragmatic method of evaluating the relative merits of conflicting opinion, the Nazi totalitarian state found it impossible to control the raging internecine struggles.

CHAPTER XI

The Reluctant Foreign Worker

FRITZ SAUCKEL'S long and bitter dispute with Speer, as important and typical of Nazi administration as it was, should not obscure the obvious fact that Nazi Germany was committed to solving her manpower shortage with foreign labor long before either Speer or Sauckel became major economic leaders. The basic decision to substitute foreign workers for drafted German workers had already been made. At the time Speer and Sauckel were appointed to their respective tasks, there were about three and one-half million foreign workers and POW's within the Reich. Regardless of their dispute, both men realized how vital foreign labor was to the war effort and both strove to make that labor more productive. On this point there was general agreement. In Sauckel's first public pronouncement as GBA, he voiced the consensus of the Nazi leaders on the importance of foreign workers in his typically brutal fashion. Sauckel called for the exploitation of foreign workers to the highest possible extent, "at the lowest conceivable degree of expenditure" for the Reich.[1]

To assess accurately the fulfillment of Sauckel's pronouncement, and thereby to measure the ultimate importance and success of the employment of foreign labor in Nazi Germany, it is necessary to answer some difficult questions. How many foreign workers were there within the Reich? How were they distributed? How effective were they? What problems did they cause? Interwoven with these questions are the problems of determining the positive role that German leadership played in utilizing foreigners and the action or reaction that was evoked from the foreigners and the German

[1] *NCA*, III, 57.

population by that leadership. In essence, the effective exploitation of foreign labor depended on the distribution and utilization of workers, their productivity, and the conditions of employment. To clarify these factors, one has to view the foreign labor program not only from its economic, but also from its social and psychological aspects. The program involved more than the economic exploitation of millions of persons by a few ranking Nazi officials; it involved the entire structure of the German government and the German people. Above all, the foreign labor program was a human story written in capital and small letters, and punctuated by countless human tragedies, disasters, triumphs, and frustrations.

THE DISTRIBUTION AND UTILIZATION OF FOREIGN WORKERS

Information compiled by the USSBS from captured German documents indicates that foreign labor played a decisive role in maintaining Germany's productive capabilities. As Table XIII shows, after the initial mobilization of four million German males by May 1940, the total civilian labor force was reduced to thirty-six million. Although an additional seven million German males were drawn from the labor force between May 31, 1940, and September 31, 1944, the total civilian labor force within the Reich was stabilized at approximately thirty-six million throughout the remainder of the war primarily by using foreign workers.

While the number of foreign workers in the Reich rose steadily until it represented one-fifth of the total civilian labor force by the autumn of 1944, the number of German women employed remained surprisingly stable. Statistical records on the employment of German women during the war support the contention of Albert Speer that this important reservoir of labor was not adequately tapped. The total number of German women employed actually decreased during the early war years, and it was not until the invasion of Russia

TABLE XIII

CIVILIAN LABOR FORCE BY NATIONALITY AND SEX, 1939-1944

(in thousands)

| Date | Germans | | Foreigners[a] | % of[b] Work Force | Total |
	Male	Female			
May 31, 1939	24,488	14,625	301	.8	39,405
May 31, 1940	20,449	14,386	1,154	3.2	35,983[c]
May 31, 1941	18,990	14,167	3,033	8.4	36,177[c]
May 31, 1942	16,864	14,437	4,224	11.7	35,526[c]
May 31, 1943	15,462	14,806	6,260	17.1	36,529
May 31, 1944	14,175	14,808	7,126	19.7	36,110
Sept. 31, 1944	13,535	14,897	7,487	20.8	35,919

[a] Including Jews and prisoners of war.
[b] Foreigners as a percentage of total labor force.
[c] Slight discrepancies in *Kraeftebilanz* for these years.
SOURCE: *Kriegswirtschaftliche Kraeftebilanz* for 1942, 1943, and 1944, as adjusted by the USSBS.

and the entrance of the United States in the war in 1941 that this downward trend was checked. By the autumn of 1944, when the supply of foreign workers was cut off and the Germans were desperately attempting to mobilize their reserve of woman-power, the total number of women employed was only a scant quarter of a million higher than the prewar figure of May 31, 1939. The belated attempts to draft women into industries in late 1943 and 1944 failed. By that time, the air war had created so many problems that the German administrative machine was overburdened. The problems of rehousing the bombed-out, repairing damaged factories, and preserving essential services and food supplies made organizing any large-scale transfer of women to industry virtually impossible. Nor could this have been done without risking further disruptions in the lives of those who were working already. The normal domestic life in the larger cities had become so precarious by late 1943 and 1944 that the task of maintaining homes and caring for children absorbed the energies of most of the women who were not employed.[2]

It might be argued that Germany had reached full employment by 1939 and an adequate reserve of women for war work no longer existed. The studies of the USSBS and Burton H. Klein emphatically refuted this argument, for both pointed out that Germany did much less to mobilize her women than did England, not to mention the Soviet Union.[3] For political and social reasons, the Nazi leadership preferred to utilize foreign workers instead of German women to solve their labor shortage.

From Tables XIV to XVII, a statistical picture of the composition, distribution, and importance of foreign labor in the Nazi war economy can be seen. As Table XIV indicates, after the invasion of Russia and the appointment of Sauckel, there was a noticeable emphasis on recruiting foreign ci-

TABLE XIV

FOREIGN CIVILIAN WORKERS AND PRISONERS OF WAR EMPLOYED
IN THE REICH AS OF MAY 31, 1939-1944
(in millions)

Year	Foreign Civilians[a]	Prisoners of War	Total
1939	0.30	—	0.30
1940	0.80	0.35	1.15
1941	1.75	1.27	3.02
1942	2.64	1.47	4.12
1943	4.64	1.62	6.26
1944	5.30	1.83	7.13

[a] Including Jews of all nationalities.
SOURCE: *Kriegswirtschaftliche Kraeftebilanz* for 1942, 1943, and 1944, as adjusted by the USSBS.

[2] Wilmot, *The Struggle for Europe*, pp. 557-558.
[3] See Chapter II of the USSBS, *The Effects of Strategic Bombing*; and Klein, *Germany's Economic Preparations*, pp. 136-146.

vilian labor rather than attempting to use more prisoners of war. In May 1941, the ratio between foreign civilian workers to prisoners of war was approximately 1.5 to 1, but the ratio increased steadily thereafter. By May of 1944, there were approximately three foreign civilian workers for each prisoner of war employed. This change in ratio reflected, in part, the deteriorating military situation of Germany, now forced to fight a defensive war in which the possibility of capturing large numbers of prisoners by encircling tactics was materially reduced. It also reflected the catastrophic loss of millions of Russian prisoners of war in the German camps during the first year of the war with the Soviet Union.[4] By necessity, then, the Germans were forced to recruit civilian workers.

Table XV indicates the distribution of foreign workers among various economic divisions and reflects their growing importance in industry as the war progressed. In 1940, 76 per cent of the POW's and 51 per cent of the civilian foreign workers were engaged in agriculture, while only 8 per cent of the POW's and 29 per cent of the civilians were in industry. By 1944, however, there were more POW's and civilians working in industry than in any other division of the German economy.

The importance of foreign labor in terms of the percentage of employed persons within the Reich economy can be seen in Table XVI. In 1940, foreign workers and POW's constituted only 3 per cent of the total labor force within the Reich. By 1944, foreign labor represented 20 per cent of the total labor force and was concentrated primarily in agriculture, industry, handwork, and transportation, or those divisions closely connected to the war effort. Although the percentage of foreign labor increased during the war in every division of the economy, the rate of increase was most rapid

[4] See Chapter IV on the "lost army" of Soviet POW's.

TABLE XV

DISTRIBUTION OF FOREIGN CIVILIAN WORKERS AND PRISONERS OF WAR AMONG MAJOR ECONOMIC DIVISIONS IN THE REICH AS OF MAY 31, 1940, 1942, AND 1944

(in percentages)

Economic Division	Foreign Workers[a]			Prisoners of War		
	1940	1942	1944	1940	1942	1944
Agriculture	51	45	34	76	54	36
Industry	29	36	45	8	31	44
Handwork	9	7	7	10	7	8
Transport	4	5	6	1	3	5
Distribution	2	3	3	1	2	2
Administration and Services	2	2	3	4	3	5
Domestic Service	2	2	1	–	–	–
	100	100	100	100	100	100

[a] Including Jews of all nationalities.

SOURCE: *Kriegswirtschaftliche Kraeftebilanz* for 1942, 1943, and 1944, as adjusted by the USSBS.

TABLE XVI

FOREIGN WORKERS (INCLUDING PRISONERS OF WAR) AS A PERCENTAGE OF TOTAL EMPLOYMENT, BY MAJOR ECONOMIC DIVISION WITHIN THE REICH AS OF MAY 31, 1939-1944

Economic Division	1939	1940	1941	1942	1943	1944
Agriculture	1	6	13	18	20	22
Industry	1	3	9	14	26	29
Handwork	1	3	8	9	13	16
Transport	1	2	4	8	13	17
Distribution	—	—	2	3	5	7
Administration and Services	—	1	3	3	5	6
Domestic Service	—	1	2	5	5	5
All Occupations	1	3	9	12	17	20

SOURCE: *Kriegswirtschaftliche Kraeftebilanz* for 1942, 1943, and 1944, as adjusted by the USSBS.

235

in industry. Within industry, foreign labor was more highly concentrated in "A," or armament, plants which were directly engaged in war production. These "A" firms were under contract or subcontract from the armed forces to produce basic materials, semi-finished, or end products. Companies that were granted the "A" designation usually found it easier to obtain allocations and priorities; thus the vast majority of weapons and munitions factories were in this category. As Table XVII shows, the percentage of foreign workers in the "A" firms was higher than the all-industry percentage.

TABLE XVII

COMPARISON OF THE NUMBER AND PERCENTAGE OF FOREIGN WORKERS[a] WITH TOTAL EMPLOYMENT IN "A" FIRMS AND ALL-INDUSTRY AS OF JUNE 1941-1944

Year	Number of Employees in "A" Firms		Percentage of Foreign Workers	
	Total	Foreign Workers	In "A" Firms	In All-Industry
	(in thousands)		(in percentage of total)	
1941	4,517	620	13.7	9.6
1942	4,894	1,201	24.5	14.3
1943	5,380	1,631	30.3	25.4
1944	5,977	2,090	35.0	29.2

[a] Including all Jews and prisoners of war.

SOURCE: *Entwicklung der Zahl der Beschaeftigten nach Berufsgruppen (in den W-Betrieben)*, Reichsminister fuer Ruestung und Kriegsproduktion Rue A/Arb. E., Wi (Stat.), on Roll 2074 in the files of the USSBS. There are slight discrepancies between Tables XVI and XVII because of the different sources.

Among the "A" firms themselves, the percentage of employed foreign workers varied widely, depending, in general, on the type of production, age of the firm, and its politico-economic status within the Reich. In those plants where production required heavy manual labor, such as mining, steel processing, and construction, the percentage of foreign workers was usually higher than the all-industry average.[5]

The percentage of foreign workers was also generally higher in plants where simply taught, routine manipulative work was required. For example, in the airplane-frame plants where assembly-line techniques were used, the percentage of foreign workers on the assembly lines was extremely high. According to Erhard Milch, by early 1944 they constituted nearly 90 per cent of the production-line workers in some of these factories.[6] The airplane-frame factories also illustrated the importance of the age factor in determining the percentage of foreign workers. Older plants possessing cadres of workers embracing all age levels were not as seriously affected by the drafting of younger men as were the recently built factories. Thus, the percentage of foreign workers in the factories built just before and during the war, such as the airplane-frame firms, was much higher than in the older, more established plants.

The best example of this age factor can be seen in the I. G. Farben combine. In Farben's older synthetic gasoline plants at Leuna and Ludwigshaven/Oppau, the percentage of employed foreign workers on October 1, 1944, was only 34.9 per cent and 36.6 per cent respectively. But in Farben's new synthetic gasoline plant at Auschwitz, built entirely during the war, foreign workers reached 55.1 per cent of the total employed by October 1, 1944. Moreover, this infamous plant, built in an unfavorable location in order to exploit the labor supply of the big concentration camp nearby, had on

[5] *Entwicklung der Zahl der Beschaeftigten nach Berufsgruppen (in den W-Betrieben)*, Reichsminister fuer Ruestung und Kriegsproduktion Rue A/Arb. E., Wi (Stat.), on Microfilm Roll 2074; and the Statistisches Reichsamt, Abteilung VI, *Reichsgruppe Industrie und Gesamt Industrie*, on Microfilm Roll 2018 in the files of the USSBS.
[6] *NCA*, viii, 178.

the same date 26.6 per cent concentration camp inmates, including foreigners and Germans, and only 18.3 per cent regular German workers.[7]

Still another factor in determining the percentage of foreign workers in the "A" firms was the relative status and position of individual firms within the Nazi state. Massive combines like I. G. Farben and the Hermann Goering Works, with their personal connections to the Nazi hierarchy and their monopolistic position in German industry,[8] employed at the height of the manpower shortage a higher percentage of foreign workers than the all-industry or "A" firm average. (Compare Table XVIII with Table XVII.) Although both of the combines increased in size and power throughout the war, their pattern of utilizing foreign workers differed sharply. The Goering Works, built just prior to the war, exhibited all the characteristics of a new, privileged plant. By the third year of the war, it already relied heavily on foreign workers. As the war progressed, the manpower in this plant was increased primarily by the addition of foreign workers until its percentage of foreign workers was double the all-industry average. The older Farben plants however, with a cadre of older workers, did not exceed the all-industry average until the last two years of the war, when the new synthetic fuel and rubber plants were opened at Auschwitz and Heydebreck. Farben's ability to triple its number of foreign workers during a period of critical labor shortage—from June 1942 to June 1943—underlined its unique position within the Reich.

Not only was I. G. Farben the dominating giant in the chemical industry, but its Chairman of the Board, Dr. Carl

[7] *Minor Trials*, VIII, 312.

[8] See *The Effects of Strategic Bombing upon the Operations of the Hermann Goering Works During World War II*, 1945; and Arthur Schweitzer, "Business Power Under the Nazi Regime," *Zeitschrift fuer Nationaloekonomie*, October 1960, on the I. G. Farben combine.

TABLE XVIII

EMPLOYMENT OF FOREIGN WORKERS[a] IN I. G. FARBEN AND
HERMANN GOERING WORKS, 1941-1944

		HERMANN GOERING WORKS			
Date		December 1941	June 1942	June 1943	June 1944
Total employed	(1000's)	306.4	317.6	372.8	416.4
German	(1000's)	176.3	175.5	182.8	172.1
Foreigners	(1000's)	130.1	142.1	190.0	244.3
Per cent foreign		42.4	44.7	51.0	58.7

		I. G. FARBEN			
Date		n.a.[b] 1941	n.a.[b] 1942	August 1943	October 1944
Total employed	(1000's)	118.7	131.7	170.6	180.8
German	(1000's)	108.3	109.4	102.8	97.5
Foreigners	(1000's)	10.4	22.3	67.8	83.3
Per cent foreign		8.8	16.9	39.7	46.1

[a] Including prisoners of war, Jews of all nationalities and, in the case of the I. G. Farben figures, inmates of concentration camps.
[b] No special month was given.
SOURCE: For Hermann Goering Works, see USSBS report, p. 134. I. G. Farben figures can be seen in *Minor Trials*, VIII, 310-311.

Krauch, had a decisive role in determining labor requirements for the whole chemical industry. As Plenipotentiary General for Special Questions of Chemical Production, head of the Reich Office for Economic Development, and originator and director of the famous Krauch Plan, or Karinhall Plan, Dr. Krauch represented the chemical industry and, more particularly, the Farben plants at the highest planning level of government.[9]

Although the type of production, the age of the plant, and political influence were general factors in determining the

[9] See the Krauch case, in *Minor Trials*, VII, 857 ff. The Krauch Plan was a comprehensive plan for increasing Germany's oil output, especially the production of synthetic oil.

percentage of foreign workers employed, the percentage of foreign workers in several plants of a similar position and kind would vary greatly because of specific circumstances. The time when labor was requested, the condition of the labor reserves, and the type and priority of contracts were some of the many specific factors which determined the percentage of employed foreign workers in any particular plant. Some plants, however, did refuse certain foreign workers because the plants were organized to handle only one specific nationality. A second nationality of foreign workers would mean additional cost and changes. Interpreters had to be hired, kitchens and housing arrangements altered (Sauckel and the DAF especially insisted on catering to individual national tastes within limits of the food rationing system), and new sets of regulations and rules had to be applied.[10] Other plants claimed that they did not have enough supervisors for additional foreign workers.

Rarely, however, did plants refuse foreign workers on moral scruples, and Schmelter claimed that there were no instances of governmental punishment meted out to plants for non-acceptance of foreign workers other than forcing those plants to wait until additional German labor was made available.[11] Although plants had some discretion in selecting foreign labor, in all probability the necessity of securing labor immediately and the general and specific circumstances at the time had more effect than choice alone in determining the percentage and composition of foreign workers in an individual plant.

THE PRODUCTIVITY OF THE FOREIGN WORKERS

Equally as important to the Germans as the quantity of foreign labor was the quality of the work produced by that

[10] Interview of Fritz Schmelter, February 28, 1947, in the files of the Nuremberg Trials Collection, pp. 1-3.
[11] *Ibid.*, June 5, 1948, pp. 2-3.

labor. The job of securing, transporting, and then effectively utilizing over seven million foreign workers, most of whom were adamantly opposed to the Nazi regime, was a herculean task. To achieve maximum utilization of the foreign workers, the Germans experimented with a variety of testing and training programs, incentive programs, and control methods. Actual productivity was carefully developed and supervised through close cooperation by all governmental and business agencies.

One of the first prerequisites for effective utilization of foreign labor was testing and training. Adequate testing of the workers was strongly recommended by both Sauckel's and Speer's agencies, but the responsibility for testing was left to the individual firms. Those firms with progressive and enlightened managements, like the Dortmund-Hoerder Huettenverein and the I. G. Farben plant at Ludwigshafen, quickly designed new tests for their foreign workers. During the war, these firms tested approximately 12,000 foreign workers each and placed them accordingly.[12]

It was not, however, until the German Labor Front established the Zehlendorf Institute for Industrial Psychology and Industrial Training (*Institut fuer Arbeitspsychologie und Arbeitspaedagogik*) in 1942, that standardized tests for foreign workers were available to most German firms. Under the direction of Drs. Joseph Mathieu and Wilhelm Lejeune, the Zehlendorf Institute devised a battery of eight tests to determine the capabilities of foreign workers.[13] The tests, which took three hours to administer, were similar

[12] Heinz L. Ansbacher, "Testing, Management and Reactions of Foreign Workers in Germany During World War II," *American Psychologist*, v (1950), p. 39.

[13] *Deutsche Berufserziehung und Betriebsfuehrung Grundlagen und Formen, eine kurzgefasste Darstellung der Aufgaben und Arbeiten des Amtes fuer Berufserziehung und Betriebsfuehrung der Deutschen Arbeitsfront* (Berlin-Zehlendorf: Lehrmittelzentrale der DAF, 1942), p. 18.

to the U.S. Army's World War I tests for illiterates. Although only an estimated 400,000 foreign workers were tested, the German officials were satisfied with the results of the testing programs.[14]

Once the purposes of the tests were carefully explained to the foreign workers, most of them were very cooperative; the eastern workers, who were used to such tests at home and anxious for further education and training, were especially willing.[15] They saw personal advantages in the testing program, such as promotions to better-paying jobs.

So successful was the program in upgrading foreign workers that German workers began to complain. For example, at the Berlin-Tegel plant of Rheinmetall-Borsig, German unskilled workers complained so strenuously about the rapid promotion of unskilled foreign agricultural workers to positions of skilled workers that the plant officials had to allow the German workers the same opportunity for advancement through the testing program.[16]

In contrast to the official party propaganda, German psychologists found through their limited testing program that the eastern workers ranked very high in general ability compared with other European nationals. Reinhold Groening, a psychologist of a steel mill which employed over 12,000 foreign workers, ranked the various European nationals in order of general ability based on testing in the following way:[17]

Rank	Men	Women
1	French	Russian
2	Russian, German, Polish	Polish
3	Yugoslav	German
4	Dutch, Norwegian	French, Yugoslav
5	Italian	

[14] Ansbacher, "Testing of Foreign Workers," p. 40.

[15] *Ibid.*, pp. 41-43.

[16] Comments by Dr. Joseph Mathieu, as quoted in Ansbacher, "Testing of Foreign Workers," p. 45.

[17] *Ibid.*, p. 43. See p. 261, on the rating of foreign workers' productivity.

The low estimation of Italian workers seems to have been widespread. Another German psychologist bluntly stated that "the Italians as a group appeared outstandingly ungifted."[18] However, the ranking of European nationals may be explained by the fact that, through heavy drafting, the most capable workers already had been drawn from, for example, the German and Italian economies.

In addition to the testing program, the Zehlendorf Institute was actively engaged in devising training programs for German supervisors of foreign workers and for the foreign workers themselves. The emphasis in the supervisor's training course was on attitude rather than technique. The Institute suggested a replacement of the "robust" or typical Nazi-inspired racial treatment of foreign workers with a more humane, paternalistic attitude. The avowed purpose of this change was to build closer rapport with the foreign workers and ultimately to increase their efficiency.[19]

The training courses for the foreign workers consisted primarily of actual demonstrations and the "learn by doing" method. Verbal-conceptual teaching was only of secondary importance.[20] The Zehlendorf training programs for foreign workers were augmented in most firms with brief courses in the principles of industrial hygiene and health which occasionally included introduction to the mysteries of modern plumbing.[21]

A second agency of the German Labor Front, the Committee for Work Studies (*Reichsausschuss fuer Arbeits-*

[18] Heinz L. Ansbacher, "The Problem of Interpreting Attitude Survey Data: A Case Study of the Attitude of Russian Workers in Wartime Germany," *Public Opinion Quarterly*, xiv (Spring 1950), 132-133.

[19] Ansbacher, "Testing of Foreign Workers," pp. 43-44; and his article, "German Industrial Psychology in the Fifth Year of War," *Psychological Bulletin*, xli (1944), 610-611.

[20] Ansbacher, "Testing of Foreign Workers," p. 44.

[21] USSBS, *The Effects of Bombing on Health and Medical Care in Germany*, Report 65a, January 1947, p. 115.

studien), was also engaged in the training programs for foreign workers. Prior to the war, this agency was primarily involved in training experts in time and motion studies. During the war, one of the major functions of the committee was to break down jobs that were formerly accomplished by skilled workers into a number of simple manipulations which could be readily taught to unskilled or foreign workers.[22] Speer's ministry, also involved in the training programs for foreign workers, collected and distributed information and suggestions dealing with their treatment and effective utilization.

When these educational techniques did not achieve the desired goals, Speer took the additional step of forming a special labor efficiency section in his ministry. In October 1943, Speer appointed Gotthard Friedrich to the new office of Reich Manpower Engineer (*Reichsarbeitseinsatz-Ingenieur*). Friedrich was to be assisted by thirty-four regional manpower engineers who were to work directly with some 5,000 plant manpower engineers. The plant engineers were nominated by management and confirmed by the government. Basically, these manpower engineers were to make investigations of labor problems and recommend immediate corrections. They could solicit the aid of the plant's physician, psychologist, time and motion experts, and management to accomplish their objectives. In brief, Friedrich and his manpower engineers were made responsible for the effective utilization of domestic and foreign workers in German industry.[23]

In addition to the testing and training programs for foreign workers, the Germans experimented with a variety of incentive programs. Among them were increases in wages and food rations, and awards of medals and rewards. Other incentives, reserved almost exclusively for eastern workers,

[22] Ansbacher, "German Psychology in the Fifth Year," p. 609.
[23] *Hamburger Fremdenblatt*, October 20, 1943, p. 4.

concerned removing discriminations, such as the *Ost* badge, and allowing eastern workers some of the freedoms enjoyed by western foreign workers.

Wage increases were logically the best method for increasing productivity. As has been pointed out, the wages for eastern workers steadily improved until they were comparable to wages received by western workers by 1944. However, with this one exception, the prevailing Nazi philosophy was to keep the general rise of wages strictly in check. The "hold the line" wage policy was so successfully employed by Nazi leadership that although nominal earnings did increase slightly during the war, real earnings showed little change.[24]

Although German leadership was reluctant to increase wages, it was eager to promote the idea of saving among the foreign workers for purely economic reasons. The millions of wage-earning foreign workers in the Reich represented a sizable proportion of the consumer public. To prevent the possible flow of their wages into the already heavily depleted consumer market, the German leadership placed artificial restrictions on spending by foreign workers. They were not given clothing rations or permission to buy other scarce items. These artificial controls and the tight restrictions over prices, however, drove the foreign workers into the flourishing black market. Moreover, some of the foreign workers with access to consumer goods outside of the Reich were important operators of the black market. The SD reported in January 1945 that a routine check of foreign workers' accounts indicated that large sums of money were being transferred among workers. Typical of this black-market operation were the following examples the SD found during a six-

[24] *Statistisches Handbuch von Deutschland, 1928-1944*, Herausgegeben vom Laenderrat des Amerikanischen Besatzungsgebiets (Munich: Franz Ehrenwirth-Verlag, 1949), p. 474; and Bry, *Wages in Germany, 1871-1945*, pp. 3-8 and 262-282.

month period ending in January 1945: 43 foreign workers
accumulated 238,350 RM; 25 workers, 99,280 RM; and 4
workers, 14,080 RM.[25]

A better solution to the problem was to encourage the
foreign workers to place their wages in accounts which
would then be transferred to the worker's family abroad,
thus easing the flow of consumer money within the Reich.
The Berlin bank in charge of foreign workers' accounts estimated that in 1943 a billion marks in cash or checks were
carried out of Germany by workers on vacations, and a total
of 958,552,500 RM were paid out through the transfer accounts. The bank reported some of the following transfers in
1943 by countries.

To France	277,046,200 RM
To Belgium	271,376,100 RM
To Italy	215,729,400 RM
To Poland	29,750,600 RM
To Russia	6,077,000 RM[26]

During the first six months of 1944, 563,013,500 RM were
transferred, with the bulk going to the following countries:

To France	258,657,700 RM
To Belgium	184,975,600 RM
To Italy	49,086,300 RM
To Bulgaria	17,191,400 RM
To Russia	2,117,600 RM[27]

The emphasis on the transfer of funds to France and Belgium, as opposed to Italy and eastern countries, reflected not
only the changing military position of Germany (most of
Russia, a part of Poland, and half of Italy were occupied by

[25] Report from *Der Chef der Sicherheitspolizei und des SD/IIID3
to Reichswirtschaftsministerium, Hauptabteilung III*, dated January
19, 1945, on T-71, Roll 79, Frames 581034-36.

[26] All figures from *Deutsche Verrechnungskasse, Hauptabteilung*,
report dated February 19, 1944, on T-71, Roll 78, Frames 580638-
642.

[27] *Ibid.*, report dated July 12, 1944, on T-71, Roll 79, Frames
581012-15.

the Allies in the first half of 1944), but the great disparity between the earning power of the eastern and the western worker.

Another incentive used by the Germans was increased food rations. Robert Ley of the German Labor Front was active in propagandizing for this method.[28] The German food ration system was already overburdened by a fantastic array of minute regulations dealing with every conceivable occupational and racial group. With regard to food rationing, there were three types of foreign workers: the preferred or western foreign workers who received regular German rations; farm workers, mainly Croats, Slovaks, and Italians, who received slightly less than German rations; and foreign workers in a special category, POW's, eastern workers, and Jews, who, except in the case of POW's (they were under the Army), received much less than ordinary German rations.[29]

Regardless of the difficulties, individual German firms began, in 1944, to augment the food rations of their foreign workers, particularly eastern ones, on the basis of their productivity and general behavior. Workers producing 100 per cent or more of the German norm were given an extra weekly ration of 1,500 grams of bread, 50 grams of margarine or butter, and 100 grams of meat. Workers producing from 80 to 100 per cent received an additional allowance of 750 grams of bread, 50 grams of margarine or butter, and 100 grams of meat. All other workers received normal rations.[30] Since the responsibility for granting incentive food rations rested with individual firms, it was impossible to determine

[28] Report from Robert Ley's office in January 1944, on T-81, Roll 65, Frames 79232-244.

[29] Guenther Pfeil, *Lebensmittelversorgung der auslaendischen Zivilarbeiter in Deutschland* (Berlin: Verlag fuer Wirtschaftsschrifttum, 1944), pp. 6, 26-27, 31-35.

[30] See report from *Koenigs- und Bismarckhuette Aktiengesellschaft und Reichsvereinigung Eisen, Herrn. Reg. Rat Dr. Ebhardt, Hauptabt. Arbeitseinsatz,* December 12, 1944, on T-77, Roll 347, Frames 1185583-586.

how widespread this practice was in the Reich. There was one case, however, of a prominent German personnel director who was arrested for buying additional food for foreign workers without adhering to racial discrimination.[31]

The practice of granting medals to foreign workers was another device employed by the Germans to increase productivity. In April 1943, Speer notified all armament offices that Hitler approved of giving the German Bronze Service Medal (*Deutsche Bronzene Verdiensstmedaille*) to outstanding foreign workers who came from countries without diplomatic representation in the Reich. Foreign workers were selected for these awards on the basis of two years of continual employment with excellent performance or special contributions to the war effort.[32]

Some incentives, reserved almost exclusively for eastern workers, sought to eliminate a few of the racial discriminations in hopes of increasing production. In the spring of 1943, the Nazi propaganda line began to emphasize that the struggle against the Soviet Union was in reality a European matter. Europe was battling for its life against Bolshevism, and from this struggle a united Europe was emerging. According to this propaganda, the foreign workers within the Reich were symbols of a new European unity.[33] They were now to be handled in a strict but just manner. To win their cooperation, the older racial attitude had to be modified. As Speer pointed out in a confidential circular, "Every person, even primitive man, has a fine sense of justice,"[34] and

[31] Louis P. Lochner, *Tycoons and Tyrant: German Industry from Hitler to Adenauer* (Chicago: H. Regnery, Co., 1954), p. 245.

[32] Letter from Speer to Armament Offices, April 2, 1943, on T-73, Roll 133, Frames 3296012-15. See also the directives for granting the awards published by the Speer ministry. This particular one, following Speer's directions, came from the Augsburg Armament Office, August 25, 1944, on T-73, Roll 119, Frames 3280309-310.

[33] *IMT*, xxv, 298-299.

[34] Speer's circular, May 25, 1943, on T-73, Roll 36, Frames 166344-361.

mishandling of foreign workers had to be eliminated. Beating eastern workers was especially forbidden. Indiscriminate name-calling was also to stop, for, after all, "from humans who are called beasts, barbarians and sub-humans one can not expect high productivity."[35] Eastern workers were to be granted privileges comparable to those of the western workers, although all Reich party officials insisted that the German public remember to keep blood lines and racial concepts in mind. By 1944, even such racial restrictions as wearing the *Ost* badges were relaxed slightly. Speer's ministry reported in March 1944 that the countless attempts by firms to secure a removal of the *Ost* badges for their good workers had finally been rewarded. For special events like movies and concerts, good eastern workers could be permitted to remove their badges.[36]

Although the incentive programs and concessions to encourage higher productivity indicated some modification of Nazi thought, the primary method of increasing production in the totalitarian Nazi state was still propaganda and coercion. Behind every incentive plan and concession was the implied threat of force. A pilot study conducted by the USSBS on foreign workers in the Reich indicated that the foreign workers believed that "rigid and terrorizing police control"[37] was basic for the maintenance of the German war effort.

German propaganda aimed toward the foreign workers sought to impress them with the invincibility of the German war machine, the need for greater effort in war production, and the futility of resistance against the Germans. These three themes were continually stressed in the weekly newspapers the Goebbels ministry published for the foreign

[35] *IMT*, xxv, 299.

[36] Directive of Theodor Hupfauer, March 13, 1944, on T-73, Roll 97, Frame 3251130.

[37] USSBS, *The Effects of Strategic Bombing on German Morale*, Vol. ii, 53.

workers.[38] Goebbels, who had fought bitterly with the DAF, SS, and Sauckel's office over cultural care of the foreign workers, felt that through this propaganda he could sap their will to resist and thereby control their actions. Nazi propaganda never aimed at indoctrinating the foreign workers with the "higher truths" of National Socialism—that was reserved for the Aryan race and was not for ordinary foreigners—rather it aimed exclusively at controlling them.[39]

Although Goebbels was one of the first ranking Nazi officials to realize the necessity of better treatment for the foreign workers, paradoxically, the propaganda he directed at the German public consistently presented the foreign worker in an unfavorable light. The foreign worker replaced the Jew as the Nazi scapegoat. The blame for looting after air raids, black market operations, and sabotage were all officially attributed to the foreign workers.[40] Goebbels even feared that they would combine with "Semitic intellectuals" and start a revolt within the Reich. With what he thought was astute Nazi foresight, Goebbels planned to use Sepp Dietrich's crack *Leibstandarte Division* to crush any such incipient revolt.[41] An elaborate operational plan for the mobilization of German police and army units in the event of a foreign workers' rebellion was organized, Goebbels thought, under the code word *Valkyrie*. Actually, Klaus von Stauffen-

[38] See Goebbel's directive on propaganda for the foreign workers' newspapers, on T-73, Roll 101, Frames 3256251-256.

[39] Rudolf Semmler, *Goebbels—The Man next to Hitler* (London: Westhouse, 1947), p. 124; and *Goebbels Diaries*, pp. 108, 157, 182, 186, 195, 197, 247.

[40] See USSBS, *Effects on German Morale*, II, 89-90; *Goebbels Diaries*, p. 197; and Speer's *Rede vor dem 3. Lehrgang der Kommandierenden General und Korpschefs, Kaserne Krampnitz*, on January 13, 1945. Speer claimed that the Allied intelligence groups knew a great deal about German production from their foreign workers' contacts. This speech is in the unpublished materials files of the USSBS.

[41] *Goebbels Diaries*, pp. 288-290.

berg and his circle were using the *Valkyrie* plan as a cover for their attempt on Hitler's life and the seizure of the state. The plan was activated only once—after the July 20 attempt on Hitler's life. Much to the surprise of Goebbels, the foreign workers were not implicated in the plot and, in fact, seemed quite docile at the time.[42]

The SS also worked in close connection with Goebbels' propaganda ministry. Since Himmler was responsible for internal security, the foreign workers were nominally under his police jurisdiction. Himmler's various police units, however, could not expect to control and regulate the daily actions of seven million foreigners. Instead, Himmler relied on the German employers, factory guards, and the local German police to maintain normal control over the foreigners. Minor offenses were handled through ordinary channels, while serious offenses and political offenses of all kinds were immediately reported to the SD and the district Gestapo office. In order to coordinate the activities of the SS with the Propaganda Ministry, the Labor Front, and the ordinary police, on June 21, 1943, Himmler appointed Otto Gohdes as Chief Inspector for foreign workers' affairs.[43] Gohdes was primarily involved with augmenting the propaganda program among the foreign workers and strengthening the counterintelligence program.

[42] Roger Manvell and Heinrich Fraenkel, *Dr. Goebbels: His Life and Death* (New York: Pyramid Books, 1960), p. 223.

[43] *Verfuegungen, Anordnungen, Bekanntgaben*, Part I, 1943, pp. 318-320. The organization of the myriad police units of Nazi Germany was sprawling and clumsy. In September 1939, the *Reichssicherheitshauptamt* (RSHA), or Central Security Office, was formed by merging the state and party intelligence and police units. The RSHA was subdivided into seven *Aemter* (sections). Amt I and II dealt with personnel and administration; Amt III was SD (home intelligence); Amt IV, the Gestapo; Amt V, the KRIPO, or criminal police; Amt VI, the SD (foreign intelligence); and Amt VII was the research and documentation section. Within the Gestapo a special subsection, Amt IV BA, was created to oversee foreign workers, with Otto Gohdes as the section head.

In addition to the SD, the *Abwehr*, the military counter-intelligence, had a program of placing informers among the foreign workers, but it was not until late 1944, after the arrest of Admiral Wilhelm Canaris, that the operations of the *Abwehr* were merged with the SD.[44] Generally, the SD collected information about the foreign workers from their paid informers among the workers, the employers of foreign labor, and Nazi party members. During the early years of the war, the SD was primarily concerned with ferreting out information about the spread of communist, pacifist, or defeatist propaganda among the foreign workers. It was not until the middle of 1944 that the SD showed any real concern about the possibility of open rebellion among the foreign workers, and even then the impetus for such concern stemmed from the German civilian population rather than the SD itself.

Beginning in August 1944, the weekly rumor reports (*Woechentlicher Stimmungsbericht*) were filled with accounts of uneasiness among the German population about the lack of protection and the danger of the large number of foreign workers in the area.[45] In response to such reports, Himmler ordered an intensification of the propaganda campaign among the foreign workers and a step-up in the training of German factory guard units in sabotage and mass insurrection counter-measures.[46] As early as March 1943, the RSHA had a secret agreement with the Labor Front, with the approval of the Speer ministry and the Army, that the factory police would be augmented by armed auxiliary forces (*Erweiterter Werkschutz*) of loyal Labor Front workers spe-

[44] See the *Abwehr*'s regulations on the placing of "V" men or informers among the foreign workers, on T-73, Roll 36, Frames 166522-525.

[45] For a typical illustration of this uneasiness, see the Gau-Baden's *Woechentlicher Stimmungsbericht* from May 1944 to December 1944, on T-81, Roll 167, Frames 306774-797.

[46] *NCA*, vi, 1088-1091.

cially trained to handle riots and sabotage.[47] Apparently the auxiliary guard units were undermanned by late 1944 because of the heavy drafting and the recruiting for Goebbels' people's army.

Although open insurrection by the foreign workers was always a latent threat to the Nazis, especially at the end of the war, a much more immediate and pressing problem throughout the entire war was labor discipline. The foreign workers were continually attempting to slow down work, feign illness, or abandon jobs. The RSHA and Speer's and Sauckel's ministries were bombarded by complaints from employers and labor offices. By late 1943, the foreign workers were becoming sullen, indifferent, and hostile.[48] The incidence of absenteeism and illness among them rose sharply. The illness rate for western foreign workers rose from 1.5 or 2 per cent to 9 or 10 per cent, whereas the rate for eastern workers climbed from 4 to 12 or 14 per cent—approximately double the rate for German workers.[49] Throughout 1944, the sick rate of foreign workers was consistently twice as high as that of Germans.[50] This was remarkable when one considers the poor physical quality of the German working population at that time.

The foreign workers were especially prone to leave their jobs. In industries such as mining, the rate of new recruitment barely covered the losses incurred by departures of foreign workers. In August of 1943, Paul Pleiger, Goering's deputy under the Four Year Plan, reported to Speer that from

[47] See Speer's letters on the auxiliary police units, the OKW's approval, and the DAF's instructions, on T-73, Roll 36, Frames 166374-398. See also in *Minor Trials*, ix, 920-922, 942-944, the organization of the auxiliaries in the Krupp plants.

[48] *Minor Trials*, ii, 607-608.

[49] *Minor Trials*, ii, 532; Arbeitswissenschaftliches Institut der DAF, *Arbeitseinsatz der Ostarbeiter*, p. 7; and reports from the Augsburg Labor Office, on T-73, Roll 98, Frame 3252216.

[50] USSBS, *Effects on Health*, p. 115.

July 1 to August 20, 1943, 54,375 new foreign workers were assigned to the mines, but that during the same period 42,477 foreigners left.[51] Pleiger was convinced that the foreigners were finding employment elsewhere in the Reich. Earlier in the month, Pleiger had declared to Sauckel that it was imperative that escaped workers be returned to their jobs. If necessary, the clothes of the foreign workers should be stamped with their name and that of their employer so that they could readily be returned. Sauckel was requested to inform the individual German employers that they were not to hire foreign workers without the local labor office's permission.

The refusal of foreign workers to return from furlough was another facet of the absenteeism problem. From late 1943 on, the foreign workers were violating their contracts by failure to return from leave with such frequency that it might be more appropriately termed mass "desertion." The Kiel labor office, for example, reported that it sent 950 foreign workers on leave October 22, 1943, and only 33 returned. A month later, the same office sent 900 on leave and only 28 returned. In the spring of 1944, the Innsbruck office allowed 203 French, Belgian, Croatian, and Slovak workers leave and 23 returned.[52] The labor offices were convinced that either the workers were receiving false ration and work cards from the underground or they were being intimidated into not returning by the underground movements. The only recourse that the German economic leaders had in combating this type of absenteeism was additional propaganda and more stringent police measures.[53]

Unknown to Pleiger and the other German economic leaders at the time was the role the SS was playing in the absentee rate among the foreign workers. Although undoubt-

[51] *Minor Trials*, xiii, 1029.
[52] Document RF 1545-1298F in the Nuremberg Trials Collection.
[53] Document RF 1545-1298F; and *Minor Trials*, xiii, 1027-1028.

edly some foreign workers escaped from their jobs, many of these workers were arrested by the SS and not returned to their former place of employment. Instead, the SS sent the workers to their own concentration camp factories. The SS, the state within a state, was rapidly developing an economic base for its *Waffen*-SS units during this period.[54] As early as September 1942, the SS had reached an agreement with Speer's ministry that from 3 to 5 per cent of the production of the SS plants was to be given directly to the *Waffen*-SS divisions.[55] At the time, this represented a victory of Speer over Himmler, for Speer still maintained general control over all SS plants which were producing armaments. Although Speer mentioned at the Nuremberg trials that Himmler never received the percentage of arms agreed on, he did state that Himmler was to receive from 5 to 8 per cent, a somewhat higher figure than was agreed upon in September 1942.[56] Apparently Himmler later deliberately chose to ignore this agreement, for there is conclusive proof that from the middle of 1943 until the summer of 1944 the SS was expanding its economic capabilities through mass arrests, especially of foreign workers.

Himmler had ordered his police units to arrest all escaping or "socially dangerous" foreign workers and to send them

[54] A few of the many accounts of the economic activities of the SS are Gerald Reitlinger, *The SS: Alibi of a Nation, 1922-1945* (London: Heinemann, 1956); Olga Wormser, "Le rôle du travail des concentrationnaires dans l'économie de guerre allemande," *Revue d'histoire de la deuxième guerre mondiale*, 15/16; Eugen Kogon, *The Theory and Practice of Hell*, trans. by Heinz Norden (New York: Berkeley Publishing Corp., 1950); Edward Crankshaw, *Gestapo, Instrument of Tyranny* (New York: Pyramid, 1956); Rudolf Hoess, *Commandant of Auschwitz*, trans. by Constantine Fitzgibbon (New York: Popular Library, 1961); and Enno Georg, *Die wirtschaftlichen Unternehmungen der SS*, Schriftenreihe der Vierteljahrshefte fuer Zeitgeschichte, No. 7 (Stuttgart: Deutsche Verlags-Anstalt, 1963).

[55] *NCA*, I, 916-917; and *NCA*, VIII, 186-187.

[56] *IMT*, XVI, 472.

to concentration camps.[57] Arrest statistics indicated the ruthless manner in which the police carried out Himmler's orders. Unfortunately, complete arrest statistics have never been found for the entire war. Those for the first six months of 1944 are available, however, and indicate the tempo and aim of the SS. During the first half-year of 1944, while 19,000 Germans were arrested for political and religious offenses and another 13,000 for labor offenses, the arrest rate of foreign workers for similar offenses was estimated by the USSBS to be proportionally fifteen times higher. Nearly 204,000 foreign workers were arrested during this six-month period.[58] When Walter Schieber informed Speer, in May 1944, of the huge losses in foreign workers to the SS, Speer questioned the SS *Fuehrer* and received the lame excuse that the SS food rations were better in concentration camps than in factories and, as a consequence, the foreign workers were more productive there.[59]

Unimpressed by Himmler's argument, Speer told *Der Fuehrer* that the armament industries were losing from 30,000 to 40,000 foreign workers a month to the SS. Speer pointed out to Hitler that this situation had to stop immediately, because the armament industries could not take a half-million loss per year and still maintain production.[60] Hitler agreed to see Himmler and the practice was stopped, or so it seemed to Speer. Once Himmler promised to cease his campaign of arresting foreign workers, Speer was satisfied and failed to check into the matter further. As Speer explained in Nuremberg, he had "no reason to distrust Himmler's promise because, after all, it is not customary for Reich Ministers to distrust each other so much."[61]

[57] *IMT*, xxxii, 246-247; and Document SD-41 in the Nuremberg Trials Collection.

[58] USSBS, *Effects on Morale*, i, 87.   [59] *IMT*, xli, 412.

[60] *IMT*, xli, 416-417.   [61] *IMT*, xvi, 474.

The SS arrest offensive seems to have had little effect on the attitude of the foreign workers. Factories, labor offices, and local police authorities reported continual trouble with the foreign workers throughout 1944. In March of that year, the German authorities introduced a mandatory 60-hour work week for all workers over sixteen.[62] The immediate effects of the new ruling were disastrous. In the Munich area alone, the production of the POW's dropped to 50 per cent and of German women to 70 per cent.[63] The rate of desertion among the foreign workers rose sharply. To cite only one labor office's experience, at Remscheid the rate of desertion rose quickly after March, while the rate of persons fined for labor contract violations remained stable, probably because the Germans tried to be lenient in order to forestall further desertions (see Table XIX). The high incidence of labor violations among German women in Remscheid was true in other districts.

In Bavaria, the local labor offices found that the rate of absenteeism and tardiness among foreign workers rose sharply in 1944. The reasons most commonly mentioned were bad treatment by factory officials and peasants (the Labor Trustee in these areas complained that the local police did not protect foreign workers adequately), broken promises about wages and housing, attempts to go home, and many successful changes to better jobs.[64] In Augsburg, the factories and labor offices reported that the foreign workers were brazenly complaining about the canteens, lack of soap, beer, and cigarettes. When one of the DAF officials cuffed a particular foreign worker because he refused to work, drank on the job, and continually caused trouble, the German

[62] *Ruestungswirtschaftliche Nachrichten*, March 1944, on T-73, Roll 119, Frames 3280452-461.
[63] USSBS, *Effects on Morale*, I, 61.
[64] *Ibid.*, 64.

TABLE XIX

LABOR VIOLATIONS OR DESERTIONS IN THE REMSCHEID LABOR
DISTRICT, BY SEX AND NATIONALITY FROM JANUARY 1944
TO FEBRUARY 1945

		Number of Persons Fined				Foreigners Deserting Jobs	
		Germans		Foreigners			
		Women	Men	Women	Men	Women	Men
Jan.	1944	49	23	0	0	0	0
Feb.	1944	26	17	0	0	0	0
Mar.	1944	33	17	0	2	0	0
April	1944	13	24	0	9	0	20
May	1944	21	18	1	5	0	65
June	1944	26	16	1	6	0	38
July	1944	20	10	0	7	0	26
Aug.	1944	35	17	0	0	0	8
Sept.	1944	14	6	0	2	0	11
Oct.	1944	16	7	0	5	2	12
Nov.	1944	24	15	0	1	1	40
Dec.	1944	29	6	0	5	0	2
Jan.	1945	25	10	0	3	4	27
Feb.	1945	17	7	0	5	4	51
	Total	348	193	2	50	11	300

SOURCE: Compiled from the Remscheid Amt-Gau Duesseldorf *Monatlicher Taetigkeitsbericht*, in the files of the USSBS.

plant decided to prosecute the foreign worker formally as an example. By the time they completed the charges, the foreign worker had run away.[65]

While the Germans had many difficulties with the foreign workers during the later stages of the war because of absenteeism, desertion, and open resentment, nevertheless it is quite remarkable how successfully they managed to control

[65] Letters from Augsburg *Arbeitsamt* and individual factories in the area, dated January through June 1944, on T-73, Roll 98, Frames 3252145-152.

and use the vast number of foreign workers. In general, the Nazi methods of intensive propaganda and coercion effectively cowed and disciplined the workers. In explaining the effectiveness of these methods, an American sociologist noted a widespread psychological regression in the foreign workers whom he interviewed after the war. They exhibited "a collapse of adult norms and standards in speech, behavior and attitude, and a reversion to less mature patterns."[66] The workers became withdrawn, apathetic, indifferent about their work, and docile. German employers generally noticed that the workers were fairly easy to manage, but their indifferent and careless attitude resulted in more losses in production than did overt sabotage.[67]

However, German managers after the war were almost unanimously of the opinion that, with proper inducement and treatment, the output of foreign workers could have been raised over that of German workers.[68] Needless to say, their productivity varied widely according to many factors, such as health, treatment, aptitude, and incentive. Yet, as a general rule, German officials found that the foreign workers were producing much less than the German workers. Sauckel reported in March 1943 that the foreigners were from 65 to 100 per cent as effective as German workers.[69] Robert Ley estimated after the war that eastern workers were only 20 per cent as effective at first as German workers, but later, through training courses, their productivity was raised to 50

[66] E. A. Shils, "Social and Psychological Aspects of Displacement and Repatriation," *Journal of Social Issues*, II, No. 3 (August 1946), 5.

[67] See report, *Meldungen aus dem Reichsgau Oberdonau*, SD-Abschnitt Linz, III D514, January 11, 1943, on T-81, Roll 7, Frames 14468-471.

[68] USSBS, *Effects on Health*, p. 115.

[69] Quoted from Sauckel's "Rundschreiben an alle Gauleiter der NSDAP als Bevollmaechtigte fuer den Arbeitseinsatz, vom 15 Maerz 1943," in Didier, *Handbuch fuer G.B.A.*, p. 65.

or 60 per cent of that of the German worker.[70] The most
extensive survey of the productivity of foreign workers completed in the spring of 1944, by the *Reichswirtschaftskammer*
for Speer, indicated similar results. The survey rated foreign
workers by percentages of the German norms in the following way:[71]

Eastern women	90-100%
Czech skilled workers	80-95%
Eastern men	60-80%
Italians	70%
Balkans, Dutch, Danish	50-70%

Judging from the complaints of the ranking German
officials, the productivity of the POW's was even lower than
that of the foreign workers. Speer lamented that many supervisors of the POW's felt their job was finished once the
POW's arrived safely and on time at their work places.[72]
Goering and Milch thought the payment which the *Stalags*
received for the use of their prisoners' labor was the "biggest
racket" in all of Germany.[73]

Paradoxically, while the German officials were endlessly
complaining about the low productivity of the foreign workers and the inferior quality of the German workers at that
time, the total productivity of the labor force in the Reich was
rising. The USSBS estimated that the Gross National Product of the Reich showed an annual increase throughout the
war years. In 1944, the increase in the GNP was 3 per cent,
while the increase in armament production was 25 per cent
over 1943. This rise in armament was accomplished with

[70] Interview No. 57 of Robert Ley, June 27, 1945, in the files of
the USSBS, p. 2.
[71] Reichsministerium fuer Ruestung und Kriegsproduktion, Planungsamt, *Zahlenangaben ueber den Einsatz deutscher Frauen*, Berlin,
1943-1945, p. 3.
[72] *Notizen fuer eine Rede des Herrn Reichsminister Speer*, un-
dated, in the files of the USSBS.
[73] *Minor Trials*, II, 613-614.

only an additional 3 per cent rise in the labor force in the armament industries, and in the face of heavy bombing, labor difficulties, and rising hostility on the part of the foreign workers.[74] The productivity of labor in industry proper—that is, in mining, manufacturing, and construction, where foreign labor was a third of the labor force—shows a similar rise. Edward O. Bassett of the USSBS estimated the rise of all labor productivity in industry, in per cent, as follows:[75]

1930—100.0	1942—116.4
1940—109.5	1943—127.2
1941—112.9	1944—122.8

Rolf Wagenfuehr, chief statistician for the Speer ministry, had even a higher estimate of labor productivity. Wagenfuehr found that in 1942, for the first time in the war, production per worker was higher by 7 per cent than in any preceding peacetime year. In 1943 and 1944, productivity was almost one-sixth higher in spite of the use of foreign workers, prisoners of war, half-time workers, untrained women, and chaotic economic conditions.[76] However, this was at a time when, by Wagenfuehr's own admission, Germany did not have very effective methods for compiling quantitive statistics or for maintaining continuous statistical control on the various branches of industry. As Wagenfuehr commented: "It is no fairy tale that even in 1944 nobody in Germany really knew how many working hours were required to produce one Tiger tank, and that at a time when labor was the bottleneck in the German war economy."[77]

The apparent contradiction between the rise in overall labor productivity and the inefficiency of the foreign workers

[74] USSBS, *Effects on Morale*, ii, 53.
[75] Edward O. Bassett, "Industrial Sales, Output, and Productivity, Prewar Area of Germany, 1939-1944," *USSBS Overall Economic Effects Division*, Special Paper No. 8, Report 134a, March 15, 1946, p. 74, Table 12.
[76] Wagenfuehr, *Rise and Fall of the German Economy*, p. 81.
[77] *Ibid.*, p. 30.

who comprised 20 per cent of the total labor force can be explained in many ways. The lengthened work week, Speer's reorganization of the German war economy, and the complete concentration on armament production during the last two years of the war undoubtedly were the major factors in the rising level of labor productivity.[78] Nor can one rule out the possibility that the Germans' evaluation of their productivity was inaccurate.[79]

Regardless of the accuracy of the wartime statistics, the amazing aspect of the German experience with foreign workers was not how little, but how much they accomplished. The foreign workers were judged continually by production norms designed for German workers. These standards assumed that the workers would be familiar with modern industrial techniques, have a language facility, and be highly motivated to work for their country. But the case of the foreign workers was just the opposite. Many of them were peasants from backward areas without any appreciable experience with industrial technology; they had language difficulties; and they certainly had much less reason to work hard for the Nazi regime than did the German worker. To apply German standards to a group of unwilling foreign workers and hope they would perform as well as Germans was wishful thinking. It ignored every tenet of modern industrial management and psychology. Yet the Germans brought millions of unwilling persons, many of whom were personally mistreated, into a strange country, presented them with grim living circumstances, and then molded them into productive workers. This alone speaks volumes for the ruth-

[78] Klein, *Germany's Economic Preparations*, p. 236.
[79] The Bassett, Wagenfuehr, and Klein studies are in agreement that German statistics for the war period are, at best, rough approximations. For an excellent discussion of some of the difficulties involved in constructing reliable statistics on the German wartime economy, see Klein's "Statistical Appendix" in *Germany's Economic Preparations*, pp. 241-258.

less efficiency of the Nazi totalitarian state and German industry.

The productivity of the foreign workers was not as high as the Germans desired, but still the results were impressive and significant. There can be no denial of the obvious fact, as the Office of Strategic Services pointed out, that the absorption of millions of foreign workers represented a "remarkable achievement" in organization and was *the* main factor in the maintenance of the German war economy during the last years of the conflict.[80]

[80] United States Office of Strategic Services, *Foreign Labor in Germany*, Research and Analysis Report, No. 1623, October 24, 1944, p. 1.

CHAPTER XII

The Foreign Worker's Life in the Reich

THE housing, feeding, and care of millions of foreign workers in the Reich during the war presented the Nazi regime with many problems that had not been anticipated. Basic to these problems was the conflict between Nazi ideology, which was so exclusively German and racially oriented, and economic reality, which dictated Germany's need for every ounce of production from its foreign workers. During the early years of the war when victory seemed imminent, the racial considerations were far more pronounced than the economic ones. However, as the war progressed and the economic needs became increasingly urgent, the ideological-economic conflict was resolved through the gradual erosion of the ideology. The status of the eastern worker, in particular, evolved from that of a hated *Untermensch* to that of a "guest worker," as Sauckel called him in late 1944. Every aspect of the foreign worker's life in the Reich reflected this shift in attitude.

HOUSING

A key principle of the Nazi foreign labor program was that the foreign workers were in the Reich only temporarily. As a result, the living facilities provided for them were of a transitory and makeshift nature. Early in the war, the Germans housed foreigners in private homes, halls, empty wings of factories, and German Labor Front camps—in short, in any building that could be converted into quarters. With the prolongation of the war, the housing problem grew more critical and complex. Basically the responsibility of housing for the foreign workers lay with the employing firms, but the German Labor Front was to supervise and inspect the construction and maintenance of all quarters. The Labor Front was also to represent the foreign workers in all other matters dealing with their employment in the Reich. The Labor Front and German management found that the housing of millions of foreigners created many new and unwelcome problems.

The mass influx of foreigners and the constant bombing of German cities after 1942 made it imperative that the Germans divert some of their resources from war production to housing construction even though wartime restrictions made the erection of new buildings more difficult. By the end of 1942, German authorities were hastily constructing mass accommodations for foreigners. At the same time, the foreign workers were prohibited thereafter from lodging in private homes.[1] It was hoped that this procedure would place more rooms at the disposal of bombed-out German families, ease the security problem, and be more economical.

On April 18, 1942, the Speer ministry sent detailed instructions to the armament plants on the construction of barracks for foreign workers. The plants were to canvass their areas for any buildings that could be converted into barracks; they were given permission to use the *Reichsautobahn* barracks, since the construction of the superhighway had been halted. The factories were also encouraged to build new barracks for their workers even though the ministry could not help the plants to procure construction materials. The plants would have to furnish their own materials from existing supplies and stand the entire cost of the barracks. Weekly reports were to be submitted by the plants to the ministry on the barracks construction.[2]

At the same time the Speer ministry circulated blueprints for the construction of three types of model barracks, thirty-three yards by ten feet in size. Type A barracks was designed to house eighteen civilian workers; Type B, thirty-six Rus-

[1] *Deutsche Bergwerks-Zeitung*, December 22, 1942, p. 2.
[2] Speer directive, dated April 18, 1942, on T-73, Roll 100, Frames 3254955-966.

sian POW's; and Type C, twelve women workers. Ideally the barracks were to be furnished with bunks, tables, benches, and a padlocked cupboard for each worker. In accordance with the Nazi racial attitude, the women workers received the best furnishings and the Russian POW's the worst. For example, women workers were issued sheets but the male workers had only blankets.[3] The Russian barracks were overcrowded, they did not have as many benches and tables, and the mattresses were made of straw.

Because of the bombing danger, the German Labor Front suggested that only small barracks be built in the immediate areas of work. Camps of 1,000 or more workers were not to be placed near residential districts, industrial sites, or military areas.[4] Sauckel's office wanted the workers housed by nationalities whenever possible, not on principle but to lessen friction.[5]

Financing the new barracks placed a strain on small firms. Speer estimated that the barracks would be self-liquidating after four years but many companies thought this was too optimistic. The *Frankfurter Zeitung* estimated that the cost per bed in new barracks would be between 600 and 1,200 RM. Many companies complained that the rental payments of .50 RM daily by the foreign workers did not cover the cost of housing.[6] As a remedy, employers were advised to reduce costs by crowding more beds into one building or by joining with other companies to use one joint camp. The total German investment in barracks was considerable. The *Voelkischer Beobachter* estimated the value of the camps and their equipment at 600 million RM in 1943.[7]

[3] Proudfoot, *European Refugees*, p. 87.

[4] Birkenholz, *Der auslaendische Arbeiter*, pp. 5-7.

[5] Sauckel directive, *Unterbringung auslaendischer Arbeitskraefte nach Volkszugehoerigkeit*, dated March 3, 1943, on T-77, Roll 243, Frames 986493-494.

[6] *Frankfurter Zeitung*, November 7, 1942, p. 3.

[7] *Voelkischer Beobachter*, October 20, 1943, p. 1.

The total number of camps in the Reich was estimated by the *Voelkischer Beobachter* to be 22,000. These camps housed two-thirds of the foreign workers, while the remaining third lived in private rooms.[8] There is no way of confirming this estimate because a camp might be anything from a shed in a rural area to a huge, swarming compound housing thousands of workers in the Ruhr area. Still, the estimate appears high. In 1944, the German Labor Front reported that it directly administered 1,000 camps with 1.1 million workers and supervised an additional 4,600 camps.[9] Since the Labor Front handled all non-agricultural workers in the Reich, this would mean that, according to the newspaper's estimate, there were approximately 16,400 rural camps.

The actual conditions in these labor camps varied from good to terrible. Prior to the Russian war, all foreign workers except POW's, Poles, and Jews lived in private rooms or camps where conditions were generally good. But the influx of Russian POW's and eastern workers changed everything. These workers were virtually prisoners; they were confined to the camps and guarded closely. The hundreds of thousands recruited during the first Sauckel action caused frightful overcrowding in the labor camps.

Adjectives like primitive, deplorable, and catastrophic were used to describe the conditions in the camps. Weekly reports in the summer of 1942 from the new Farben plant at Auschwitz were filled with comments about the lack of washing facilities and the pitiful hygienic installations.[10] Conditions in the Krupp plants were just as bad. Krupp's chief physician, Dr. Wilhelm Jaeger, reported that the eastern workers arrived in the Reich half-starved and then were subjected to beatings and other cruel treatment. The conditions

---

[8] *Ibid.*

[9] Deutsche Arbeitsfront (DAF), *Die Deutsche Arbeitsfront, Wesen, Ziel, Wege* (Berlin: Verlag der DAF, 1943), p. 45.

[10] *Minor Trials*, viii, 449-451.

in their barracks were termed deplorable. In some camps there were twice as many workers in barracks as health standards allowed. In one camp on Kraemerplatz in Essen, an old elementary school was converted into a barracks for 1,200 eastern workers. Ten children's toilets serviced them, and the doctor reported excretion covered the floor of the bathroom. Similar conditions were reported in other converted barracks, but they became even worse after heavy air raids began.[11] Of the fifty-seven Krupp camps subjected to repeated air raids, twenty-two were destroyed, twenty-two others were twice destroyed, and three camps were partially destroyed.[12]

Max Ihn, the personnel director at Krupp, admitted the mistreatment and the deplorable living conditions in his plant, but he maintained that the management was striving to correct it.[13] In May 1942, for example, Krupp's Cast Iron Works suspended further labor allocation until the necessary billeting space was made available.[14] Conditions in other plants must have been similar to the Krupp camps, because Sauckel asked plant managers to "see with their own eyes" that the directives for care of the eastern workers were enforced. Lest he be considered too soft on the easterner, Sauckel tempered his instructions to the plant managers by stating that he also wanted to prevent "politically incompetent plant supervisors from giving overly much care to the eastern workers on the other hand, thus provoking a justified discontent among the German workers."[15]

By October of 1942, Sauckel's office had received so many complaints from labor offices, plant officials, the East Ministry, and the police that Sauckel sent a confidential order to

[11] *IMT*, xxxv, 57-63.   [12] *Minor Trials*, ix, 678-679.
[13] *NCA*, vi, 1113-1114.   [14] *Minor Trials*, ix, 687.
[15] *Verfuegungen, Anordnungen, Bekanntgaben*, Vol. II, 1942, p. 567.

all labor offices to inspect the factories for compliance with government regulations and especially to see if the factories were cutting too many cost corners at the expense of their foreign workers.[16] By December, Sauckel put some muscle behind his pleas to factory managers by pointedly threatening to refuse further labor allocations to factories that did not correct the living conditions of their foreign workers.[17] How successful Sauckel was in his threats is debatable. Inspection reports would seem to indicate that not much was done. Typical of these reports was one conducted in the Dortmund area by the DAF, SS, and the local labor office in March 1943, and forwarded by Sauckel's office to the Reich Iron and Coal Association. The inspectors found the barracks partially inadequate. In some cases they were lousy and filthy, and there was one instance where a camp was still enclosed by barbed wire.[18] The cleanliness of the sanitary installations left much to be desired. In general, the inspection team blamed the plant authorities for not having the necessary understanding, insight, and good will toward the foreign workers to correct the situation.[19]

In June 1943, at the suggestions of Franz Mende of the DAF and Max Timm, Sauckel's principal advisor, a central inspection agency for the care of foreign workers was set up by the DAF and GBA. The new agency was to issue directives in Sauckel's and Ley's names, and its inspection teams had the power to make on-the-spot corrections of living conditions in the factories. The agency was to report directly to the DAF, GBA, and the regional labor offices. An additional clause in the agreement allowed the East and Propa-

[16] *IMT*, xxii, 213-215.

[17] Document D-196, a memo from Sauckel, dated December 21, 1942, in the files of the Nuremberg Trials Collection.

[18] See Chapter VI for the decision to remove barbed wire from around Russian camps.

[19] *Minor Trials*, vi, 743.

ganda Ministries representation in the inspection teams whenever these ministries deemed it necessary.[20] The East Ministry became very active after the June 1943 agreement and visited from eight to ten thousand camps per year. Rosenberg's ministry also established a welfare agency with a budget of 5.3 million RM to help improve the living conditions of eastern workers in the Reich.[21]

In spite of the best intentions of some German agencies, the housing of foreign workers deteriorated markedly in the last two years of the war, especially in the urban areas. The bombing raids, the continual flow of new foreign workers, and the acute shortage of building materials made it impossible to check the decline in housing. Conditions became so alarming in some camps that Speer's office ordered factory managers to take precautions to insure a minimum of seven cubic meters of air space per person in the barracks, and Sauckel's office openly discussed the disastrous spread of vermin in the camps.[22] By late 1944 governmental and party agencies were swamped with reports about irregularities in the barracks, ranging from stopped-up plumbing to wild parties.[23]

In all fairness to the German authorities it must be admitted that generalizations about conditions throughout the

[20] *Reichsarbeitsblatt*, 1943, Part 1, 588.
[21] Braeutigam, *Ueberblick*, p. 94.
[22] See Speer directive of August 16, 1943, on T-73, Roll 133, Frame 3295997; and the *Reichsarbeitsblatt*, 1944, Part III, 35-37.
[23] Typical of some of these were the *Augsburger Waagenfabrik* report of November 10, 1944, dealing with two women in a barracks for Russian male workers, on T-73, Roll 98, Frame 3252207; Regensburg *Kreisobmann* reports on mishandling of water and electricity, on T-81, Roll 68, Frames 77837-849; Item RMFRUK/83, *Maschinelles Berichtwesen*, a group of letters and reports about the barracks in 1944 that cited cases of German military personnel spending nights in the barracks of foreign women and of loud drinking parties, on T-73, Roll 5, Frames 1050381-394.

Reich are difficult to make. In some areas the authorities found the barracks were clean, orderly, and satisfactorily maintained.[24] Western workers in particular confirmed the fact that their housing in the Reich varied with the employer, but was by no means poor.[25] However, the bulk of the German evidence suggests that the eastern peoples suffered terrible privations during their stay in the Reich.

FOOD

The Nazi attitude toward feeding the foreign workers went through three phases: during the first period, from the beginning of the war until the spring of 1942, racial considerations were important; in the second period, from 1942 until the summer of 1944, many of the inequalities were removed; and in the third period, from the summer of 1944 to the end of the war, the Germans tried selective feeding. During the first period, the *Untermensch* philosophy was applied to the feeding of Polish and eastern workers. Inspired by Nazi racial concepts, this *Untermensch* policy was administered by Goering, Himmler, and Backe. As has been noted,[26] it was a complete disaster and by the spring of 1942 the lunacy of the policy was apparent to all. The second period began with the appointment of Sauckel and the huge influx of eastern workers; the Germans altered their food plans to meet the new situation. Prior to that time, many of the western workers received individual ration cards while the rest were catered to in mass canteens. Now, as a matter

[24] A few of the favorable reports are Remscheid Labor Office's Monthly Reports from April 1942 to March 1943, in the files of the USSBS, and the SD/Aussenstelle Aachen reports, on T-175, Roll 249, Frames 2741153-158.

[25] G. Jacquemyns, *La Société belge sous l'occupation allemande, 1940-1941* (Brussels: Nicholson et Watson, 1950), III, 31-33.

[26] See Chapters II and VIII on the feeding of the Poles and Russians.

of principle, all foreigners were to be fed as far as possible in canteens.[27]

On March 22, 1942, the Reich Minister of Food and Agriculture established a standard weekly ration for civilian foreign workers (except eastern workers) lodged and fed in camps, irrespective of age and sex.[28] The weekly ration consisted of 450 grams of meat, 225 grams of fats, 2,800 grams of bread, and 5,250 grams of potatoes (10 grams = 3.53 oz.; 500 grams = 1.1 lbs.). Foreigners performing "heavy," "exceptionally heavy," or mining tasks were to receive additional rations. Eastern workers received about 200 grams less of bread and meat and 100 grams less of fats per week than did other foreigners.[29] In addition, the factory and camp canteens were authorized to draw small weekly amounts of flour, soup ingredients, *Naehrmittel* (nutritious food products, such as potato flour, barley, and oatmeal), and vegetables for each foreigner. However, all vegetables except turnips were to be issued only if the supplies for German civilians permitted it. In reality, this meant that the foreign workers rarely received them.

The German decision to establish a standard diet was prompted by the disastrous physical condition of many eastern workers and the realization that they were useless to German industry unless sufficiently nourished. The first large contingents of Russian POW's and civilians in the spring of 1942 were in such poor health that the factories could not put them to work immediately.[30] One firm even notified its labor office that it was not interested in receiving any more

[27] Foreign workers who did not take their meals in factory or camp canteens received special ration cards, but to control them application for the cards had to be made through the employer.

[28] Birkenholz, *Der auslaendische Arbeiter*, p. 222. This diet was increased slightly in October 1942.

[29] *IMT*, XLI, 218-222.

[30] *NCA*, VII, 9-20; and *Minor Trials*, VI, 707-709.

Russians unless they were able to work.[31] Nor was the standard diet sufficient to build up the natural strength of many of the eastern workers.[32] German managers invariably described the eastern workers as inefficient because of insufficient food.[33] Commenting on this after the war, Ley claimed that Sauckel and he tried to eliminate the differences in food rations between the eastern workers and everyone else. However, he said, "We simply could not feed everybody; we did not have enough food, but anyway, the food was far better than these people had at home."[34]

The German authorities made slight adjustments in the standard rations based on the food preferences of various nationalities. Thus, Italian workers might receive more spaghetti and less bread, while French workers might get more cheese and fewer potatoes.[35] In the larger camp and factory canteens, foreign workers were allowed to have their food prepared by cooks of their own nationality.

Some foreign workers were able to supplement their inadequate rations with food parcels from home. Customs procedures were simplified so that gift parcels could be sent.[36] It must be assumed however, that parcels from home brought no relief to any great number of foreigners in the Reich.[37]

[31] *Minor Trials*, IX, 875.

[32] *Minor Trials*, IX, 895-896.

[33] USSBS, *Effects on Morale*, I, 64.

[34] Interview of Robert Ley on October 2, 1945, p. 21, in the files of the USSBS.

[35] Mende, *Die Beschaeftigung*, p. 230.

[36] Birkenholz, *Der auslaendische Arbeiter*, p. 211.

[37] German peasants were especially indignant about the food parcels. The peasants thought, for example, that their Italian workers were overfed (because of the food parcels from home) and overpaid (at .26 RM per hour plus room and board). Then, too, they could not understand why such husky young men were not in the Army. See their complaints to the local labor offices, on T-81, Roll 537, Frames 5306927-958, and T-81, Roll 645, Frames 5448510-565.

Often western workers were caught selling the contents of their gift parcels to eastern workers at exorbitant prices.[38]

To further supplement diets, Sauckel encouraged the foreign workers to plant gardens around their camps to raise vegetables. Camp leaders were instructed to provide tools and seeds. Apparently this garden program was not very successful. Shortages of seeds, land, and tools made the cultivation of the garden plots difficult. Even when possible, the foreign workers often did not enjoy the fruits of their labor because of pilferage. Sauckel even suggested that camp directors organize mass hunts for wild vegetables and fruits.

Eastern workers, in particular, added to their provisions by continually begging for food and ration coupons. German newspapers frequently admonished the population not to give foreigners ration coupons.[39] As far as non-rationed foods were concerned, the foreign workers were at a distinct disadvantage for the German authorities employed other control measures, such as identification cards and housekeeping permits, to limit the sale of these foodstuffs to Germans only.

The actual distribution of the food rations was done by the camp or factory canteen. Usually the food consisted of one cold meal in the morning and one warm meal in the evening. Foreigners working over ten hours per day were given a thin soup during the middle of the day at their place of work. Special regulations were issued allowing canteens to draw additional rations for this extra midday soup.[40] The foreign workers paid 1.00 RM daily for the standard ration and .20 RM extra for the soup. Usually employers made a straight deduction of 1.50 RM per day for room and board (this was set by law).

The canteens were sharply criticized by the foreign work-

[38] See reports of SD-Ab, Koblenz III, B2, on T-175, Roll 269, Frames 2765415-422.

[39] Fried, *Exploitation of Foreign Labour*, p. 98.

[40] Birkenholz, *Der auslaendische Arbeiter*, p. 208.

274

ers and German authorities. A spokesman for the Reich Ministry of Agriculture and Food argued that some workers were underfed not because of an insufficient amount of food but because of faulty food preparation by the camps. He hinted that the canteens were not using all the food they received.[41] Sauckel's inspection teams corroborated this view for they found that the food in many camps was poor and inadequate, primarily owing to incompetent kitchen management. All too often, the canteens were run as profitable concessions, which gave rise to considerable objections.[42] That some canteens were interested in profits seems inevitable, considering the enormous amounts of money involved. The German press estimated the annual turnover in foreign workers' canteens at 360 million RM.[43]

From mid-1942 on, the German authorities were actively propagandizing the need for better treatment of the foreign workers. More than anything else, the German military defeats in Russia forced the Nazis to change their methods of handling the foreigners. After Stalingrad the official party line was that the struggle against communism was an all-European matter, and out of this struggle a united Europe was growing. The foreign worker in the Reich was a symbol of the new Europe, and the Nazis were instructed to show the foreign worker by words and deeds how important European cooperation was.[44] It was imperative that the foreign workers receive sufficient rations. Every hour of work lost through illness or undernourishment was compared to a lost battle.

During the last year of the war, the Nazi authorities emphasized that differences in food rations between foreign

[41] Fried, *Exploitation of Foreign Labour*, p. 95.
[42] *Minor Trials*, VI, 743.
[43] *Voelkischer Beobachter*, October 20, 1943, p. 1.
[44] See Bormann's confidential memo to all party offices, dated May 5, 1943, in *IMT*, XXV, 298-301.

workers and German workers had been abolished. However, evidence indicates that the eastern workers never did receive the same amounts of food as German and non-eastern workers. Soviet workers were not given extra night rations, and they even received smaller rations for heavy work.[45] As late as August 1944, Sauckel had to remind employers that it was a punishable offense to reward foreigners with food or clothing for extra work.[46]

After Goebbels received the appointment as Plenipotentiary for Total War, the Nazi authorities tried a selective feeding policy. Employers were granted full authority over all their workers, German as well as foreign, and they were encouraged to use the food ration as a means to reward and punish workers on the basis of their production. Additional rations of cold food for good workers were to be deducted from the rations of the less willing workers.[47]

The changes in the Nazi food policy reflected the erosion of the Nazi racial philosophy throughout the war. The longer the war dragged on, the less important racial considerations became. Although the eastern workers derived slight advantages from the changes in the food policy, it is noteworthy that even then these gains came at the expense of their fellow foreign workers. The amount of suffering the Nazi food policy caused can never be estimated.

The price Nazi Germany paid for her foreign labor program in terms of the food supply was enormous. The inadequate diet reduced the productivity—the quality and quantity of work—of the foreign workers, and the burden of supplying even a minimal diet to eight million foreigners reduced the effectiveness of the German work force by de-

[45] *Minor Trials*, ix, 940; and interview of Robert Ley on October 2, 1945, p. 21.

[46] *Essener National-Zeitung*, August 31, 1944, p. 2.

[47] See RuKo Augsburg directive, dated August 5, 1944, on T-73, Roll 83, Frame 3230059; and *Deutsche Bergwerks-Zeitung*, August 26, 1944.

pleting their own foodstuffs. Even the Speer ministry criticized the foreign labor program because it had brought about a slow deterioration in the German food supply with a corresponding decrease in the output of German workers.[48] The annual food requirements for eight million foreign workers alone amounted to 700,000 tons of bread grains, 90,000 tons of fats, and 150,000 tons of meats,[49] or about the total amount of food imported from the Soviet Union during the last year before the invasion. To this must be added the additional cost of transportation, handling, and shortage. The total expenditure was a high price indeed to pay for unwilling workers but a price that most Nazi leaders refused to consider.

CLOTHING AND HEALTH

Foreign workers were required to bring their own clothing with them, including shoes, underwear, coats, and work clothes. The workers were not entitled to ration cards for clothing or shoes.[50] Only in cases of dire necessity could foreign workers acquire articles of clothing. While most of the western workers were reasonably outfitted when they arrived in the Reich, many of the eastern workers arrived in tattered rags. German authorities had to set up a system of renting clothes to these workers. Companies were allowed to rent clothing to their foreign workers at a fee deducted from their wages. The fee was fixed at a rate slightly higher than the expenses borne by German workers who did not participate in this scheme. Rented clothes were to be returned upon termination of work even if they had become unwearable.[51] Additional regulations allowed foreigners to receive, every three months, a ration coupon enabling them to buy .20 RM worth of sewing materials to repair their clothes.

[48] *Minor Trials*, XIII, 1124.
[49] Brandt, *Germany's Agricultural and Food Policies*, I, 612.
[50] *IMT*, XXXII, 207.   [51] *Reichsarbeitsblatt*, 1943, Part V, 75.

By the autumn of 1942, the clothing situation of the eastern workers had become desperate. The Remscheid Labor Office reported that only a quarter of its eastern workers had good working shoes and the rest of their clothes were in bad condition. Shortages in stockings, coats, underwear, and shirts were critical.[52] In some plants eastern workers had to work in their bare feet or in sandals with wooden soles.[53] Sauckel termed it an "emergency situation" (*Notstand*) and asked Funk, the Reich Minister of Economics, to allot to the foreign workers a considerable portion of the clothes collected by civilians for the *Wehrmacht* on the eastern front. At the same time, Sauckel organized a special campaign in the occupied areas to send clothes to eastern workers in the Reich.

After the publication of Bormann's decree of May 5, 1943, ordering strict but correct handling of foreign workers, clothing drives were organized in the Reich. The office of the *Gauleiter* in Baden, for example, reported that 21,000 pairs of shoes were collected for its 46,000 foreign workers.[54] In Vienna, 3,000 clothing coupons were donated to the foreign workers in the area.[55] But devices of this sort were not nearly enough. The East Ministry and Sauckel finally had to organize a special program to manufacture low-quality clothing for eastern workers. The uniform agreed upon consisted of a lined jacket and trousers for men and a lined jacket, skirt, and blouse for women. It was made from rags or a cellulose material.[56] Overcoats were not produced, although some eastern workers were supplied with them from existing stocks of old clothes. By October 1944, foreign workers were issued new clothes only if they turned in their old ones, since

[52] Remscheid Labor Office's monthly reports for 1942, in the files of the USSBS.
[53] *IMT*, xxxv, 58, 65-66, 74.
[54] *IMT*, xxxv, 646.   [55] *Minor Trials*, viii, 342.
[56] Braeutigam, *Ueberblick*, p. 94.

the production of clothing depended on the supply of rags collected.

The shortage in shoes among the eastern workers was never really solved. Initially, the eastern workers were to be supplied either with wooden shoes, or with shoes made of wooden soles and two straps and galoshes with wooden soles. The upper part of the galoshes and the shoes were made from material other than leather. Regulations for the easterner's shoes were issued by Goering in November 1941.[57] Goering had hoped that some of the eastern workers might be employed in their own workshops, which would construct the wooden shoes. However, the shoes were so poorly made that many eastern workers preferred going barefoot to injuring their feet by wearing them.

Strict penalties were imposed on foreign workers who stole or deliberately damaged clothes so that they could be turned in for new ones. Camp directors were continually cautioned that every article of clothing was of importance to the war economy. Foreign workers employed in plants using concentration camp inmates ran additional risks, because inmates often escaped by stealing civilian clothes. In the I. G. Farben plants at Leverkusen, four Polish workers were sent to a concentration camp because they had left their clothing in an unlocked hut, from which some concentration camp inmates had stolen them and escaped.[58]

The clothing policy followed by the Nazis was exactly like their feeding and housing policy. The employer was given complete authority over his workers within the general guide lines established by governmental offices. Clothes were requested, issued, collected and, in the case of eastern workers, often owned by the employer. The foreign worker without ration cards or the means of purchasing food and other

[57] *IMT*, xxxix, 500.
[58] *Minor Trials*, viii, 403.

279

necessities was literally controlled by his employer. By refusing to give the foreign workers ration cards and making
them completely dependent on their employers, the Germans
hoped to cut down on the amount of job switching and
escapes.

The Nazi health policy for the foreign workers varied as
much as the feeding policy. Originally foreign workers, except Poles, Russians, and Jews, were brought under the
German social insurance system. Foreigners were eligible
for unemployment, sickness, accident, and social security
benefits. They paid the same compulsory contributions of 9
per cent of their wages to German social insurance funds as
the Germans did and, in principle, they were to receive equal
treatment. In reality, the Nazis rigged the system so that the
foreigner received far less for his contribution. This was done
in a variety of ways. German authorities limited the benefits
to the foreign worker and his dependents in the Reich, and
they systematically directed that claims for insurance benefits and services be paid from the foreign fund, not the German one. The Germans also induced the occupied areas to
extend services to the dependents of their nationals employed
in the Reich.

Even when the foreign workers applied for services they
encountered difficulties. Foreigners' chances of receiving
medical treatment or hospitalization while in the Reich were
slim. Whenever possible, foreigners were to be treated in
their camps, while hospitalization was possible only in "quite
extraordinary cases."[59] Doctors were scarce and often skeptical of the ills of foreign workers, for the doctors were under
constant pressure to prevent unwillingness to work. Until
March 1943, the German authorities employed another control over foreigners' sickness benefits by transporting sick
and disabled workers back to their own countries. Sick foreigners whose recovery was not expected within two weeks

[59] Birkenholz, *Der auslaendische Arbeiter*, p. 96.

were to be sent back as soon as they were certified to travel. This procedure, plus many other legal, bureaucratic, and political difficulties, sharply reduced the foreign worker's chances of receiving his legitimate benefits under the German social insurance system.[60]

Polish and Soviet workers were not originally eligible for German insurance benefits, although a social assistance scheme was initiated by the Germans with the understanding that benefits were granted as privileges and the eastern workers were not legally entitled to them. Gradually, however, the eastern workers were given benefits similar to those of other foreigners. An order of August 1, 1942, allowed eastern workers medical and dental treatment necessary for the maintenance of labor efficiency. Workers were granted hospitalization and sick pay of 1.50 RM per day to cover their room and board. The workers' dependents in the Reich were granted similar medical care. The cost was to be borne by the employer alone.[61] In March of 1943, a special injury-accident insurance plan was introduced for eastern workers. Administrated by the Reich accident insurance fund, the order creating this program clearly stipulated that benefits could not be claimed as a right; they were granted only at the discretion of the Reich accident insurance fund. The special regulations dealing with eastern workers were repealed by a decree of March 25, 1944. After April 1, 1944, eastern workers were included in the general German social insurance system and had to pay the regular contributions.[62]

Although the eastern workers eventually received most of the benefits that other foreigners were entitled to, racial considerations blocked their full participation in the German

[60] For a detailed description of the operation of the German social insurance system, see Fried's *Exploitation of Foreign Labour*, pp. 208-238.

[61] Sauckel Defense Document 60, in the files of the Nuremberg Trials Collection.

[62] *Reichsgesetzblatt*, 1944, Part i, 68.

social insurance system. For example, maternity benefits were never paid to eastern women. The basic rules concerning pregnant foreign workers were established in August 1941, and stipulated that pregnant foreigners were to be sent home. In March 1943, these regulations were changed, allowing pregnant as well as sick and disabled foreign workers to remain in the Reich. Decrees by Sauckel in May 1943 and January 1944 extended the provisions of the Maternity Protection Act to cover Italian, Spanish, Bulgarian, Croatian, Slovak, Hungarian, Danish, Dutch, Norwegian, Rumanian, Swedish, Swiss, Latvian, Estonian, Finnish, and Flemish women. Benefits under the act provided for weekly subsidy equal to the average wages for six weeks before and six weeks after childbirth. Services of a midwife, contribution toward the expenses of confinement, medicine, medical care, and admission to a nursing home (hospitalization was not provided) were other services granted under this act. Polish, Soviet, French, and the majority of Czech and Yugoslavian women, as well as Belgians of Walloon origin and Jewish women of all nationalities, were excluded from this act.[63] These excluded foreign women were obligated to notify their employers of pregnancy as soon as they knew of their state so that they could claim certain exemptions from work, such as lighter assignments.

In some instances, Nazi officials encouraged or ordered abortions for eastern women. *Gauleiter* Karl Wahl of Swabia reported that in 1944 he received an abortion order but ignored it.[64] In Bayreuth, the health office reported that some doctors of the "reactionary Catholic clique" refused to perform abortions on eastern women who gave their permission.

[63] See "Gesetz zum Schutze der erwerbstaetigen Mutter," May 17, 1942, in *Reichsgesetzblatt*, 1942, Part i, 321, and amendments in *Reichsarbeitsblatt*, 1943, Part v, 58; 1943, Part iii, 141; and 1944, Part ii, 60.

[64] *IMT*, xlii, 35.

The health office wanted these cases reported to the SD so that they could keep the doctors under observation.[65]

Children of foreign workers in Germany were not to be returned to their homelands. Himmler sent special instructions that they were to be separated from German children. The *Reichsfuehrer SS* also wanted a thorough examination of the blood lines of children who were part German. Severe penalties were to be imposed if the racial laws were violated.[66] If the children were of the correct racial stock, they were to be "Germanized."

Eastern workers were prohibited from using public mineral baths, while the rest of the foreign workers were discouraged from using them unless they had a doctor's permission.[67] Even in death the eastern workers were discriminated against. Early in the war, Reich Minister of Labor Seldte prohibited the transportation of foreign workers' bodies back to their homeland. Funeral services for eastern workers were to be reduced to an absolute minimum.[68] Public cemeteries were ordered to make plots available for eastern workers at an ample distance from those intended for German graves.[69]

Although foreigners were entitled to medical care, frequently they were unable to obtain it because of the shortage of doctors and medical supplies. As a rule, foreigners were not to be treated by private doctors. They were to go to either the camp doctors or the health insurance doctors. To remedy

[65] Document RF 1542-1753 PS from the Bayreuth Health Office, dated October 25, 1943, in the files of the Nuremberg Trials Collection.

[66] Himmler's letter to all authorities, dated July 27, 1943, on T-175, Roll 409, Frames 2933143-144.

[67] Directive from the Reich Minister of the Interior, dated September 27, 1944, on T-175, Roll 416, Frames 2941594-595.

[68] *Reichsarbeitsblatt*, 1940, Part i, 528, and 1941, Part i, 326, 399. Late in 1944 the special regulations dealing with the burial of eastern workers were amended.

[69] *Reichsarbeitsblatt*, 1943, Part i, 455.

this situation Sauckel began to recruit foreign physicians and surgeons to care for the foreign workers in the Reich. Numerous inducements, such as nice homes, private practices, and the use of autos, were used to attract foreign doctors. Sauckel's attempts were only partially successful. A number of Ukrainian doctors came, but few others.[70] By the spring of 1944, there were only 2,500 foreign doctors in the Reich.[71]

Medical care for some of the POW's and eastern workers was practically non-existent. In Essen, for example, shortages of bandages, medicines, and professional help doomed many foreign workers to inhuman suffering and death.[72] Even favored nationalities complained about the inadequate medical care. The doctors were only interested in keeping the foreigners on the job; often, in their haste, they overlooked serious cases of illness.[73]

There can be little doubt that the foreign workers were guilty of malingering. Insufficient food, long hours of work, and harsh treatment forced many of them to try to get out of work in spite of the severe penalties if they were caught. Some workers went to two or more doctors in search of extra food rations, while others, more desperate, tried self-mutilation.[74]

The Nazis frequently emphasized that foreigners were accorded equal treatment with Germans. However, the health policy, like every other aspect of the foreign labor program, indicates that racial considerations and exploitation of subjected peoples were important ingredients in the Nazi attitude.

[70] USSBS, *Effects on Health*, p. 115.
[71] Fried, *Exploitation of Foreign Labour*, p. 215.
[72] See affidavits of Drs. Apolinary Gotowicki and Wilhelm Jaeger in *IMT*, xxxv, 57-66.
[73] Fried, *Exploitation of Foreign Labour*, p. 212.
[74] USSBS, *Effects on Health*, pp. 115-116.

FREE-TIME ACTIVITIES

Although there were no legal restrictions barring participation in German life, probably social and psychological
factors limited the foreign worker's desire to associate with
the German population. The difficulties that any foreigner
has in a strange country were magnified in wartime Germany. The war mood of the population, the propaganda
which made the German public suspicious of foreigners, and
the natural reluctance to share the few non-rationed goods
and the few remaining pleasures of life with members of
"enemy" nations must have sharply reduced the foreign
workers' opportunities for normal leisure activities. After
1942, with the intensification of the war, the closing of many
public amusements, and the billeting of foreigners in camps
instead of private quarters, the difficulty of finding suitable
free-time activities for the non-eastern worker was comparable to that of the eastern worker.

Political, racial, and police considerations dictated the extent to which eastern workers were able to enjoy their free
time. Shortly after the first large group of Polish workers
arrived in the Reich, the Nazi authorities imposed the
Untermensch concept on the Poles. Following the pattern
already established for the Jews, Poles were systematically
excluded from participation in German life. This meant barring them from all cultural, religious, and social functions
and limiting their contacts with the German population to
those that were absolutely necessary for their work. Separate
and distinctly unequal facilities were developed for the Poles.
Special Polish church services, inns, movies, sports events,
and social affairs were organized.[75]

After the appointment of Sauckel as GBA, more emphasis
was given to the free-time activities of the foreign worker.
Sauckel encouraged German authorities to organize sporting

[75] *NCA*, viii, 258-262.

events and other amusements for them. He also insisted that they have more freedom of movement. As a reward, eastern workers were to be allowed outside their living quarters, provided they had adequate German supervision. Sauckel also stopped the practice, which had begun with the Poles, of separating individual members of families working in the Reich. As far as possible, families were to be kept together and separate quarters were to be made for them. However, Sauckel maintained the racial policy of forbidding marriage among easterners within the borders of the Reich.[76]

In 1943, with the help of the DAF, 18,000 meetings, 4,000 sports events, 3,800 language courses, and 5,750 "Strength Through Joy" gatherings were organized in the 22,000 camps housing foreign workers. This meant that, on an average, there was one language course, one sports event, and one "Strength Through Joy" gathering in every fourth or fifth camp. During the same year, some 235,000 books, 4,940 radios, and 11,000 pieces of sporting equipment were distributed—an average of 11 books, 0.23 radios, and 0.5 pieces of sporting equipment per camp.[77]

Employers and camp directors were encouraged to set up entertainment rooms and recreational areas. In many camps this was impossible because of the crowded living conditions. Much more common in urban areas was the gradual takeover of German cafes and inns by foreign workers. Everywhere in Germany certain cafes became known as "foreign workers' cafes." German authorities reluctantly recognized this situation, but often they tried to stop German soldiers and women from visiting them, with little success. In Regensburg, for example, the district party leader warned Germans not to visit the Cafe Central because it was for French and other foreign nationals. In spite of his warning, Germans continued to visit the cafe because of the "alluring

[76] *IMT*, xxxviii, 427.
[77] *Voelkischer Beobachter*, October 20, 1943, p. 1.

Mediterranean music" they heard there. The party official even mentioned that the local Gestapo was thinking about allowing a cafe for the eastern workers.[78]

Vacations and furloughs had been promised foreign workers, usually after six or twelve months of work in Germany. During the first years of the war, foreigners received periodical leaves if their work proved satisfactory. However, with the mass importation of foreigners after the first Sauckel action in 1942, the German authorities decreed a maze of regulations to hinder and discourage foreigners from taking leaves. Originally eastern workers were not eligible for leaves, but this policy was modified, in theory at least, in 1943.[79] Incidentally, Polish industrial workers were allowed leaves until the Russian war, when German regulations aimed at Soviet workers were also applied to Poles. On July 23, 1943, new regulations were passed allowing eastern workers one week's vacation in the Reich after the completion of one year of satisfactory work, and two weeks at home after three years of work. In March of 1944, eastern workers were accorded the same leave privileges as German workers. All of these regulations were, of course, academic, since eastern workers seldom were given permission by German authorities to take their leaves.

Leaves for western foreign workers also became rarer after 1942. The great strain on the transportation system and the difficulty in obtaining permission of the labor offices, employers, and military authorities decreased interest in them. Then, too, the mass desertion of foreign workers on leave led to a drastic curtailment of furloughs. Although the Germans avoided announcing a complete and uniform halt to all leaves up to the summer of 1944, when Goebbels, in his position as Plenipotentiary for the Total War Effort,

[78] Letter from Regensburg *Kreisobmann*, dated January 12, 1944, on T-81, Roll 68, Frames 77835-836.

[79] *Reichsgesetzblatt*, 1942, Part i, 419.

ordered a ban on all holidays and furloughs, it was very doubtful if many western foreign workers had the chance to exercise their prerogative of taking leave after 1942.

Although the Nazis paid relatively little attention to most of the free-time activities of the foreign workers, they gave lavish attention to those activities which could be useful in influencing the workers ideologically. Movies, books, and especially newspapers were produced in large quantities for the foreigners. For example, by late 1943, there were fifteen foreign-language weekly or bi-weekly newspapers published for the workers. In addition, there were three special papers for miners in Russian, Ukrainian, and Croatian and two papers for agricultural workers in Dutch and Slovak. Circulation for some editions of these newspapers was as high as 80,000, while the combined total circulation for all the foreign-language newspapers was 750,000.[80] All of these newspapers were published by the *Fremdsprachen Verlag G.m.b.H.*, Berlin-Charlottenburg, by agreement with Goebbels' ministry. Foreign workers were also urged to buy Nazi-controlled newspapers and magazines published in their

[80] *Voelkischer Beobachter*, October 20, 1943, p. 1. The following newspapers were published: *Domovina Hrvatska* ("Homeland Croatia"), Croat; *Slovensky Tyzden* ("Slovak Week"), Slovak; *Broen* ("The Bridge"), Danish; *Van Honk* ("Away from Home"), Dutch; *Il Camerata* ("The Comrade"), Italian; *De Vlaamsche Post* ("Flemish Post"), Flemish; *Enlace* ("The Link"), Spanish; *L'Effort Wallon* ("Walloon Effort"), French; *Le Point* ("The Point"), French; *Cesky Delnik* ("The Czech Worker"), Czech; *Rodina* ("Homeland"), Bulgarian; *Trud* ("Labour"), Russian; *Ukrainez* ("The Ukrainian"), Eastern Ukrainian; *Holos* ("The Voice"), Western Ukrainian; *Bielaruski Rabotnik* ("The White Russian Worker"), White Russian. The special papers for miners were: *Schachtjor* ("The Miner"), Russian; *Na Schachti* ("In the Mine"), Ukrainian; and *Sretno* ("Welcome"), Croat. The paper for agricultural workers in Dutch was *De Landbauwer* ("The Farmer"), and in Slovak, *Uroda* ("The Product of the Soil"). See also Oron J. Hale's book, *The Captive Press in the Third Reich* (Princeton: Princeton University Press, 1964), pp. 279-283.

home countries. A number of such papers were on sale in the urban areas of Germany.

All of the foreign workers' newspapers were blatantly propagandistic, but since they were semi-official in nature they were widely read. Announcements dealing with wages, leaves, tax deductions, and social welfare benefits were published in them. In addition, the newspapers carried carefully screened articles on the war, Germany, and news from the home country, as well as the popular question-and-answer columns and letters to the editor. Politically, the newspapers stressed the community of interest between Germans and non-Germans by calling attention to the socialist intentions and achievements of the Third Reich, while degrading the social accomplishments of the workers' former governments. Needless to say, pronouncements from collaborationists from their own countries were played up. After May Day, 1942, the official line of propaganda emphasized that by their participation in the war effort the foreign workers were helping to build a "new and better Europe" which would respect the rights of the worker and guarantee him a higher standard of living.

A number of short one-reel films were produced for the foreign workers. Usually the contents of the films were the same—the necessity of the German victory, the advantages of working in the Reich, and the postwar prosperity of an European common market presided over by Germany.[81] Films produced for viewing by the peoples in the occupied areas were also shown in the camps, as well as some German films and newsreels.

Aside from books obtained from the occupied areas, the only other books published for foreigners in the Reich were technical and vocational ones. Sauckel encouraged labor

[81] See *Reichsring fuer Volksaufklaerung und Propaganda Hauptamt*, folder RPL 120, on T-81, Roll 673, Frames 5481380-420, for instructions dealing with propaganda for foreign workers.

offices to distribute foreign-language technical books as a part of his training program, but very little was done to translate German manuals because of the cost and the shortage of professional translators.

FOREIGN WORKERS AND THE GERMAN PUBLIC

The utilization of foreign workers in the Reich ran contrary, in many respects, to the ideology of the Nazis. One of the major war aims of the Nazis was the establishment of clearer racial separation. Yet, by necessity, the Nazis brought millions of foreigners into the Reich to work. Many of the earlier pronouncements of Nazi officials, after the inception of the foreign labor program, were defensive in attitude and apologetic in tone. The German people were told that this was only a temporary wartime condition and that after the war the foreigners were to be sent home. Germans were continually warned that they should guard themselves against any intimacies which might lead to violation of the purity of the German race. Although Nazi propaganda concerning the use of foreigners in the Reich gradually changed through the war from resentment to grudging acceptance, it never varied from the original concept of racial purity. Even in the last few catastrophic months of the Third Reich, in true Mad Hatter form, Nazi officials were firing off directives reminding the German people of the necessity of maintaining the racial laws.[82]

The *Blut und Boden* concept of Nazism was also undermined by the use of foreigners because the Nazis wanted eventually to create a peasant state based on modern industrial techniques. The sturdy, biologically pure, and strong peasantry was always considered the racial repository of the German *Volk*. The mystique of *Blut und Boden* dic-

[82] See directives of Himmler and others from November 1944 to April 1945, on T-73, Roll 97, Frames 3251031-34, 3251049-53, and 3251086-94.

tated that nothing should break the sacred relationship between the German peasant and his soil. The German farmer
and worker was never to be allowed to become a master, over-
seeing the work of foreigners in the hard manual occupations.
The importance that Nazi circles attached to maintaining the
flow of German workers to such hard manual labor as agriculture and mining was significant. Franz Seldte expressed
these sentiments in a broadcast on October 23, 1940. He
said:

> We must never reach a point where mining and agricul-
> ture, any more than any other occupations, become occu-
> pations for foreign workers. Both agriculture and mining
> will remain in the future spheres in which the German
> worker is supreme, and our young people have every
> reason to look for training and advancement in these
> particular industries.[83]

Friedrich Syrup echoed the same ideas when he told the
German people that after the war the foreigners would be
dismissed from these occupations because the soil could only
belong to the people who plow it and the coal to those who dig
it. The conditions in France, where foreigners did much of
the hard manual labor, must be considered a "horrible
lesson" for the German people.[84]

Although during the war it was not possible to reconcile
the national and racial doctrines of Nazism with the need
for millions of foreign workers, the Nazis did satisfy some
of their racial doctrines by discriminating and segregating
foreigners, particularly the eastern workers. The policy of
segregation and discrimination was organized, in a sense, to
assuage the Nazi conscience and to show the German worker
that the regime was still trying to uphold its racial and po-

[83] *Reichsarbeitsblatt*, 1940, Part v, 519.
[84] Friedrich Syrup, *Arbeitseinsatz im Krieg und Frieden* (Essen:
Essener Verlagsanstalt, 1942), p. 15.

litical doctrines. In other words, the policy of methodical, harsh treatment of the foreigner was organized in part for the psychic benefit of the German worker. Dr. Ley, who made it a point to shake hands only with German workers while inspecting factories, clearly perceived the necessity of this policy. Ley told Braeutigam once that the "trusting German worker would not understand it if the contrast between him and the eastern worker disappeared."[85]

The political and racial doctrines of the regime, as well as considerations of military security, militated against the development of genuine social relations between foreign workers and Germans. The years of racial indoctrination, the war hysteria, and the sheer magnitude of the foreign labor program created uneasiness which increased as the war proceeded. As German farms and factories, cities and countryside, resounded more and more with the babble of foreign tongues, the problem of social relationships between foreigner and German became more acute.

The foreign worker's most immediate contact with the German populace came through their jobs. Working alongside of Germans day after day, it was inevitable that in spite of Nazi admonitions and dire newspaper accounts of Germans who were punished for fraternizing with foreign workers, some friendships would develop. Judging from Nazi and western sources, the German peasants, in particular, paid too little attention to official policies of discriminations toward foreigners, much to the distress of Nazi officialdom. Frequently foreign workers ate at the same table with the peasants and received the same treatment as German farm hands.[86] As *Gauleiter* Wahl of Swabia reported, it was impossible to enforce the segregation instructions in the rural

[85] Braeutigam, *Ueberblick*, p. 95; and Ley's interview of October 2, 1945, p. 14.

[86] *IMT*, xxxv, 635-636; and David Rodnick, *Postwar Germans* (New Haven: Yale University Press, 1948), pp. 12-13.

areas; the peasants simply were ignoring them.[87] The prevailing attitude in the rural areas was one of sympathy toward the foreigners, and by 1944 this was true in urban areas as well.[88]

Evidence of German workingmen's sympathy for foreign workers was, however, contradictory. David Rodnick, in *Postwar Germans*, mentioned the lack of peasant hostility toward the foreigners, yet he felt that only six out of one hundred German workers could identify themselves with the foreigners, despite traditional indoctrination by the socialists before the Hitler period. Rodnick explained this attitude by claiming that the German worker felt himself to be as much a victim of unfair treatment as was the foreign worker, hence he had little sympathy to spare.[89] A political scientist with the U.S. Army felt that there had been little contact between the foreigners and Germans, although certain favored nationalities like the French were well treated.[90] A pilot study of French workers by the USSBS indicated that the French, as might be expected, showed considerable understanding of the German population and especially the working class of the Reich.[91]

A detailed study of Belgian workers in the Reich made after the war reported that the rapport between the Belgian and German workers was normal.[92] Perhaps the best summation of the western foreign worker's relationship with the German worker was given by a Frenchman who told a reporter, "We worked hard, too. The German workers liked us, and we got along with most of them. But we had so little to eat."[93]

[87] *IMT*, XLII, 35.   [88] Shils, "Aspects of Displacement," p. 8.

[89] Rodnick, *Postwar Germans*, p. 4.

[90] S. K. Padover, *Experiment in Germany* (New York: Duell, Sloan and Pearce, 1946), pp. 17-19.

[91] USSBS, *Effects on Morale*, II, 60-61.

[92] Jacquemyns, *La Société belge sous l'occupation*, III, 31-34.

[93] Percy Knauth, *Germany in Defeat* (New York: Alfred A. Knopf, 1946), p. 73.

The case of the eastern peoples was different. The literally hundreds of documents submitted at the Nuremberg trials attested to the fact that the eastern worker received little sympathy from the German working class. The deep-seated fear of the easterners, coupled with the Nazi racial propaganda about their inferiority, made it difficult for the Germans to achieve any empathy with them. Then, too, the obvious mistreatment of the eastern workers evoked the usual syndrome of guilt in the Germans. German behavior toward the easterners was capricious, ranging from ferocity to affection. The following examples clearly illustrate the point. When a Russian worker named Gagiel told some German workers that ". . . everything will soon be ruined in Germany, then all officials, foremen, masters, plant chiefs, . . . will have their throats cut. Then we (Russians) will live in good houses; you Germans will live in barracks," the Germans beat him and turned him over to the SD, which sentenced him to death.[94] On the other hand, in an I. G. Farben plant, the German workers were so incensed at the sight of concentration camp inmates being flogged that they joined with Polish workers in walking off the job.[95] In a Krupp plant, SS *Scharfuehrer* Grollius refused to bring Russians to work when they were not fed, even though his fellow guards insisted that the workers should receive a beating instead of food.[96]

In part, the German worker's attitude toward the foreign worker was colored by his perfectly natural desire to be a good patriotic citizen of the Reich. The government made a consistently strong effort to enlist the aid of the worker in watching the foreigners for any signs of sabotage or insubordination. Being loyal and German, they took their responsibility seriously. Very little missed their attention. Although

[94] *Minor Trials*, IX, 910.
[95] *Minor Trials*, VIII, 403.
[96] *Minor Trials*, IX, 875-877.

the USSBS reported that 86 per cent of the Russians, 50 per cent of the French, and 34 per cent of the Italians who were interviewed thought they saw some form of resistance activity among foreign workers, the German employers, workers, and officials uniformly reported little or no resistance during the war.[97] There was only one instance of open mutiny by foreign workers, excluding, of course, the last days of the war, when all order broke down. This involved some Russian workers in Hamburg in the summer of 1943, and the mutiny was promptly crushed by Himmler's police units. It was indeed remarkable that the foreigners showed so little open defiance, considering their predicament.

The foreign worker's relationship with his employer was also varied. Generally the western workers found their German employers no more difficult to work for than their employers at home. Also many plants quickly saw the advantages of promoting some foreigners to foremen over work gangs of the same nationality. Often members of these work gangs were given special wages, rest periods, and other privileges commensurate with their efficiency. This technique received the encouragement of various Reich officials.[98]

The biggest single factor affecting the foreign worker's relationship with his employer was the security problem. Nazi police and labor regulations granted the employer a wide range of powers over his employees, especially the foreign workers. Employers were obligated to determine the attitude of their workers and report every instance of violation of the prescribed regulations. Needless to say, in wartime Germany there were a host of things that could be construed as labor, political, or economic violations. Such things as spreading rumors and defeatist propaganda, handling tools so roughly that they might be damaged, failing to work

[97] USSBS, *Effects on Morale*, II, 22 ff.
[98] Otto K. Krauskopf, *Der Auslaendische Arbeiter in Deutschland* (Berlin: Verlag fuer Wirtschaftsschriften, 1943), Vol. I, p. 173.

hard enough, and malingering all came under the heading of offenses. Such offenses were dealt with by the employers, who were granted police powers by Sauckel and Himmler. For example, employers' rights to punish workers ranged from leveling small fines to sending workers to labor education camps for six weeks. These camps (*Arbeitserziehungslager*) were constructed by the employers under directives sent by Himmler. Foreign workers confined to these camps were to work hard ten hours but not more than twelve hours every day of the week. They received .50 RM per day and could be confined for six weeks at the utmost, since a longer duration might have an adverse effect on the worker's capability.[99] In one of the Krupp plants, the guards for Russian camps were ordered to deal ruthlessly with the slightest sign of resistance, insubordination, or disobedience. In the event that the Russians tried to escape, the guards were ordered to shoot to hit them.[100] That these harsh methods of handling foreign workers did not set very well with some Germans can be inferred from comments made by Nazi officials. Sauckel said once of the harsh treatment of Soviet POW's and the need for obtaining more work from them, ". . . the thought that POW's through their work primarily fill the wallets of the entrepreneur, and hence must be protected from him, is erroneous."[101] Field Marshal Milch, commenting on the difficulties with foreign workers, blamed the misguided bureaucracy of overfed teachers, sports leaders, and other "academic types" for complaining too much that foreigners could not be handled as decently as they would be in peacetime.[102]

The foreign workers' contacts with the German general public were limited. Again the peasants seemed to accept them while the urban population became increasingly uneasy

[99] See Himmler's circular on labor camps, dated May 28, 1941, on T-175, Roll 197, Frames 2737116-123; and *Minor Trials*, XIII, 1027-1028.
[100] *Minor Trials*, IX, 890.
[101] *NCA*, III, 227.   [102] *Minor Trials*, II, 534.

about the lack of protection and the large number of foreigners. Naturally the foreigners were blamed for many things, such as looting after air raids, hogging seats on trains and buses, writing nasty slogans and words like "Boche" in public places, and laughing about air-raid damage.[103] One of the most prevalent rumors about the foreigners concerned an organization which was to set fire to buildings during air raids. Yet a composite affidavit of 15,433 Germans submitted at Nuremberg mentioned specifically that there were no instances of foreigners involved in setting fires, and in fact many foreigners freely helped out in air-raid work.[104]

Of course, it would be impossible to give a definitive answer to the problem of the foreign worker's relationship with the German public. But in view of the depersonalized, atomized society of Nazi Germany, it is easy to assume that life was grim for the foreigner. Wrenched from his native homeland, often in a brutal manner, the foreigner found himself dumped into an alien, sometimes hostile society. He was scrutinized by Germans for any sign of resistance, and even spied upon by informers among the foreign workers. For every small kindness, there was probably a humiliation and often much worse. One can be only amazed at the silent courage and determination of these foreign workers.

In summary, for most of the eastern workers and some of the western workers, life in the Reich was one long, continual nightmare of hard work, insufficient food, inadequate quarters, personal discrimination, and cruelty. The Germans' fear of eastern workers who went berserk was typical. Cases of entire German families who were slaughtered by foreign workers were not rare.[105] Yet, when the final collapse of the Reich occurred, the foreigners showed remarkable restraint, for there was no general jacquerie, only widespread random

[103] See correspondence to SD/Aussenstelle Aachen, on T-175, Roll 249, Frames 2741153-161, for some typical examples of German complaints about the foreign workers.

[104] *IMT*, XLII, 350-351.

[105] Shils, "Aspects of Displacement," p. 9.

looting and some individual murders.[106] After years of oppression, the foreign workers were primarily interested in returning home as quickly as possible.

The first western observers in the Reich after the war thought it remarkable that the foreign workers did not seek revenge.[107] After the shock of finding the concentration and extermination camps, it was only natural that western observers would assume that all foreigners had been subjected to considerable mistreatment. Although this study has not been primarily concerned with the individual treatment of the foreign worker, it can readily be surmised that the stereotype of "slave labor" applied at the Nuremberg war trials to the foreign labor program was too inclusive. Undoubtedly, there was "slave labor" in the concentration camps, and undoubtedly forced labor was an extermination device practiced by the Nazis against peoples they considered inferior. Undoubtedly racial considerations and the desire to exploit foreigners were important for the Nazis, yet it would be a gross error to assume that the single term "slave labor" could accurately describe a complex and constantly changing labor program involving millions of foreign workers over a six-year period.

To the overwhelming majority of German people who worked side by side with the foreign workers and endured the same rigors of air bombing, food shortages, and long hours of work, the foreign labor program was only an economically expedient device to win the war. That some of the foreign workers concurred with this German view can be surmised from the fact that nearly three-quarters of a million of them, mostly eastern workers, refused repatriation to their homelands after the war.[108]

[106] USSBS, *Effects on Morale*, II, 60-61.
[107] Cf. Knauth, *Germany in Defeat*, p. 12; Padover, *Experiment in Germany*, p. 343; and Shils, "Aspects of Displacement," p. 14.
[108] Shils, "Aspects of Displacement," p. 15.

CHAPTER XIII

Microcosm of the Nazi World

C ONQUERORS from the pharaohs of ancient Egypt to the totalitarian dictators of our own century have dreamed of, planned, and tried to use the human resources of their conquests. The Nazi foreign labor program was no exception, but this twentieth-century example does illustrate the scope, methods, results, and weaknesses of a totalitarian regime. The entire Nazi world was reflected in the program—the inherent anomalies in the Nazi ideology, the fierce struggle for power among the leaders, the ever-changing war strategy, and the vicious in-fighting between governmental agencies.

The pattern of the foreign labor program had its origins in German history, Nazi philosophy, and immediate requirements of the blitzkrieg strategy. Historically, Germany had a long and continuous experience with seasonal foreign workers in the Reich, and although the Nazis did not have a preconceived plan for the utilization of foreigners at the outbreak of the war, they certainly were aware of the possibilities of using their conquered human resources. Then, too, Germany's experiences in World War I were well known. The Kaiser's feeble and futile attempts at recruiting foreigners and the importance of the labor shortage during the last two years of that war were constant reminders to the Nazis that the German domestic manpower supply was not adequate for any protracted war. Even the first area conquered in World War II reminded the Nazis of the possibilities of using foreigners, for western Poland was traditionally the major recruiting area for German agriculturalists who were seeking seasonal workers.

The influence of Nazi philosophy on the origins of the foreign labor program is less clear. Granting the obvious fact that the Nazi philosophy, impregnated with racialism, opportunism, and collectivism, could easily lend itself to exploiting the labor of others for its own goals, the decision to set up a foreign labor program should have led the Nazis into a logical quandary. Yet once the war started, circumstances favored a practical solution to the manpower shortage—drafting foreigners—rather than concern about the more theoretical considerations of what effect mixing foreigners with Germans would have on the Reich in the future.

Still, the decision to use foreign workers in the Reich definitely compromised a part of the Nazi ideology and many Nazis were uneasy about it. As a result, German handling of the foreign labor program was never as resolute as it might have been. The Nazis were continually plagued by the ensuing tension that developed between their ideology and the expediencies of war. Even routine administrative decisions concerning the foreign workers took on ideological overtones; nothing could be settled on a completely pragmatic basis. As a general rule, however, as long as the Nazis were confident that they were winning the war, ideology took precedence over expediency; but once the Nazis sensed that the war was going to be a long one, the reverse was true as far as the foreign workers were concerned. The major exceptions to this rule, as is commonly known, were the Jews and other groups condemned as racially undesirable by the SS.

The Hitlerian blitzkrieg strategy swung the balance in favor of the foreign labor program in spite of obvious Nazi philosophical objections. In the early days of the war, the Nazi leaders were by no means convinced of the infallibility of the blitzkrieg concept. The rapid but poorly coordinated mobilization of the German Army which tore gaping holes in the manpower economy—already considered taut—and the muted enthusiasm of the German populace toward the opening of the war seemed to bode evil for the Reich. The reluctance of Hitler and the Gauleiters' circle to prepare for total mobilization by drafting German women for work, slashing consumer goods, subordinating racial and political considerations to further economic and military ones, precluded any subsequent help in those areas. The timing of the attack on Poland at the height of the harvest season intensified the apprehensions that existed in the minds of Goering and Backe. The combination of all of these factors inevitably led these two Nazi leaders to the same conclusion: foreigners had to be used immediately. Reluctantly, the two leaders decided to ignore some of the racial tenets of Nazism and begin the task of improvising a foreign labor program for the Reich.

As soon as the blitzkrieg strategy was vindicated by the military triumphs in Poland and France, the Nazi leaders—their confidence now restored—showed a positive preference for the foreign labor program as opposed to the less attractive alternative of complete mobilization. The successes of the blitzkrieg indicated to the Nazis that they could be allowed all things at once, including a "peacelike war economy." Moreover, they need not make difficult choices between racial and political considerations on one hand, and economic and military ones on the other.[1] The Nazis could pursue all of them simultaneously. As a result, the labor program became characteristically a fusion of Nazi objectives that were in reality dichotomous. The Nazis were going to use the foreign labor program to strengthen their economic might; yet at the same time, they were going to use it as a

---

[1] For instance, the SS did attempt at times to link their extermination campaign with the foreign labor program in Poland. See the letters of Dr. Wilhelm Hagen, chief German physician in Warsaw, to Hitler protesting the murder of 70,000 Poles during a planned resettlement of 200,000 Poles in Germany as war workers, on T-175, Roll 38, Frames 2547999-8011. The SS accused Hagen of Social Democratic party loyalties and a complete lack of understanding of Nazi policies. The SS sent him to a concentration camp in March 1943.

3 0 1

means of enforcing racial and political ideas on their subject peoples.

During the first two years of the war, German officials experimented with the foreign labor program. The early stages were plagued by unclear lines of authority, bureaucratic confusion, and indecisiveness. The first draft of over a million Polish workers, in January 1940, was handled by Dr. Werner Mansfeld, Goering's Chief of Labor Allocation in the Four Year Plan. Without any specific authorization, precedence, or guide lines, Mansfeld had to direct and coordinate into a smooth operation the activities of his own office, the Reich ministries of the Interior, Labor, Food, Munitions, and Transportation, the Army, and Frank's General-Government office in occupied Poland.

The *Untermensch* philosophy was applied to the Polish workers without particular success. Racial, wage, and working discriminations used by the Germans against the Poles only complicated the tasks of effectively recruiting and utilizing these eastern workers. The imposed restrictions bore heaviest on the German administration in occupied Poland. In spite of growing evidence that the racial policies of the Nazi party were hindering the foreign labor program in the East, the Germans did manage to meet their urgent labor needs from the Polish reservoir; what they lacked in finesse, they compensated for in force. The Polish experience had become, by 1940, a forerunner of the later mass recruitment drives by Sauckel.

The foreign labor program in the East, characterized by forced recruitment, racism, and massive scale, sharply contrasted with the program extended to the newly occupied western areas of Europe. In the West, the program was voluntary, devoid of stringent racial overtones, small-scaled, and sporadic in operation. At first, Germany capitalized on the widespread unemployment and the vast number of prisoners of war in order to fulfill its labor requirements. In a sense, these groups of workers were mobilized by their former governments and turned over to the Germans, ready to be used. Only later, when it was realized that all the resources of the conquered areas were needed for the war effort, did Germany confront a complete set of problems. Decisions had to be made on the basis of priorities; programs had to be organized which would not conflict; and, most important of all, the resistance of an alien population had to be overcome.

The contribution of Germany's allies and the neutral nations to the foreign labor program was modest during the first two years of the war. All of Germany's allies signed a series of agreements with the German Foreign Office calling for the recruitment of their nationals to work in the Reich, but the total number of workers involved was small, and the concessions that the Germans gave these workers indicated that the agreements were token. Only Italy, a land of chronic unemployment, seemed willing to recruit a substantial amount of labor. The neutrals were understandably reluctant to allow many of their workers to leave for the Reich, although German private firms were able to recruit some specialists from the unemployed of these countries through wage inducements.

The real turning point in the foreign labor program—and, for that matter, in the entire German war economy—came after the first winter of war in Russia. The failure of the *Wehrmacht* to crush the Red Army in a swift campaign and the entrance of the United States into the war altered German economic policies completely. The death of Reich Minister Todt and the appointment of Speer to his position coincided with the abandonment of the blitzkrieg strategy and the entry of economically oriented realists, rather than political-minded doctrinaires, in the highest echelons of the Reich's economy. Speer, a proponent of armament in depth, launched a series of reforms aimed at broadening the industrial base of the Reich, rationalizing production procedures,

and centralizing the administration of the economy. To supply the necessary labor for the Speer reforms, Hitler picked
Sauckel, the *Gauleiter* of Thuringia. Speer and Sauckel were
to revamp the war economy.

From the beginning, however, Speer and Sauckel clashed
incessantly; their personalities, philosophies, and methodol-
ogies were fundamentally opposite. Speer was the young,
ambitious, brilliant technocrat, suspicious of and impatient
with the bombastic, plodding Nazi functionaries who surrounded him. Shielded by his personal friendship with Hitler, Speer, a relative newcomer to the ranks of the Nazi top
echelon, thought and acted boldly after his appointment as
Munitions Minister. Immediately sensing the fluidity and
drift of the German economic administration, Speer deliberately plotted to make himself master of the war economy.
He planned to marshal all of Germany's human and material
resources under his command and give the Reich a coher-
ent, well-directed war economy—but Sauckel and the Gauleiters opposed Speer's grand design.

Sauckel, the long-time *Gauleiter* and typical Nazi doctrinaire, fought to gain control over labor and to remain independent of Speer. Speer thought that Sauckel was
legalistic, dogmatic, and a born intriguer, representing everything wrong with the German administration. Sauckel, on
the other hand, thought Speer overimpulsive, reckless, and
vain. But Sauckel had other reasons for disliking the young
architect. The *Gauleiter* came from the atavistic pro-labor,
anti-capitalistic wing of the party that took seriously what
little was left of socialism in National Socialism. Along with
most of the other Gauleiters, Sauckel identified Speer with
the pro-business, aristocratic, *nouveau riche* element in the
party that had gained prominence after 1930, much to the
displeasure of the *Alter Kaempfer*. In many ways, then, the
Sauckel-Speer feud was the externalization of the internal

contradictions in the nature of National Socialism that had plagued the party throughout its existence.

Another root of the Speer-Sauckel dispute was Hitler's indecisiveness, which encouraged empire-building among his lieutenants. When Hitler appointed Sauckel and Speer to new positions in the spring of 1942, he did not delineate clearly their authorities and responsibilities. Both were to serve under the Four Year Plan Office, but Speer had assumed that Sauckel was to be his subordinate, while Sauckel felt that his position was equal to Speer's. Both of these ambitious men had arrived at the same conclusion independently; Germany needed an absolute czar to coordinate and direct the war economy. Each felt at the time of his appointment that Hitler had given him the mandate for power. Conflict was inevitable, but Sauckel was no match for Speer. Within six months, Speer had wrestled control of the economy from the other grasping Nazi leaders and was rapidly becoming Goering's heir apparent.

The general lack of a tight administrative system also encouraged friction between Sauckel and Speer. Their respective administrative organizations were conglomerates of parts of the old Reich ministries, bits of Goering's Four Year Plan offices, and newly established wartime agencies. Sauckel's organization, for example, consisted of three sections of the Reich Labor Ministry, Goering's Labor Allocation Office, and the newly created GBA Office. Later in the war, Sauckel grafted the Gauleiters' party administration and the regional and local labor offices' administration to his organization. Yet, in spite of the creeping spread of his organization, Sauckel was never close to being supreme in the labor field. The Army had control over drafting policies; the German Labor Front supervised the welfare and training of German workers; the *Zentrale Planung* distributed labor to industry; the Food Ministry handled agricultural labor; and, of course, SS *Reichsfuehrer* Himmler had undisputed jurisdiction over security and racial policies dealing with all workers and absolute control over a sizable group of workers in the concentration camps. Speer's organization was hardly any better. It consisted of the Ministry of Armament and War Production, two sections of Goering's Four Year Plan offices, parts of the Ministry of Economics and, later in the war, the Armament Inspectorates and Commissions of the Army, Navy, and Air Force. It was no wonder that in this atmosphere of blurred lines of administration, authority, and responsibility, bitter struggles for power occurred.

Although Speer established himself as virtual economic dictator by the middle of 1943, Sauckel never accepted Speer's supremacy and continually sought to undermine the young architect. Through his close connections with Bormann and the Gauleiters' circle, Sauckel sought, until the last days of the war, to subvert the work and position of Speer.

Sauckel's vendetta with Speer did not, however, prevent him from accomplishing his major mission of gathering millions of foreigners for the Reich. By being eminently successful in recruiting foreign workers, Sauckel hoped to enhance his own claims for leadership of the economy. What distinguished Sauckel's handling of foreign labor was not the addition of new techniques of recruitment or utilization of foreigners, but the scope, attitude, and intensity of the program under his management.

The foreign labor program under Sauckel's predecessor, Mansfeld, was a mere adjunct to the Four Year Plan designed to supply additional labor to the war plants and farms of the Reich. When the foreign labor program was reorganized in the spring of 1942, with Sauckel as its head, he was given charge not only of foreign, but also of domestic labor. In a sense, the labor in the occupied areas was integrated in the Reich economy and treated as a part of an organic entity. Sauckel's first actions in office indicated this shift in attitude.

Immediately, Sauckel issued and enforced compulsory work regulations in occupied areas similar to those used in the Reich. Sauckel also began to call up age classes in the East. Later, after he had pressured the Vichy-styled governments in the West, he began to call up age classes there, too. Nazi Germany's labor resources, stretching from the Volga to the English Channel, were finally brought under a program with some degree of uniformity.

Sauckel's appointment coincided with a change in attitude among some ranking Nazi officials toward the foreign workers. Goebbels, Speer, and Sauckel, in particular, realized that if they expected effective work from the foreigners, many of the earlier Nazi policies would have to be relaxed, living conditions improved, and more time and energy expended in training, placing, and utilizing the foreigners. Of equal importance was the necessity of convincing the rank and file of the Nazi party and the masses of Germany that the supply of foreign workers was not inexhaustible and that Germany had to have maximum use of every German within the Reich as well as every foreigner under its control.

However, the long years of Nazi indoctrination were not so easily reversed. Racial hatred, constant claims of victory, and sheer inertia made it difficult to change the prevailing manner of using foreigners. Speer remarked after the war that, sealed off from all sources of criticism and free comment, the Nazi state became a victim of its own propaganda,[2] and the handling of Germany's manpower supply was a case in point. The Nazi ideology, like all ideologies, had blinded its devotees to reality. The Nazis exhibited a truly schizophrenic attitude toward foreigners. At the same time that Goebbels, Speer, and Sauckel were calling for maximum utilization of foreign labor, other Nazis were allowing millions of Russian POW's to die in open camps in Russia,

[2] Interview of Albert Speer, May 22-23, 1945, in the files of the USSBS, p. 5.

and the SS was busily engaged in its grisly task of mass extermination. In spite of constant exhortations by Goebbels and Sauckel, it was not until the closing months of the war that all foreign workers except the Jews were treated in a manner comparable to that accorded the German workers in the Reich. But even then, while the extermination camps were operating at top speed, Goebbels and Sauckel failed to see the inconsistency of an extermination program and a foreign labor program.

Regardless of ideological confusion, administrative floundering, and personality clashes, one thing emerged clearly; Sauckel was extremely successful in securing foreign labor for the Reich. In four recruiting campaigns, from the spring of 1942 until December of 1944, Sauckel managed to procure over five million new foreign workers for the German war economy. When one considers the tremendous difficulties encountered, this was a remarkable achievement. Indeed, the ability of the Nazi state to recruit and assimilate millions of foreigners into its sophisticated and complex economy is an ominous portent of the efficiency and productive capabilities of a ruthless totalitarian regime.

By the end of 1944, one out of every five workers in the Reich was a foreigner. They constituted the only supply of manpower for industries that demanded heavy labor, and by the last two years of the war the foreign workers had become the backbone of the mining, steel, and chemical industries. Without these millions of foreign workers, it is doubtful that Nazi Germany could have remained in the war as long as she did. In fact, by using foreigners in her factories and fields, Nazi Germany was able to draft thirteen million German men into the military services, which not only held out for years against overwhelming odds, but came very near to winning the war.

But the statistical record of the number of foreign workers in the Reich does not tell the entire story. Undoubtedly, they were less efficient than the German workers. How much more efficient they could have been had conditions been different can be only a matter of idle speculation. Of more importance is an evaluation of the advantages of eight million foreign workers against the disadvantages of the program itself. In other words, was the foreign labor program worth while?

The use of foreign labor was certainly a contributing cause of the alienation of the peoples in the German-occupied areas. In places like the Ukraine where the Germans could have capitalized on their initial reception, their brutal policies were a major factor in the destruction of every vestige of local sympathy. After a few months of German rule in the Ukraine, the flow of volunteer workers for the Reich ceased because, as Speer reported after the war, "immense mistakes were made in their treatment by us."[3] Once forceful recruitment started, German occupational difficulties in the Ukraine were only compounded. Antagonized by Nazi racial policies, misrule, and forced recruitment, the Ukrainians responded with passive and, later, open resistance to their conquerors.

In every other area where the Germans instituted forced labor drafts for the Reich, the results were the same— sabotage, partisan movements, and resistance. Everywhere, the foreign labor program placed a heavy additional burden on the German occupation authorities and the Army. Each time the Germans removed a worker from the occupied areas, they generated more hostility toward their own rule and, incidentally, diminished by one productive worker the agricultural or industrial potential of that area.

Within the Reich itself, the foreign labor program had more subtle and damaging effects on the German war effort. The program was too successful, too soon. To Germans within the Reich, the apparent ease and speed with which Sauckel managed to recruit three million foreigners in 1942

---

[3] Pre-trial interrogations of Albert Speer, October 18, 1945, in the files of the Nuremberg Trials Collection, p. 8.

and the beginning of 1943 perpetuated the complaisant Nazi propaganda attitude that "victory is at hand." The program also obscured the obvious defects (obvious at least to Speer, Thomas, and others) in the mobilization and utilization of domestic German labor. By supplying enough labor to German industry in this period, Sauckel was merely delaying or, better perhaps, postponing the eventual day when Germany would be obliged to tackle the much more difficult problem of thorough mobilization, with its many unpleasant aspects, such as drafting more German women into industry and drastically reducing consumer production.

Sauckel's program was producing effects diametrically opposed to the Speer reforms. By seeming to supply the necessary labor for Germany, by ignoring the dictates of the Speer-dominated *Zentrale Planung* on labor distribution, and by constantly intriguing at the *Gauleiter* level against Speer, Sauckel was able to slow down or nullify most of Speer's manpower reforms. Furthermore, Sauckel's success in recruiting foreigners certainly stiffened the Gauleiters' opposition to Speer's plan for total mobilization. Thus, in the critical period from spring of 1942 until the close of 1943, Sauckel, his foreign labor program, and those persons in the Nazi leadership who so energetically supported it managed to block the Speer reforms long enough to make them too late. It was for this reason that Hans Kehrl, at Nuremberg, characterized Sauckel's foreign labor program as "the biggest of all mistakes made by the leadership."[4]

That Sauckel and other political leaders could effectively check the well-designed plans of the economic arbiter of the Reich for such a long period of time indicated the inherent weaknesses of the Nazi totalitarian state. In such a state, which espoused the twin doctrines of blanketed secrecy and the omniscient leader, the art of governing was lost. Without the benefits of open discussion and orderly methods of hand-

[4] *Minor Trials*, XIII, 1127.

ling conflicts, it proved impossible to make self-correcting moves. In such a state, where power was concentrated in one man who was not always rational, minister was pitted against minister and personal friendship with the leader, or his secretary, or his doctor might be of more value to a minister than the most expertly conceived plans.[5] In such a state, decision-making was arrived at through a process of savage, personal, and political in-fighting with the inevitable result of demoralizing everyone concerned.

In particular, the history of the foreign labor program illustrated the weaknesses of the Nazi brand of totalitarianism. Administratively, the foreign labor program exemplified the near-chaos in the Nazi state. Torn by personal dissension and intrigue, and racked by a conflict-ridden organizational structure, the foreign labor program was never able to function smoothly. Ironically, the very fortes of the Nazis—their activism, their flair for the dramatic, their emotionalism, in short, all the elements that had made them into a successful mass political movement—turned into liabilities when transplanted into the more prosaic and orderly realm of governmental administration.

The foreign labor program was, after all, a microcosm of the Nazi world—a curious mixture of improvisation, ideology, and opportunism. From its inception in September 1939 until its collapse in May 1945, the program offered an instructive example of how the Hitlerian state tried to answer the complex economic question of complete utilization of the total manpower potential available to Germany.

[5] For one of many accounts of the bitter personal intrigues within Hitler's inner circle, see *The Bormann Letters; The Private Correspondence Between Martin Bormann and His Wife from January 1943 to April 1945.* Bormann thought Speer was attempting to undermine his position with Hitler through Dr. Morrell, *Der Fuehrer's* private physician.

Bibliographical Essay

SPECIALIZED STUDIES such as this one do not readily lend themselves to conventional bibliographies. The monotonous listing of individual documents, legal handbooks, monographs, articles, and books dealing with the foreign labor program would serve little purpose, except to reassure the general reader and the specialist that my duty to scholarship had been faithfully executed. Rather than compiling such a bibliography, I thought it would be more valuable to include a selective bibliographical essay which would allow an explanation and evaluation of some of the materials currently available on the foreign labor program. It was also my hope that this approach might serve as an incentive for others to plunge into the remarkable collections of Nazi materials in this country.

To reduce needless repetition, literature on special problems discussed in the footnotes of this study have been omitted, as well as materials which have only a tangential relationship to the foreign labor program. Thus, general histories of the Third Reich, biographies of Nazi leaders, and prewar accounts of the German economy, for example, have not been discussed in this essay.

A. COLLECTIONS OF CAPTURED GERMAN DOCUMENTS

The three large collections of captured German documents and the published reports based on them are: the files, working papers, and reports of the United States Strategic Bombing Survey (USSBS); the files and published sets of the Nuremberg Trials; and the voluminous collection of documents microfilmed at Alexandria, Virginia. All three collections are deposited in the National Archives, Washington, D.C.

(1) United States Strategic Bombing Survey

The published reports and collections of documents of the USSBS is the best single collection of materials on the overall economic life of Nazi Germany during the war years. Since 1954, the *Index to Records of the United States Strategic Bombing Survey* (Washington, 1947) has been declassified and made available to scholars. The files are organized loosely around numbers corresponding to the published report numbers. In many instances, the original German documents, their translations, the working papers of the USSBS, and a great deal of extraneous material are grouped together. Consequently, the researcher must examine every item in the index that pertains to his subject, and then physically handle each numbered bundle. In general, the files contain a rich collection of interviews of major German economic leaders; periodical reports from various levels of the German government; factory, police, Army and Allied Intelligence reports; administrative handbooks; statistics from various Reich offices; and the preliminary working papers of the USSBS. Many of the original German documents seem to be from the collection made by Speer at the interrogation camp "Dustbin" at Kransberg. Most of the files are incomplete; apparently many of the documents were sent to Nuremberg for the various trials.

Especially valuable for this study were the collections of interview reports of Fritz Sauckel, No. 71, June 2, 1945; Robert Ley, No. 57, June 27 and October 2, 1945; Fritz Schmelter, May 26, 1945; and the Speer interviews of May 15, 17, 18, 22, 23, 28, and 31, 1945. Understandably, these interviews have a degree of frankness about them that is missing in the pre-trial interrogations at Nuremberg. Two indispensable manuscripts in the files are General Georg Thomas, *Grundlagen fuer eine Geschichte der deutschen Wehr- und Ruestungswirtschaft*, 1945, and Rolf Wagenfuehr, *The Rise and Fall of the German War Economy, 1939-1945*, 1945. Both are decidedly pro-Speer in their interpretations. The complete stenographic minutes of the 21st, 53rd, and 54th meetings of the Central Planning Board, all dealing with the labor program, are valuable accounts of the operation of the board in relationship to the labor program. *Memorandum on Organization/Speer* prepared by Dr. Gerhard Fraenk, 1945, and *Who's Who in Germany and Austria*, n.d., are important in untangling the administrative knot of the Third Reich.

Some of the individual documents in the files have been microfilmed. Those most helpful with statistics were *Arbeitseinsatz* (*Arbeitsbuchinhaber*) *20.3.45.*, from the G. B. Ruest./Planungs-amt/Statistische Leitstelle, on Microfilm Roll 2075; *Entwicklung der Zahl der Beschaeftigten nach Berufsgruppen* (*in den W-Betrieben*), from the Reichsminister fuer Ruestung und Kriegs-produktion (Speer's ministry), on Microfilm Roll 2074; and *Indexziffern der Deutschen Ruestungsendfertigung, Juni 1944*, also from the Reichsminister fuer Ruestung und Kriegsproduktion. Two basic documents from the Statistisches Reichsamt are *Kriegswirtschaftliche Kraeftebilanz, 1939-1944,* on Microfilm Roll 2074; and the *Reichsgruppe Industrie und Gesamt Industrie* reports, on Microfilm Roll 2018. The complete set of the Remscheid Labor Office's *Monatlicher Taetigkeitsbericht,* from March 1942 to March 1945, offers an instructive view of the operation of the foreign labor program in one district. There are other *Monatlicher Taetigkeitsbericht* from scattered labor offices throughout the Reich also in the files.

Of the 208 published reports of the USSBS, the two from the Morale Division, *The Effects of Bombing on Health and Medical Care in Germany,* 65a, January 1947, and *The Effects of Strategic Bombing on German Morale,* Vol. II, December 1946, are important because they were based on interviews with German officials and industrialists, and on a pilot study of foreign workers conducted by the USSBS. The four most useful reports from the Overall Economic Effects Division are *The Effects of Strategic Bombing on the German Economy,* October 31, 1945, which is the summary report of the USSBS; Edward O. Bassett, *Industrial Sales, Output, and Productivity, Prewar Area of Germany, 1939-1944,* Special Paper No. 8, Report No. 134a, March 15, 1946; *The Effects of Strategic Bombing upon the Operations of the Hermann Goering Works During World War II* (mimeographed, 1945), which illustrates the labor program in a privileged industrial firm; and *The Gross National Product of Germany, 1939-1944* (mimeographed, 1945).

(2) Nuremberg Trials Collection

The second collection of documents examined in the preparation of this study was the published Nuremberg Trials Documents and the United States government's preparatory files for the Nuremberg cases. The United States edition of the published Nuremberg Trials Documents is comprised of three sets of volumes. The first set, *Trial of the Major War Criminals Before the International Military Tribunal,* 42 vols. (Nuremberg, 1947-1949), is a complete account of the proceedings of the main trial and most of the documents presented in evidence. The second set, *Nazi Conspiracy and Aggression,* 10 vols. (Nuremberg, 1947-1949), contains translations of most of the documents used by the Western allied prosecutors and of some of the defense docu-

ments. The third set, *Trials of War Criminals Before the Nuremberg Military Tribunals under Control Council Law No. 10*, 15
vols. (Washington, 1951-1953), is a partial record of the proceedings and documents of the subsequent trials of minor Nazis
held at Nuremberg, including the I. G. Farben, Krupp, and
foreign office cases. All three sets show the marks of hasty
translation and editing. A comparison of some of the translated
documents with the original ones in the files at the National
Archives indicates textual differences. Another limitation regarding information concerning the foreign labor program in these
sets is that they were written primarily from the viewpoint of
the prosecution rather than the defense. As a consequence, many
of the longer defense documents of the Speer and Sauckel cases
were not included. Moreover, one has the distinct impression
that only one side of the case has been adequately presented. It
is this researcher's opinion that these published sets should be
used more cautiously than heretofore.

The files of the Nuremberg Trials at the National Archives
have not been extensively utilized by scholars because of the difficulties of finding specific materials in this large collection. One
index to the documents is 14,000 one-page legal summaries drawn
up by the American prosecution as a quick reference to individual documents. These briefs contain the code number (e.g.,
PS-1406 or RF 1507-810F), the origin, and a brief summary
of the document. The individual documents are filed by the code
number. The second, more limited index contains some important pre-trial interrogations and defense documents listed under
the name of those involved. For example, Sauckel's name-folder
has a rather complete set of his defense documents plus the very
valuable pre-trial interrogations of September 15, 18, 19, 20,
21, 24, 28, and October 5 and 8, 1945. In these interrogations,
Sauckel, who was not a highly articulate person, gave a much
more candid and better-organized account of the operation of
the labor program than he did at the trial. The name-folders of
Albert Speer, Fritz Schmelter, Max Timm, Carl Goetz, and
Franz Seldte yielded similarly valuable information.

The proceedings and documents in the minor trials of Nazi
industrialists are very important because the charge of using
"slave labor" was a principal one. However, much of the evidence submitted was from the first Nuremberg trial. One interview of Fritz Schmelter on February 28, 1947, dealing with
the distribution of foreign workers to German firms, is essential

in understanding the differences between the policies of Speer and Sauckel in 1943 and 1944.

(3) Microfilmed German Records

By far the most ambitious and voluminous collection of documents cited in this study is the German records microfilmed at Alexandria, Virginia. In 1955, a group of scholars privately organized the American Committee for the Study of War Documents; a year later, the committee became part of the American Historical Association. Late in 1956, with the approval and support of the United States government and a number of private foundations, the committee began to microfilm captured German records and return the original documents to the West German Federal Republic.

The scope, depth, and volume of the microfilmed collection offer an unparalleled opportunity to the researcher. Rarely have the innermost workings of a state been more carefully preserved and exposed. Insofar as this study is concerned, it is this collection of documents which affords the best insight into the foreign labor program. Although much of the USSBS and the Nuremberg Trials Collection is included in this microfilmed material, however, I have preferred to refer to the Nuremberg documents whenever possible because those volumes were more accessible than the microfilmed rolls.

The microfilmed German records were collected under a general classification and assigned a coded "T" number. The records were then filmed in rolls under this general classification. For example, the code number of "T-71" is used to identify materials and records of the Reich Ministry of Economics, while "T-76" identifies materials from the Organization Todt. The indices for the general classification and the individual rolls of microfilm appear in *Guides to German Records Microfilmed at Alexandria, Virginia* (Washington, 1958—). At this time of writing, forty-nine guides are available. The guides are organized to give the serial, roll, item marking, provenance, filming information, and notes. The serial and roll refer to the sequence of the film; the item marking is the identification symbol of the original folder; while the provenance indicates, when ascertainable, the German archival origin of the documents. The filming information includes the amount of material filmed and the first frame number of each folder. The notes give a general description of the materials filmed.

Materials on the labor program are scattered throughout the microfilmed collection, because every administrative office involved with the foreign workers made a collection of labor decrees, notices, or memos that were germane to its own activities. Then, too, the very nature of the foreign labor program, the conscious attempts of Sauckel to propagandize it, and his fondness for important-sounding proclamations and manifestoes resulted in widespread distribution of labor materials. For example, the "T-175" series, *Records of the Reich Leader of the SS and Chief of the German Police*, Parts I and II, in Guides 32 and 33, contain a rather complete collection of Sauckel's general pronouncements as well as materials directly related to the exercise of police power over the foreigners.

In addition to the SS reports on "T-175," the series numbers and guides to the microfilmed documents most important to this study follow: "T-71," *Records of the Reich Ministry of Economics*, Guide 1. Materials from this ministry include some excellent reports from the Reich Statistical Office, accounts of Sauckel's recruiting trips, and some very interesting reports dealing with the payment of foreign workers, the transfer of funds to their homelands, and the SS investigations of their black-market activities in Germany. "T-81," *Records of the National Socialist German Labor Party*, Parts I, II, and III, Guides 3, 20, and 35, furnished, primarily, reports from party organizations dealing with the behavior of foreigners, instructions for the German populace in dealing with foreigners, and related problems. Most useful were the reports from regional and local German Labor Front (DAF) offices concerning every phase of the program's operation. Reports of the *Gau* offices illustrate the role of the party in the program, but these reports tend to exaggerate the influence and importance of the *Gauleiter*. An excellent source of information about the German population's attitudes toward the foreigners as well as the best description of the *Zeitgeist* in wartime Germany can be found in the weekly canvass of opinion reports (*Woechentlicher Stimmungsbericht*) emanating from the *Gau* offices.

"T-77," *Records of Headquarters, German Armed Forces High Command*, Parts I, II, III, and IV, Guides 7, 17, 18, and 19, are extremely important because they contain the *Wehrwirtschafts- und Ruestungsamt* (*Wi Rue Amt*) records. A wide range of subjects was covered in this collection, including such things as rearmament, the domestic economy, war production, and related economic, military, political, and cultural matters. The *Ruestungsamt* became a part of Speer's ministry in 1942. As a result, materials covered in the "T-77" series are closely related to the "T-73" materials, *Records of the Reich Ministry of Armaments and War Production*, Guide 10. To list the subjects covered by these two series would demand another index, for every aspect of this study is related to material in "T-77" and "T-73." These two series will remain the most important sources for the German war economy and the foreign labor program until such time as the Russian and East German holdings of the records of the Labor Ministry and Sauckel's offices in Berlin and Weimar become more accessible to Western scholars.

Of less importance were "T-84," *Miscellaneous German Records Collection*, Parts I, II, and III, Guides 5, 8, and 36, and "T-83," *Records of Private Austrian, Dutch, and German Enterprises, 1917-1946*, Guide 23. A rather good account of the operation of the foreign labor program in the East can be gathered from the *Monatsbericht Wi Stab Ost/Abt. Arbeit*, in "T-178," *Fragmentary Records of Miscellaneous Reich Ministries and Offices*, Guide 11, and the materials on "T-454," *Records of the Reich Ministry for the Occupied Eastern Territories, 1941-1945*, Guide 28. Although there are materials on the foreign workers in many of the remaining guides, those cited are most important.

The collections from the USSBS, the Nuremberg Trials, and the records microfilmed at Alexandria, Virginia, were the primary ones used in this study. However, there are numerous other collections of German documents presently available in this country on nearly every facet of Germany's history since 1914. The best description of this country's holdings of German documents is the *Guide to Captured German Documents* prepared by Gerhard L. Weinberg and the War Documentation Project Staff under the direction of Fritz T. Epstein in 1952, and the *Supplement to the Guide to Captured German Documents*, prepared by the same staff in 1959. Both are indispensable for anyone interested in Germany in the twentieth century. It is to be hoped that in the future the National Archives will have the financial means to compile a world-wide guide to the Nazi records such as Weinberg and Epstein have prepared for the United States holdings.

B. OFFICIAL GERMAN GOVERNMENT AND NAZI PARTY PUBLICATIONS DEALING WITH FOREIGN WORKERS

Throughout the war, German governmental and party agencies published a variety of manuscripts dealing with every facet of the employment of foreigners in the Reich. Many of these publications fall under the general classification of handbooks for employers, labor officials, and German Labor Front (DAF) administrators. Wages, legal rights, housing, medical benefits, productivity, and general experience with foreigners are just some of the countless subjects covered by these materials. One of the earliest publications which clearly anticipated the massive employment of foreigners was by the labor official Walter Stothfang, *Der Arbeitseinsatz im Kriege* (Berlin, 1940). In 1941, the first collection of decrees appeared from the Deutsche Arbeitsfront, Amt fuer Arbeitseinsatz, *Sammlung der Bestimmungen ueber den Einsatz auslaendischer Arbeiter in Deutschland* (Berlin, 1941). Two articles by members of the Labor Ministry in the same year indicate the slow rate of German utilization of foreigners in industry. Both Dr. Letsche, "Der Einsatz gewerblicher auslaendischer Arbeitskraefte in Deutschland," *Reichsarbeitsblatt*, v, 1941, and Walter Stothfang, "Der Arbeitseinsatz an der Jahreswende," *Monatshefte fuer NS-Sozialpolitik*, v, 1941, stress the necessity of transferring more foreigners from agriculture to industry.

After the appointment of Sauckel in 1942, two of the first all-inclusive administrative handbooks to appear were Carl Birkenholz, ed., *Der auslaendische Arbeiter in Deutschland, Sammlung und Erlaeuterung der arbeits- und sozialrechtlichen Vorschriften ueber das Arbeitsverhaeltnis nichtvolksdeutscher Beschaeftigter* (Berlin, 1942); and Franz Mende, *et al.*, *Die Beschaeftigung von auslaendischen Arbeitskraeften in Deutschland* (Berlin, 1942). Some of the other handbooks which appeared later in the war were Otto K. Krauskopf, *Der Auslaendische Arbeiter in Deutschland*, 2 vols. (Berlin, 1943); Hans Kuppers and Rudolf Bannier, *Arbeitseinsatz und Arbeitsrecht*, 2 vols. (Berlin, 1942); Wolfgang Siebert, *Das Deutsche Arbeitsrecht, Sammlung der arbeitsrechtlichen Bestimmungen mit Einleitung, Vorbemerkungen und Hinweisen*, 4 vols. (Hamburg, 1943); Hermann Frohn and Paul Lipkow, *Handbuch ueber die Heeresstandortlohn-*

*stellen, Einrichtung, Geschaeftsbetrieb, Aufstellung der Lohn-
rechnungen und Rechnungslegung, Abfindung der auslaendischen
Arbeitskraefte* (Berlin, 1943); and the Deutsche Arbeitsfront,
*Der auslaendische Arbeiter in Deutschland, eine tabellarische
Uebersicht* (Berlin, 1943).

The most useful, and by far the most comprehensive, survey
of the entire foreign labor program was Friedrich Didier, ed.,
*Handbuch fuer die Dienststellen des G.B.A. und die interessierten
Reichsstellen im Grossdeutschen Reich und in den besetzten
Gebieten* (Berlin, 1944). Most of the important decrees pertain-
ing to the program which appeared in various governmental
journals such as the *Reichsarbeitsblatt, Reichsgesetzblatt,* and
the party's official *Verfuegungen, Anordnungen, Bekanntgaben*
are also included in Didier's handbook.

The utilization of the eastern worker, his productivity, and his
slow rise in status can be traced in the following: from the Labor
Ministry, L. Hass and F. Tschepur, *Arbeitseinsatz der Ostarbeiter* (mimeographed, 1942), and Hans Kuppers and Rudolf
Bannier, *Einsatzbedingungen der Ostarbeiter sowie der sowjetrus-
sischen Kriegsgefangenen, Sonderveroeffentlichung des Reichsar-
beitsblattes* (Berlin, 1943); from the German Labor Front,
*Arbeitseinsatz der Ostarbeiter in Deutschland: Vorlaeufiger Be-
richt zur Untersuchung des Arbeitswissenschaftlichen Instituts
ueber Arbeitseignung und Leistungsfaehigkeit der Ostarbeiter*
(Berlin, 1943), and *Die Leistungsfaehigkeit von Ostarbeitern in
Deutschland im Vergleich zur Leistung deutscher Arbeiter an
Hand von Akkordunterlagen* (mimeographed, 1943); from
Speer's ministry, *Einsatz von Ostarbeitern in der Deutschen
Maschinenindustrie* (Essen, n.d.), L. Hass, *Auswahl und Einsatz der Ostarbeiter, Psychologische Betrachtungen, Leistung
und Leistungssteigerung* (Haus der Technik, Gau Westmark,
n.d.), Theodor Hupfauer, *Mensch, Betrieb, Leistung* (Berlin,
n.d.), and K. Hempel, *Der Arbeitseinsatz-Ingenieur, Sammlung
aller Bestimmungen und Richtlinien in laufenden Fragen* (Berlin,
1944).

The German Labor Front published a number of materials
related to the integration of foreign labor in the German administration such as *Die Deutsche Arbeitsfront, Wesen, Ziel, Wege*
(Berlin, 1943); *Deutsche Berufserziehung und Betriebsfuehrung,
Grundlagen und Formen* (Berlin-Zehlendorf, 1942); and *Der
Einfluss der Arbeitseinsatzbestimmungen auf das Arbeitsverhaeltnis* (Berlin, 1942); but their monthly publications, *Amt-*

liches Nachrichtenblatt, Monatsbericht ueber die deutsche Sozial-ordnung, and especially *Lagerfuehrer-Sonderdienst,* offered a more immediate view of the DAF problems in housing and handling millions of foreigners.

The relationship between Germany's failure to use more of its own women and the recruitment of foreigners was covered in two pamphlets from the Reichsministerium fuer Ruestung und Kriegsproduktion, Planungsamt, *Soll-Ist-Vergleich* (mimeo-graphed, 1943-1945), and *Zahlenangaben ueber den Einsatz deutscher Frauen* (Berlin, 1943-1945), while Martha Moers, *Industrielle Frauenarbeit; ein psychologisch-paedagogischer Beitrag zur Aufgabe der Leistungssteigerung* (Berlin-Zehlendorf, 1941), anticipated the need to bring more women into industrial work. The tone as well as the title of W. Lejeune's pamphlet, *Voraussetzungen und Wege des richtigen Einsatzes fremdvoelkischer Arbeitskraefte* (Berlin, 1944), indicates the remarkable change in German attitudes late in the war, especially toward foreign women workers.

The problem of the foreign workers and the German food supply was covered by Johann von Leers, *Bauerntum,* 9 Aufl. (Berlin, 1943), and Guenter Pfeil, *Lebensmittelversorgung der auslaendischen Zivilarbeiter in Deutschland* (Berlin, 1944), and of course was often commented on in government periodicals, such as the *Landswirtschaftliches Ministerialblatt.*

C. OTHER PRIMARY AND SECONDARY SOURCES

The number of memoirs, secondary works, and collections of documents on Nazi Germany during the war continues to grow enormously each year. Therefore, only a fraction of the materials related to the foreign labor program can be mentioned. The books listed below represent a highly selective bibliography on the significant aspects of the labor program.

Two provocative accounts of the German war economy are *Germany's Economic Preparations for War* by Burton H. Klein (Cambridge: Harvard University Press, 1959), and *The German Economy at War* by Alan P. Milward (New York: Oxford University Press, 1965). Klein's work is based on his experience with the USSBS and emphasizes the failures of the German blitzkrieg economy. While Milward substantiates Klein's general conclusions, he argues that the economic policy was a success. He also stresses the role of Dr. Todt in beginning reforms in the economy that Speer received credit for after the war. William N. Medlicott, *The Economic Blockade*, 2 vols. (London: H.M.S.O., 1952, 1959), generally follows the USSBS failure interpretation, but has an explanation of the labor program in terms of the blockade. An interesting series of articles by H. W. Singer, "The German War Economy in the Light of German Economic Periodicals," *Economic Journal*, L, 534-546; LI, 519-535, 192-215, 400-421; LII, 18-36, 186-205, 377-399; LIII, 121-139, 243-259, 370-380; LIV, 62-74, and 206-216, stresses the flexibility of the German economic leaders. In spite of the title, a virtual economic history of the period from a Marxian viewpoint is Juergen Kuczynski, *Die Geschichte der Lage der Arbeiter unter dem Kapitalismus: Studien zur Geschichte des staatsmonopolistischen Kapitalismus in Deutschland 1918 bis 1945*, Vol. 16 (Berlin: Akademie-Verlag, 1963), which interprets the developments under Speer during the war as logical consequences of the German form of capitalism.

Four wartime books about the German economy that remain valuable are Otto Nathan and Milton Fried, *The Nazi Economic System: Germany's Mobilization for War* (Durham, N.C.: Duke University Press, 1944); Franz Neumann, *Behemoth* (New York: Oxford University Press, 1943); Joseph Borkin, *Germany's Master Plan: The Story of Industrial Offensive* (New York: Duell, Sloan and Pearce, 1943); and Adolf Weber, *Kurzgefasste Volkswirtschaftspolitik* (Berlin: Duncker und Humblot, 1942).

The fascinating and difficult question of the relationship between German business and Nazism is discussed by George W. F. Hallgarten, *Hitler, Reichswehr und Industrie* (Frankfurt: Europaeische Verlagsanstalt, 1955); Louis P. Lochner, *Tycoons and Tyrant: German Industry from Hitler to Adenauer* (Chicago: Henry Regnery Co., 1954); Norbert Muhlen, *The Incredible Krupps* (New York: Henry Holt, 1959); and Josiah E. Du Bois' book on the I. G. Farben Company, *The Devil's Chemists* (Boston: The Beacon Press, 1952). Hjalmar Schacht defends his role in the Reich in his *Confessions of "the Old Wizard"* (Boston: Houghton Mifflin, 1955), but a more balanced account is *Hjalmar Schacht: For and Against Hitler* by Edward Norman Peterson (Boston: Christopher Publishing House, 1954). The best account of the business problem—although, like Hallgarten's book, it emphasizes the early years of the Nazi regime—is *Big Business in the Third Reich* by Arthur Schweitzer (Bloomington: Indiana University Press, 1964).

The general labor policies of Nazi Germany are explained in the following books: Gerhard Bry, *Wages in Germany, 1871-1945* (Princeton: Princeton University Press, 1960); Evelyn Anderson, *Hammer or Anvil: The Story of the German Working-class Movement* (London: Gollancz, 1945); Clarence D. Long, *The Labor Force in War and Transition—Four Countries* (New York: National Bureau of Economic Research, 1952); Fritz Steinberg, *German Manpower: The Crucial Factor* (Washington: The Brookings Institution, 1942); and Eberhard Trompke, *Der Arbeitseinsatz als Element deutscher Wehr- und Kriegswirtschaft* (Rostock: Carl Hinstorffs, 1941). The foreign labor policies are discussed by John H. E. Fried, *The Exploitation of Foreign Labour by Germany* (Montreal: International Labour Office, 1945); United States Office of Strategic Services, *Foreign Labor in Germany*, Research and Analysis Report, No. 1623, October 24, 1944; and two articles by Eduard Willeke, "Der Arbeitseinsatz im Kriege," *Jahrbuecher fuer Nationaloekonomie und Statistik*, CLIV (1941), 177-201 and 311-348. Apologetic explanations for the use of foreigners by Germany because of allied warfare tactics can be found in *The Nuremberg Trials* by August von Knieriem (Chicago: Henry Regnery, 1959), and *Die wirtschaftlichen Kriegsmassnahmen Deutschlands im 2. Weltkrieg in voelkerrechtlicher Betrachtung* by Ernst-Guenter Zumach (Erlangen, 1955, mimeographed).

A basic analysis of the Nazi perversion of traditional German policies, with an interesting discussion of the use of foreign agricultural workers during the war, is found in Frieda Wunderlich, *Farm Labor in Germany 1810-1945: Its Historical Development Within the Framework of Agricultural and Social Policy* (Princeton: Princeton University Press, 1961). The books by Karl Brandt, *et al.*, *Germany's Agricultural and Food Policies in World War II*, Vol. I, and *Management of Agriculture and Food in the German-occupied and Other Areas of Fortress Europe*, Vol. II (Stanford: Stanford University Press, 1953), explain the economic consequences of the foreign labor program on the food supply available to Germany.

The social and psychological aspects of the foreign labor program are treated by Heinz L. Ansbacher in "Testing, Management and Reactions of Foreign Workers in Germany During World War II," *American Psychologist*, v (1950), pp. 38-49, and "The Problems of Interpreting Attitude Survey Data: A Case Study of the Attitude of Russian Workers in Wartime Germany," *Public Opinion Quarterly*, xiv (1950), pp. 126-138, in which Ansbacher disagrees with the USSBS conclusions. E. A. Shils, in "Social and Psychological Aspects of Displacement and Repatriation," *Journal of Social Issues*, ii, No. 3 (August 1946), pp. 3-18, found that regressive behavior was common among the foreign workers.

The demographic consequences of the war and the foreign labor program are discussed by Eugene M. Kulischer, *Europe on the Move: War and Population Changes, 1917-1947* (New York: Columbia University Press, 1948); Joseph B. Schechtmann, *European Population Transfers, 1939-1945* (New York: Oxford Press, 1946); Malcolm J. Proudfoot, *European Refugees, 1939-1945* (London: Faber, 1957); and Grzegorz Frumkin, *Population Changes in Europe Since 1929* (New York: Kelly, 1951).

The operation of the labor program in the East and the heavy burden it placed on the German occupational administration are described best in the works of Alexander Dallin, *German Rule in Russia, 1941-1945* (London: Macmillan, 1957), *Odessa, 1941-1944: A Case Study of Soviet Territory Under Foreign Rule* (U.S.A.F. Project Rand, 1957), and *Reactions to the German Occupation of Soviet Russia* (Maxwell Air Force Base, Ala.: Air University Human Resources Research Institute, 1952). Gerald Reitlinger, *House Built on Sand* (New York: Viking, 1960), covers the same material as Dallin, but particularly noteworthy are two chapters on labor recruitment in Russia. More specialized studies are Vladimir Samarin, *Civilian Life Under the German Occupation, 1942-1944* (New York: Research Program on the U.S.S.R., 1954); Ihor Kamenetsky, *Hitler's Occupation of the Ukraine, 1941-1944* (Milwaukee: Marquette University Press, 1956); and Oleg Anisimov, *The German Occupation in Northern Russia During World War II* (New York: East European Fund, Series No. 56, 1954). The effect of the labor program on the partisan movement is explained by Edgar M. Howell, *The Soviet Partisan Movement, 1941-1944* (Dept. of the Army Pamphlet 20-244, August 1956), and John A. Armstrong, ed., *Soviet Partisans in World War II* (Madison: University of Wisconsin Press, 1964).

Writings from members of the East Ministry include Otto Braeutigam, *Ueberblick ueber die Besetzten Ostgebiete waehrend des 2. Weltkrieges* (Tuebingen: Studien des Instituts Besatzungsfragen zu den deutschen Besatzungen in 2. Weltkrieg, 1954); Peter Kleist, *Zwischen Hitler und Stalin* (Bonn: Athenaeum, 1950); and Alfred Rosenberg's sketchy *Letzte Aufzeichnungen* (Goettingen: Plesse, 1953).

For other eastern areas, the most useful accounts were Martin Broszat, *Nationalsozialistische Polenpolitik, 1939-1945* (Stuttgart: Deutsche Verlags-Anstalt, 1961); Robert Herzog, *Grundzuege der deutschen Besatzungsverwaltung in den ost- und suedosteuropaeischen Laendern waehrend des zweiten Weltkrieges* (Tuebingen: Studien des Instituts Besatzungsfragen zu den deutschen Besatzungen in 2. Weltkrieg, 1955); and Lutz Ewerth, *Der Arbeitseinsatz von Landesbewohnern besetzter Gebiete des Ostens und Suedostens im Zweiten Weltkrieg* (dissertation, Tuebingen, 1954).

In the West, there is surprising unanimity about Laval's Fabian tactics against German labor officials in the following books: Robert Aron and Georgette Elgey, *The Vichy Regime, 1940-1944*, trans. by Humphrey Hare (London: Putnam, 1958); Pierre Tissier, *I Worked with Laval* (London: William Reineman, 1949); *The Diary of Pierre Laval*, trans. by Josée Laval (New York: Charles Scribner's Sons, 1948); Alfred Mallet, *Pierre Laval*, 2 vols. (Paris: Amiot-Dumont, 1955); Otto Abetz, *Das Offene Problem* (Cologne: Greven, 1951); and the very important *France During the German Occupation, 1940-1944: A Collection of 292 Statements on the Government of Maréchal Pétain and Pierre Laval*, 3 vols., trans. by Philip W. Whitcomb, Hoover Institution on War, Revolution, and Peace (Palo Alto, Calif.: Stanford University Press, 1957).

For the other western countries, the following works are vital: Werner Warmbrunn, *The Dutch Under German Occupation, 1940-1945* (Stanford: Stanford University Press, 1963); G. Jacquemyns, *La Société belge sous l'occupation allemande*, 3 vols. (Brussels: Nicholson et Watson, 1950); and Walter Herdeg, *Grundzuege der deutschen Besatzungsverwaltung in den west- und nordeuropaeischen Laendern waehrend des 2. Weltkrieges* (Tuebingen: Studien des Instituts Besatzungsfragen zu den deutschen Besatzungen in 2. Weltkrieg, 1955). The rationale behind German rule, as well as many of the German decrees, can be seen in the book *Axis Rule in Occupied Europe: Laws of Occupation, Analysis of Government, Proposals for Redress* by Rafael Lemkin (Washington: Carnegie Endowment for International Peace, 1944), but it should be read in conjunction with *Die deutsche Besetzungsgerichtsbarkeit waehrend des 2. Weltkrieges* by Guenther Moritz (Tuebingen: Studien des Instituts Besatzungsfragen zu den deutschen Besatzungen in 2. Weltkrieg, 1954). For an excellent analysis of the differences between German rule in the East and in the West, see *Das Dritte Reich und Europa* (Munich: Institut fuer Zeitgeschichte, 1957).

The friction generated between Italy and Germany by the foreign labor program can be seen in Dino Alfieri, *Dictators Face to Face*, trans. by David Moore (New York: New York University Press, 1955), and in *The Ciano Diaries, 1939-1943*, ed. by Hugh Gibson (Garden City, N.Y.: Doubleday and Co., 1946).

Last, but not the least important, are two books that I strongly recommend for any student of the Nazi period: Heinz Paechter, *Nazi-deutsch Glossary* (New York: Frederick Ungar, 1944), and Cornelia Berning, *Vom "Abstammungsnachweis" zum "Zuchtwart," Vokabular des Nationalsozialismus* (Berlin: Walter de Gruyter, 1965). Both are indispensable guides to the, occasionally, almost impenetrable thicket of Nazi jargon.

INDEX

329

employed in, 49; wages in, 246
Berlin, 59, 134-135
*Bezirksgruppe Steinkohlenberg-
bau Ruhr*, 52
Bichelonne, Jean, 182, 190-91,
193, 197
Bismarck, Otto von, 45
black market, 50, 53, 245-46
blitzkrieg strategy, 14-15, 45, 67,
99-100, 299-301, 303
Blut und Boden concept, 290-91
Bohemia-Moravia: labor quota
for, 145; workers recruited
from, 16-17, 138, 148, 195
bombing, 265, 268, 270
books for foreign workers, 289-90
Bormann, Martin: and appointment of labor czar, 103; cen-
tralizes state and party, 117; in
Committee of Three, 210; his
directive on foreigners, 278;
and living conditions of eastern
workers, 124, 172; and Sauckel,
106, 205, 208, 214, 306; his
search for power, 128; and
Speer, 220, 227, 311; and total
war mobilization, 210; trans-
mits instructions from Hitler to
Rosenberg, 79
Boyez, Emile, 197
Braeutigam, Otto, 84-85, 156,
165, 173, 292
Britain, 14-15, 67, 233
British prisoners of war, 49
Bulgaria, 57, 246

Canaris, Admiral Wilhelm, 252
Central Planning Board, *see
Zentrale Planung*
Central Reich Employment Office,
115
Central Security Office (RSHA),
251-53
chemical industry, 237-39, 308
children (German), 12, 35, 150-
52

Chinese workers, 112
Ciano, Count Galeazzo, 63, 80-81
civil government chiefs, 114, 117,
141, 224
civil servants, 149, 219, 225-26
civilian administrative agencies,
141
civilian workers, 148-49; by nationality and sex, 232; number
of, 56
clothing, 52, 277-80
coal production, 139
combing commissions in France,
142-43, 184, 197
Commandant of Kharkov, 156
Committee for Social Peace, 197
Committee of Three, 210
Compulsory Labor Decrees, 11-
12, 45, 135, 140, 145, 154,
156, 186-87, 200
concentration camp labor, 48,
237-39, 298, 306
construction industry, 21
consumer goods: elimination of,
212, 218, 300-301; Gauleiters
opposition to, 219-220; industries, 17, 68; production of, 97-
98, 209, 222, 310
contracts, 222
control methods for foreigners,
53, 241, 249-55, 259
Corrière della sera, 60
crane operators, 223
Croatians: compulsory labor laws
for, 200; desertion of, 254; food
rations for, 247; number recruited, 138, 148
Czechoslovakia: crisis in, 17;
liaison men for, 55; ranking of
nationals, 260; supply of workers from, 212

DAF: care of foreigners, 240; and
Committee for Work Studies,
243-44; and cultural affairs,
250; on eastern workers, 170-

workers from, 79; war in, 38, 89, 234. *See also* Russia
Spain, 57, 64
Special Plenipotentiary for Labor, *see* Sauckel, GBA
Speer, Albert: and allocation of labor, 103, 121; appointment of, 20, 89-90, 303; and armament commands, 226-27; and armament offices, 95-96; and armament plant personnel, 212; his attitude toward Gauleiters, 117; his attitude toward GBA, 205; and Bormann, 311; on civilian production, 218; on combing German factories, 208; and Committee of Three, 210; his concept of total war, 144, 212; criticism of administration, 98-99, 216, 219; criticism of consumer production, 97-98; and defects in mobilization, 310; on desertion rate of foreign workers, 253-56; his differences with Nazi party, 227; early career of, 87-88; and economy of Germany, 89, 301; and foreign labor program, 212-16, 307; on foreign workers, 135, 230; and France, 184, 190; and Gauleiters, 105-106, 219-20; on GBA appointment, 105-107; on German food supply, 216; on German war production, 150-51, 204ff; and Goering, 98, 106-107
    and Hitler, 98-99, 221, 304; on industry in occupied areas, 142; on iron ore production, 149; labor allocation records of, 206, 209-11; and labor control, 204-205, 207-208, 211; and labor offices, 8; and Ley, 98, 222; on manpower distribution, 213, 220-23; and medals for foreign workers, 248; on Nazi propaganda, 101-102; number of foreign workers recruited by, 153; opposition to forceful recruitment, 150-51; personality of, 88-89; his plans for Nazi party, 218; power of, 227-28, 306; productivity of foreign workers recruited by, 260; and public construction, 21; and racial attitudes, 248-50; his recommendations for recruitment of foreign workers, 151; records of, 208-209; reforms of, 89, 97-98, 127, 210, 214, 303-304; representatives of, 150, 224-25; resignation of, 228; and Russian workers, 122, 208; and S-plants, 190-99, 203, 218, 223-24; and Sauckel, 107, 143, 204-29, 304-306; special factory guards needed by, 252-53; statistical office of, 151-53; and steel distribution and production, 92-93, 212-13; and Ukrainians, 309; and use of women in war effort, 101-102, 214-15, 231; on utilization of labor, 147; and *Zentrale Planung*, 93-94, 96-97, 206-209
Speer's Ministry: apportionment of workers by, 223; attitude toward foreign workers by, 173-74; and combing commission in France, 184; and construction of barracks, 265-66, 270; control of deferred workers by, 225; control of employment by, 120; criticism of foreign labor program by, 277; and destruction of recruitment program, 224; and Gauleiters, 117, 227; labor statistics of, 208-209; and labor supply, 224; and training program for foreigners, 241, 244
sponsorship system, 192

Yugoslavia, 65, 148, 242

Zehlendorf Institute, 241-43
Zeitzler, General Kurt, 158
Zentrale Planung: creation of, 93-94; and labor allocation system, 206-209, 305, 310; on labor in France, 142-43; labor priorities of, 121; labor requirements of, 131; on labor shortage (skilled), 142; on labor supply,

212, 224; and problems with red slip program, 225; quota for 1943, 145; and recruitment program, 149, 163; and Reich leaders, 207; and S-plant program, 224; and Sauckel, 149-150, 187, 213; and Speer, 96-97

Zwangsmassnahmen, see Compulsory Labor Decrees